Latinos
in a
Changing
U. S. Economy

SAGE SERIES ON
RACE AND ETHNIC RELATIONS

Series Editor:
JOHN H. STANFIELD II
College of William and Mary

This series is designed for scholars working in creative theoretical areas related to race and ethnic relations. The series will publish books and collections of original articles that critically assess and expand upon race and ethnic relations issues from American and comparative points of view.

SERIES EDITORIAL BOARD

Latinos in a Changing U. S. Economy

Comparative Perspectives on Growing Inequality

Rebecca Morales
Frank Bonilla
editors

Sage Series on Race and Ethnic Relations

v o l u m e   7

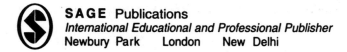

SAGE Publications
International Educational and Professional Publisher
Newbury Park   London   New Delhi

Research and editorial support for this book was provided by the Inter-University Program for Latino Research of the Ford Foundation. Editorial support was also provided by the Tomás Rivera Center and the Claremont Graduate School.

For information address:

 SAGE Publications, Inc.
2455 Teller Road
Newbury Park, California 91320

SAGE Publications Ltd.
6 Bonhill Street
London EC2A 4PU
United Kingdom

SAGE Publications India Pvt. Ltd.
M-32 Market
Greater Kailash I
New Delhi 110 048 India

Printed in the United States of America

Library of Congress Cataloging-in-Publication Data

Latinos in a changing U.S. economy : comparative perspectives on
  growing inequality / edited by Rebecca Morales, Frank Bonilla.
      p.   cm.—(Sage series on race and ethnic relations ; v. 7)
    Includes bibliographical references and index.
    ISBN 0-8039-4923-5.—ISBN 0-8039-4924-3 (pbk.)
    1. Hispanic Americans—Economic conditions.   I. Morales, Rebecca.
  II. Bonilla, Frank.   III. Title: Latinos in a changing U.S. economy.
  IV. Series.
  E184.S75L369   1993   92-40081
  330.973'09'08968—dc20   CIP

93 94 95 96 10 9 8 7 6 5 4 3 2 1

Sage Production Editor: Judith L. Hunter

Contents

Foreword

Latino Studies is a central concern of the Sage series on Race and Ethnic Relations. *Latinos in a Changing U.S. Economy: Comparative Perspectives on Growing Inequality,* by Rebecca Morales and Frank Bonilla, is the first of a subseries that we foresee as being on the cutting edge of Latino issues in the United States and in the world at large. Morales and Bonilla have organized and edited essays by an emerging generation of Latino scholars offering original theoretical insights regarding the economic plight of Latino populations in major U.S. cities.

There are at least two reasons why this volume will be a source cited for many years to come. First, its contributors share a conceptual framework in presenting, testing, and comparing three major theories of economic inequality as applied to Latino experiences: economic restructuring, human capital, and racial discrimination. We hope this comparative conceptual work will encourage other scholars in Latino Studies to enhance the needed development of a deep, sophisticated theoretical base in this critical field of studies of people of color. Second, through the various urban case studies the contributors present, the complex and paradoxical ethnic diversity that constitutes Latino experiences in the United States should encourage researchers and policymakers alike to develop a more comprehensive sense of the sociological, political, cultural, and economic meaning and consequences of being Latinos in the United States.

John H. Stanfield II
Series Editor

1

Restructuring and the New Inequality

Rebecca Morales
Frank Bonilla

It is now widely understood that one of the economic consequences of the unprecedented expansion of the 1980s in the United States is that the rich got richer while the middle class stagnated and the poor fell farther behind. This growing economic division left a deep imprint on society. Aggregate measures document not only growing income inequality, but also a massive transference of wealth. White family incomes and net worth rose, even as these indicators fell among African Americans and Latinos. The resources available to individuals more narrowly defined their ability to improve and invest in communities, thereby reinforcing spatial demarcations in the spread of economic and social inequality.

The reality that opportunities for upward mobility in the United States were not part of the economic boom of the 1980s raises serious questions. This reversal of an historical trend toward equality is leading some to ask whether it is the product of a decade of excess. The absence of tangible improvements, despite efforts to stimulate the economy, leads others to question whether the polarization is instead a harbinger of other more enduring problems. These are troubling prospects. We pose these questions from the perspective of Latinos, a group that realized demographic growth at nearly 10 times the rate of non-Hispanic whites and more than 5 times that of African Americans between 1980 and 1990. Members of this large and expanding segment of society are having to come to terms with the possibility that they may never reach parity with the average American without concerted efforts to change their circumstances that must involve the nation as a whole.

The problem lies in how to interpret the dilemma confronting Latinos in light of recent trends. There are several competing views. One is that the disparity felt by Latinos is a function of their own attributes, such as English language and educational limitations, or what is widely referred to as their human capital. Another is that the situation is the product of institutional constraints, such as failures of the educational system or of protections for workers' compensation or benefits reflected in a weakened social safety net. Yet a third line of reasoning is that structural barriers such as occupational shifts place enormous obstacles in the path to economic advances. The geographical distribution of wealth and poverty arguably adds another dimension. Urban segmentation is seen by some as generating the growth of an urban underclass, a dynamic that is compounded by international trends. Within minority neighborhoods, environmental blight and social disorganization further erode the prospects for economic recovery. To come to terms with these views, we begin our examination of the reality confronting Latinos with a question: To what can we attribute the persistent and growing inequality facing Latinos today?

THE PARADOX OF GROWTH AND INEQUALITY

Two significant developments add urgency to the question at hand: the nature of Latino population growth in the last decades, and qualitative aspects of job creation over the same period of time. Stated in other terms, recent changes in the supply and demand for labor have redefined the labor market. A systematic examination of Latinos in the United States reveals a high rate of population increase, from 6.4% of the population in 1980 to 9% by 1990 (Table 1.1). This is the result of above average rates of immigration and reproduction during the last two decades. The largest subgroup of Latinos are of Mexican origin (64%), followed by Central and South Americans (14%), Puerto Ricans (10%), others of Hispanic origin (7%), and Cubans (5%) (Table 1.2). Though Mexicans have traditionally dominated, the emerging prominence of Central and South Americans reflect recent migratory flows. As a whole, Latinos account for approximately 30% of the nation's population gain from 1980 to 1990.

Table 1.1 Resident Population Distribution for the United States by Race and Hispanic Origin, 1980 and 1990 (in thousands)

	1980		1990		Change	
	Number	*Percent*	*Number*	*Percent*	*Number*	*Percent*
Total Population	226,545.8	100.0	248,709.9	100.0	22,164.1	9.8
White	188,371.6	83.1	199,686.1	80.3	11,314.4	6.0
Black	26,495.0	11.7	29,986.1	12.1	3,491.0	13.5
Am. Indian*	1,420.4	0.6	1,959.2	0.8	538.8	37.9
Asian**	3,500.4	1.5	7,273.7	2.9	3,773.2	107.8
Other	6,758.3	3.0	9,804.8	3.9	3,046.5	45.1
Hispanic***	14,608.7	6.4	22,354.1	9.0	7,745.4	53.0

SOURCE: U.S. Bureau of the Census, *Current Population Survey* (March 1991).
* American Indian, Eskimo, or Aleut.
** Asian or Pacific Islander. The 1980 number for Asians or Pacific Islanders shown in this table is not entirely comparable with the 1990 count. The 1980 count of 3,500,439 Asians or Pacific Islanders based on 100% tabulations includes only the nine specific Asian or Pacific groups listed separately in the 1980 race item. The 1980 total Asian or Pacific Islander population of 3,726,440 from sample tabulations is comparable to the 1990 count; these figures include groups not listed separately in the race item on the 1980 census form.
*** Persons of Hispanic origin can be of any race.

The growth of Latinos has coincided with an unusual increase in labor supply due to high numbers of women, youth, and immigrant entrants. The labor force participation rates of women rose from 42% in 1969 to 57% in 1989 nationwide. Women comprised 45% of the nation's civilian labor force in 1989, and account for 59% of the net growth experienced since 1969. Baby boomers, or the generation born after World War II, constitute another major group of new entrants into the labor force.

Table 1.2 Persons of Hispanic Origin, 1980 and 1990 (in thousands)

	1980		1990	
	Number	*Percent*	*Number*	*Percent*
Total Hispanic Population	14,608.7	100.0	22,354.1	100.00
Mexican Origin	8,736.0	59.8	13,305	64.00
Puerto Rican Origin	2,016.0	13.8	2,180	10.49
Cuban Origin	803.5	5.5	1,014	4.87
Central and South American Origin	1,051.8	7.2	2,842	13.67
Other Hispanic	2,001.4	13.7	1,437	6.91

SOURCE: U.S. Bureau of the Census, *Current Population Survey* (March 1991).

Fewer than 10 million workers between the ages of 20 and 24 entered the labor force in 1969, in contrast to nearly 16 million in 1979 (by 1987 this group had declined to 15 million). A third major group enlarging the work force are recent immigrants. Immigrants comprised 19% of the net addition to the labor force between 1970 and 1980. This level of contribution compares to the last century, when immigrants entered the industrial economy at rates of 23% in the 1850s, 21% in the 1880s, and 20% during the 1900s (Greenwood & McDowell, 1986). Throughout the 1980s, the U.S. population grew by over one-half million additional immigrants each year.

As recent immigrants and others entered the work force, they were until recently absorbed into a growth economy. Throughout the 1970s, the number of jobs increased by one fourth (28%) from 70.4 million in 1969 to 89.8 million in 1979. During the 1980s, total jobs grew by another 21%, reaching 108.6 million in 1989—an expansion unparalleled in any other industrialized nation. In contrast to prior decades, the 1990s opened with threatening intimations of prolonged recession and unemployment. Yet based on past performance, a renewed impetus toward a robust economy was not foreclosed.

The issue is not the sheer number of jobs, however, but the quality of employment, opportunities for upward mobility, and the nature of economic well-being. One early indicator of a troubled job market came when unemployment began to stabilize at higher than expected levels. In contrast to the 1970s, when 5% unemployment was considered high, the average annual unemployment rate in the 1980s was more than 7%, a rate higher than for all but 2 of the nearly 30 years between 1950 and 1979 (Mead, 1991).

Research also indicates that since the 1970s, national low-wage employment rose and middle-strata jobs declined (Carnoy, Daley, & Hinojosa Ojeda, 1990b; Harrison, 1988; Harrison & Bluestone, 1988). The change in employment structure occurred in the wake of a sectoral shift (Table 1.3). Manufacturing employment dropped 3% from 1969 to 1989 even as jobs in the service sector grew by 93%.[1] The net result is that manufacturing declined in relative importance from 29% of all jobs to 19% while services increased from 42% to 54%. The structural changes adversely affected white men, minority men and women, youths, and full-time as well as part-time workers in all parts of the country (Harrison & Bluestone, 1988).

Table 1.3 U.S. Employment Structure, 1979 and 1987

	1979	*1987*
Total (thousands)	95,387	109,854
Agriculture/Mining	4.0%	3.6%
Industry	29.0%	24.8%
Construction	6.1%	6.2%
Nondurable Manufacturing	7.2%	6.0%
Durable Manufacturing	12.3%	9.4%
Information & Knowledge	3.4%	3.2%
Services	67.0%	71.6%
Information & Knowledge	25.2%	27.7%
Other Services	41.8%	43.9%

SOURCE: Based on categories and data tabulated by Applebaum and Schettkat (1989, Table 2.1, p. 428).

The nature of jobs coming out of the restructuring disadvantaged the newest groups to enter the work force. In part, this is because casual, part-time jobs, or those defined as less than 35 hours per week, constituted nearly one quarter of net job creation (Applebaum & Schettkat, 1989). Much of the increase in part-time employment since 1979 has been involuntary. In March 1991, approximately 6 million persons, or 29% of the 21 million part-time workers (comprising 17% of the U.S. work force), held part-time jobs involuntarily. U.S. Labor Department statistics indicate that the number of involuntary part-time workers rose by 75% over the last 15 years and accounted for more than 40% of the growth of part-time labor in the 1980s. Part-time employment was particularly noticeable in social welfare services, personal and recreation services, and retail trade, where nearly one third of employment was part-time, and in eating and drinking places and hotels where the proportion was 40% (Applebaum & Schettkat, 1989). The growth of jobs in service industries with a high concentration of part-time work, combined with a decline in full-time work in manufacturing, led to an overall rise of part-time employment. Among those most highly affected by the expansion of part-time work have been women, who constitute 52.8% of the service industry work force, along with youths, minorities, and immigrants (Table 1.4).

Employment throughout the 1980s has also been characterized by a sharp decline in real wages (Figure 1.1). Lower wages resulted from the

Table 1.4 Labor Force Characteristics, 1987

	Percent Less Than 35 Hrs	Percent Female
Total	18.2	45.0
Agriculture/Mining	18.7	18.7
Industry	6.1	16.9
Construction	9.6	8.4
Nondurable Manufacturing	4.9	40.8
Durable Manufacturing	3.6	25.1
Information & Knowledge	16.5	40.7
Services	22.4	52.8
Information & Knowledge	16.5	54.5
Other Services	26.1	51.6

SOURCE: Based on categories and data tabulated by Applebaum and Schettkat (1989, Tables 2.4 and 2.5, pp. 431, 432).

replacement of high-wage manufacturing by lower paying service employment and increase of less stable jobs, but also from a stationary minimum wage. In 1981, the federal minimum wage was set at $3.35 per hour, and did not change until 1990. Because the minimum wage is set in nominal terms, inflation eroded its value over time. In 1991, a full-time minimum-wage worker earned $8,840 per year, which was 3% below the federal poverty level for a family of three and 26% below the poverty level for a family of four. From 1973 to 1990 the average weekly wage dropped from $315 to $258 (inflation-adjusted to 1982 dollars), thereby erasing half of the gains in real wages made since World War II (Mead, 1990, 1991).

Real wages fell more rapidly during recessions and never fully recovered during expansions (Burtless, 1991). With each setback, wages became more unequally distributed. The growing inequality of wages is captured in statistics that show that from 1979 to 1987, real wages of male workers between the ages of 25 and 64 declined an average of 2% per year among the bottom one fifth of the wage distribution, but increased by 0.5% among those in the highest one fifth (Burtless, 1991). For females the data are slightly less negative, but similar in outcome.

The nature of the new employment structure has hurt both whites and minorities, though the burden has been far greater for people of color.

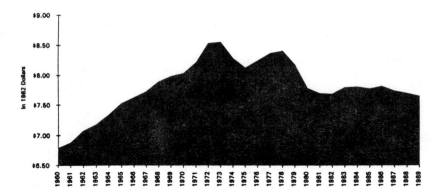

Figure 1.1. Real Wages, United States, 1960-1989
SOURCE: Bureau of Labor Statistics, Bulletin 2370, March 1991.

Nearly 60% of net new employment since 1979 held by all workers paid poverty level wages, yet at the other extreme, 17.6% of net new white employment was in jobs that pay three times the poverty level, as opposed to only 5.4% of the black increment of employment (Harrison, 1988).[2] Racial differences are also apparent among displaced workers. Blacks were displaced or permanently laid off for economic reasons at a much higher rate than whites (Hamermesh, 1987), and spent twice as much time without a job (Addison & Portugal, 1987). Among those who found work, minorities lost more ground in terms of earnings than whites (Ong, 1990).

With lower overall returns to employment, family incomes have become more unequal. From 1979 to 1989, families in the lowest one fifth of the income distribution faced a decline of real income while those in the top 20% enjoyed an average annual income growth of 12%, and 17% among the top 5% (Burtless, 1991). The net worth of these income groups translated into a growing wealth gap. Measured as the difference between families' total assets (including real estate, checking and savings accounts, certificates of deposit, and stocks and bonds) and total debts, the net worth of upper-income Americans rose from 1983 to 1989 but fell among the poor (Table 1.5). Those earning $50,000 or

Table 1.5 The Widening Gap

| | 1983 | | 1989 | |
Family Income	Percent of Families	Net Worth Median*	Percent of Families	Net Worth Median*
Less than $10,000	19	$3,800	20	$2,300
$10,000-19,999	23	$19,300	20	$27,100
$20,000-29,999	19	$36,000	17	$37,000
$30,000-49,999	23	$67,700	23	$69,200
$50,000 and up	17	$176,100	20	$185,600

* Half the families lie above and half the families lie below the this figure.
SOURCE: Federal Reserve Board.

more per year saw their net worth rise from $176,100 in 1983 to $185,600 in 1989; those earning less than $10,000 saw it decline from $3,800 to $2,300. Affluent Americans with money to invest in certificates of deposit paying high interest, growth stocks, or appreciating homes made significant gains. According to a 1992 study of the Federal Reserve Board, the value of homes among the well-off rose more rapidly than for others. For families earning $50,000 or more, the average value of their home rose from $112,100 in 1983 to $130,000 in 1989, even as those earning between $30,000 and $50,000 realized almost no gain, as their home value rose from $74,700 to only $75,000 in the same period (Kennickell & Shack-Marquez, 1992). Thus, the inequality of family incomes intensified the inequality across communities.

The concentration of wealth has been mirrored by a rise in poverty. In 1990, 13.5% or 33.6 million persons lived below the poverty line (U.S. Bureau of the Census, 1991). Poverty throughout the 1980s approximated levels evident in the mid-sixties when the "war on poverty" was declared in the United States (Figure 1.2). For the most part, the poor consist of minimum-wage earners unable to make subsistence wages, involuntary part-time workers, and the unemployed.

This profile of economic distress might have been relieved through income transfer payments, but instead it was reinforced by a decline in social program expenditures. Throughout the 1980s, a 55% cut of budgetary allocations to federal social programs sharply reduced the

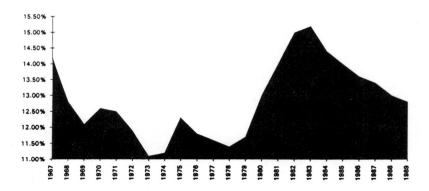

Figure 1.2. Persons Below Poverty, 1967-1989
SOURCE: U.S. Department of Commerce, Poverty in the United States, 1988-1989, No. 171.

social safety net for low-income persons (Table 1.6), even as deregulation made the remaining jobs more hazardous and less secure.

The problem has been further compounded by locational patterns.
Finding their way into the job market has become harder for many urban
dwelling poor and minorities due to the suburbanization of both ser-
vice-oriented and goods-producing industries; a lack of replacement of
entry level, low-skill, or blue-collar employment in central cities; and
an increase of managerial, professional, technical, and administrative
jobs in city centers (Kasarda, 1989). The resulting spatial mismatch of
jobs to the skill level of the work force has meant that poorly educated
minorities residing in city centers have less access to employment,
thereby leading to an increase in unemployment rates (Farley, 1987a;
Kasarda, 1989). The selective out-migration of better educated minorities from the city center compounds the urban concentration of those
least able to take advantage of the changing job patterns (Grier & Grier,
1988).

The paradox of economic growth and income inequality is multi-
dimensional. At one level it is an outcome of economic restructuring.
When probed deeper, the situation appears to be tied to problems of
greater job instability, lower wages, declining social services, the urban

Table 1.6 Changes in Low-Income Discretionary Programs, FY 1981-1989 (in millions of dollars)

Discretionary Low-Income Programs	FY 1981 Budget Authority*	FY 1981 Levels, Adjusted for Inflation**	FY 1989 Budget Authority	Change FY 1981-89 After Inflation	Percent Change After Inflation
Child Welfare Services	$173	$239	$247	$8	3.5%
Commodity Supplemental Food Program	27	37	50	13	34.3
Community Development Block Grant	3,695	5,096	3,000	−2,096	−41.1
Community Services Block Grant	525	724	378	−346	−47.8
Compensatory Education (Chapter 1)	3,545	4,889	4,579	−310	−6.3
Emergency Food and Shelter	0	0	114	114	NA
Financial Aid for Needy Students	3,802	5,244	5,814	570	10.9
Food Donations	129	178	199	21	11.9
Head Start	814	1,123	1,235	112	10.0
Health Care Services					
Community Health Centers	325	448	415	−33	−7.4
Health Care for the Homeless	0	0	15	15	NA
Immunizations	31	43	142	99	232.1
Infant Mortality Initiative	0	0	21	21	NA
Maternal & Child Health	457	630	554	−76	−12.1
Migrant Health	43	59	46	−13	−22.4
Higher Education Programs (TRIOs)	160	221	219	−2	−0.8
Homeless Shelter Programs	0	0	128	128	NA
Housing Assistance for the Elderly	797	1,099	480	−619	−56.3
Indian Education	355	490	341	−149	−30.4
Indian Health	692	954	1,082	128	13.4
Legal Services	321	443	309	−134	−30.2
Low-Income Energy Assistance	1,850	2,552	1,383	−1,169	−45.8
Low-Income Weatherization	175	241	161	−80	−33.3
Older Americans Employment	277	382	344	−38	−10.0
Public Housing Operating Subsidies	1,071	1,477	1,618	141	9.5
Social Services Block Grant (Title XX)***	2,991	4,125	2,700	−1,425	−34.5
Subsidized Housing	30,170	41,610	7,539	−34,071	−81.9
Temporary Emergency Food Assistance	0	0	50	50	NA
Training and Employment Services	9,106	12,559	3,786	−8,773	−69.9
Work Incentive Program (WIN)	365	503	91	−412	−81.9
WIC	900	1,241	1,929	688	55.4

continued

Table 1.6 Continued

Discretionary Low-Income Programs	FY 1981 Budget Authority*	FY 1981 Levels, Adjusted for Inflation**	FY 1989 Budget Authority	Change FY 1981-89 After Inflation	Percent Change After Inflation
Total discretionary programs with subsidized housing	$62,796	$86,608	$38,969	−$47,639	−55.0%
Total discretionary programs without subsidized housing	$32,626	$44,998	$31,430	−$13,567	−30.2%

SOURCE: Center on Budget and Policy Priorities, "Shortchanged: Recent Developments in Hispanic Poverty, Income and Employment," Washington, DC, November 1988.

*FY1981 budget authority levels at the start of the Reagan administration, prior to rescissions implemented by the administration in spring 1981. Budget authority is the total amount of funding that is appropriated by Congress each year. In some cases, funds that are appropriated may not be entirely spent in that year and may be spread out over a number of years.

**Inflation from FY1981 to FY1989 is calculated using CPI-U, FY1988/FY1981, and assumes a 4.8% inflation factor for FY1989, as reflected in the Congressional Budget Office's August 1988 forecast. Total inflation adjustment for FY1981 to FY1989 is 37.92%.

***Although the social services block grant (SSBG) is sometimes regarded as a "capped entitlement," the SSBG are limited to those actually appropriated. If Congress appropriates less than the authorized level, only the amount appropriated is actually provided.

concentration of less educated minorities and immigrants, a spatial mismatch of jobs to workers, and a process of environmental deterioration. In the face of these trends, Latinos entering the labor market in the last decade have encountered difficult conditions. For many, the outcome has been unstable employment, diminished job opportunities, and extreme impoverishment.

THE LATINO PROFILE

Latinos in the United States display several distinct characteristics: high rates of immigration and reproduction, low levels of education, high rates of urbanization, concentration in low-paying jobs, and high levels of poverty. These traits are both cause and consequence of the restructuring.

The U.S. Bureau of the Census reports that during the 1980s the Hispanic population increased by 34%, as opposed to 7% for the non-Hispanic population. Immigration is a major contributor, with approximately one half of the growth resulting from net migration (U.S. Bureau of the Census, 1988a). Reproduction is also high, as shown in an overall fertility rate among Hispanic women of 106 births per 1,000 women as opposed to 67 for non-Hispanic women (U.S. Bureau of the Census, 1988b). The high rates of immigration and reproduction are reflected in a population that is younger than that of the nation as a whole. Latinos maintain a median age of 25 years against a national median of 32 years.

Youth and immigrant status have contributed to a less educated population. In 1986, only half of adults 25 and older were high school graduates, as compared to more than three fourths of all whites and more than three fifths of African Americans. Only 1 in 10 Latinos was a college graduate (National Council of La Raza, 1990a). In the decade from 1980 to 1990, the white population realized an increase in college enrollment from 31.8% to 39.4%, and African Americans saw a gain from 27.6% to 33.0%, but Latinos suffered a decline from 29.8% to 29.0% (Carter & Wilson, 1992). Therefore, this group has entered the labor force with fewer acquired skills than the average for the nation.

Latinos are also an overwhelmingly urban population. Their rates of urbanization (90%) far exceed those for the nation as a whole (75%), and they are clustered in the most dynamic metropolitan areas of the United States, such as Los Angeles and New York, and those areas most exposed to international influences, such as Miami (Table 1.7). As a consequence, their concerns are integrally tied to those of the nation's metropolises, though agro-rural issues remain important (Rochin & de la Torre, 1992).

Within these labor markets, Latinos reveal low occupational attainment. In 1988, Latino men were more likely to be employed as production workers and less likely to be managers than the population as a whole, and Latinas were more likely to be operators or in service occupations and less likely to be employed in managerial or technical occupations than the general population (Table 1.8). Low-wage occupational concentration is particularly evident among Mexicans and Puerto Ricans, though it exists among all subgroups. Latinos are not only low-wage workers, but after adjusting for inflation, they have lost ground with respect to wages in recent years. Latino men averaged $49 per year *less* in 1987 than in 1978. In part this was because 23.8% of these Latino men were minimum-wage workers (Center on Budget and Policy Priorities, 1988).

Table 1.7 Population of Hispanic Origin Ranked by Metropolitan Area, 1980 and 1990 (in thousands)

	1980	*1990*
Los Angeles	2,766	4,779
New York	2,045	2,778
Miami	627	1,062
San Francisco	649	970
Chicago	620	893
Houston	446	772
San Antonio	485	620
Dallas	248	519
San Diego	275	511
El Paso	297	412
Phoenix	199	345
McAllen	230	327
Fresno	151	237
Denver	174	226
Philadelphia	158	226
Washington, D.C.	95	225
Brownsville	162	213
Boston	92	193
Corpus Christi	148	182
Albuquerque	155	178
Sacramento	106	172
Tucson	111	163
Austin	94	160
Bakersfield	87	152
Tampa	80	139
Laredo	91	125
Visalia	73	120
Salinas	75	120
Stockton	67	113
Santa Barbara	55	98
Orlando	26	96
Detroit	77	91
Las Vegas	35	83
Modesto	40	81
Las Cruces	50	76
Hartford	44	76
Seattle	45	76
West Palm Beach	29	67
Salt Lake City	45	62
Milwaukee	42	60

SOURCE: U.S. Census, *Statistical Abstract of the United States*, 1991, p. 32-36. For consolidated metropolitan areas where applicable.

Table 1.8 Occupational Characteristics of All Persons and Persons of Hispanic Origin, March 1988 (in thousands)

Occupation	Total Population	Total Hispanic	Mexican	Hispanic Subgroups Puerto Rican	Cuban	C. & S. American	Other Hispanic
Males	61,538	4,719	2,945	458	319	624	373
Percent	100.0	100.0	100.0	100.0	100.0	100.0	100.0
Manag/Prof.	26.2	13.0	10.3	15.1	23.7	12.1	23.5
Tech/Sales/Adm.	19.9	15.4	12.3	16.6	27.8	20.5	18.9
Service Occ.	9.4	14.8	13.3	19.0	10.7	21.8	13.6
Farm/For/Fish.	4.1	8.2	11.5	1.8	1.6	4.1	2.0
Prec. Prod/Craft	19.2	20.5	22.1	17.5	15.0	19.7	17.8
Oper/Fabr/Lab.	20.9	28.1	30.4	30.0	21.1	21.9	24.2
Females	51,027	3,224	1,831	337	230	538	287
Percent	100.0	100.0	100.0	100.0	100.0	100.0	100.0
Manag/Prof.	25.3	15.7	12.6	20.5	27.3	14.1	23.2
Tech/Sales/Adm.	45.1	41.1	41.7	44.7	41.8	37.9	37.8
Service Occ.	17.7	21.7	21.9	15.3	13.0	28.4	22.5
Farm/For/Fish.	0.9	1.5	2.1	—	—	0.2	2.6
Prec. Prod/Craft	2.3	3.5	3.6	3.6	3.2	3.4	2.9
Oper/Fabr/Lab.	8.8	16.6	18.0	15.8	14.7	16.0	11.0

SOURCE: U.S. Bureau of the Census (1988a).
NOTE: Data on occupational groups reflect characteristics of the population for March of the respective survey year and are not adjusted for seasonal change. Data released by the U. S. Department of Labor, Bureau of Labor Statistics, may not agree entirely with data shown due to differences in methodological procedures and seasonal adjustment of the data.

These forces translate into low average incomes. The average family income among Latinos fell by 12.7% from 1978 to 1982 after adjusting for inflation (a drop of $1,585), compared to 9.5% among white families, and 15.5% among African Americans. In the period of economic recovery from 1982 to 1987, the average income of white families grew by 11.4%, and 13% among African Americans, but only 6.3% among Latinos (Center on Budget and Policy Priorities, 1988). In 1987, 6 out of every 10 Latino families were among the poorest two fifths of the total population, but only 1 in 10 was among the wealthiest one fifth (Center on Budget and Policy Priorities, 1988). Latinos are clearly overrepresented at the economic bottom.

Poverty has thus become a pressing issue. From 1978 to 1987, Latino poverty rose nearly one third, from 21.6% to 28.2%. By contrast, the poverty rates for both whites and African Americans reflected a much smaller increase (from 8.7% to 10.5% for whites and from 30.6% to 33.1% for African-Americans). With each recession, Latinos fell further into poverty (Center on Budget and Policy Priorities, 1988).

Though poverty and inequality are concerns shared by all Latinos, they are of greatest immediacy for Puerto Ricans, Mexicans, and certain recent immigrant groups such as Dominicans. Puerto Ricans display the greatest distress with 40.3% classified as poor in 1987, the highest rate for any racial or ethnic group in the nation. This was followed by Mexicans at 28.3%, up from the 1978 level of 20.6%. Family poverty rates were 37.9% for Puerto Ricans, and 25.5% for Mexicans, followed by Other Hispanics (26.1%), Central and South Americans (18.9%), and Cubans (13.8%).

Against this profile, we can start to construct a logic for Latino impoverishment and low economic standing. According to prevailing views, impoverishment among many is the result of unemployment. In 1991 when the unemployment rate for the nation as a whole was 6.7%, it was 9.4% for Hispanics. Among the subgroups, these figures were 11.8% for Puerto Ricans, 9.6% for Mexicans, 8.5% for Cubans, and 8.2% for Other Hispanics. Labor force participation rates, a rough proxy for discouraged workers, present a mixed picture because they are higher than the national average among all subgroups except Puerto Ricans, for whom work force attachment has become a serious issue. In addition, poverty is increasingly linked with single-parent families. Approximately half of the Hispanic families living below the poverty level are headed by women. This problem is most apparent among Puerto Ricans, with the highest rate of families headed by females (43%).

For those still in the work force, persistent poverty appears to be directly linked to the erosion of wages, the nature of Latino employment, and cutbacks in government assistance—or structural and institutional causes—in concert with certain specific attributes of this population that shape their employability—or aspects of human capital. These factors interact to disadvantage Latinos as they enter the work force and provide few options for improving the situation.

Thus, because of Latino concentration in low-wage jobs, erosion of the minimum wage affected Latinos more severely than the general population. The proliferation of low-wage employment and loss of opportunities for upward mobility created structural barriers to advancement (Harrison

Table 1.9   Size of Budget Cuts in Nonentitlement Programs With High Hispanic
Participation

Program	Reductions in Appropriations Levels FY1981-FY1989	Percentage of Participants Who Are Hispanic
Public Service Employment (CETA)	−100.0%	14.3%
Subsidized Housing	−81.9	11.0
Work Incentive Program (WIN)	−81.9	9.0
Training & Employment Services	−69.9	10.5
Low-Income Energy Assistance	−45.8	9.0
Legal Services	−30.2	17.8

SOURCE: Center on Budget and Policy Priorities, "Shortchanged: Recent Developments in Hispanic
Poverty, Income and Employment, " Washington, DC, November 1988.

& Bluestone, 1988). These barriers were aggravated by unresolved
problems of wage discrimination (Ong, 1990).

Further, layered upon the problematic transformation of an economy
and society are the limitations of the people themselves. Low educational status has been repeatedly linked to poor economic performance
among Latinos (Carnoy et al., 1990a). The influx of new immigrants
with low educational attainment, combined with the failure of schools
to meet the needs of Latino students and inadequate on-the-job training,
all contribute to wage and income polarization.

And because Latinos are largely urbanized, they disproportionately
feel the effects of the suburbanization of better paying jobs, and loss of
support from government programs and social expenditures upon urban
areas. Sharp federal program cuts throughout the 1980s had their most
detrimental effect on low-income households. As Latinos constitute
9%-17% of the beneficiaries of low-income programs (or twice their
level of representation in the population) they were about twice as likely
to feel the loss as the population as a whole (Table 1.9) (Center on
Budget and Policy Priorities, 1988). Though the burden of cushioning
extreme impoverishment was increasingly transferred to the local level,
cities were less equipped to handle the problem, so needs went largely
unmet.

Although seeking to unravel the contributing factors provides significant insight into the situation, many questions remain unanswered.
Specifically to be addressed in this volume are: (a) Is there evidence of
a *persistent* and *growing* inequality in the socioeconomic position of

Latinos after controlling for demographic and other differentials such as cyclical movements in the economy? (b) To what extent can the changing socioeconomic position of Latinos be attributed to the way in which they participated in the *recent* transformations of industrial and occupational structures in the United States? The primary issue as posed in these terms is whether the interaction of industrial restructuring and massive immigration resulted in a onetime economic setback, or whether the problem is actually more enduring. Here the history of Latino migration and immigration offers some needed points of reference.

A LEGACY OF MIGRANTS AND IMMIGRANTS

Each of the major Latino groups may be said to exemplify a particular dimension of the polarizing impact of the ongoing economic restructuring. To simplify the distinctions, Mexicans, especially recent immigrants, typify a pattern of high participation with low wages, generally at earnings below official poverty standards. Puerto Ricans, with the highest proportion of persons living in poverty, exemplify exclusion or withdrawal from formal labor markets and the highest rates of welfare dependency and family disruption. Cubans embody a privileged migration in terms of class, occupational composition, and the extraordinary support for the postrevolution exodus, though they increasingly reflect the composition of other Latino groups with successive immigrant waves. The means of incorporation into the labor market for the different groups are outcomes of distinct histories of migration and immigration.

Mexicans. The modern history of Mexican immigration can be understood as consisting of two broad periods. The first began at the turn of the century and continued to the mid-sixties. The second began in the mid-sixties and continues to the present. The first period was one of extreme fluctuations, with population flows peaking during periods of high labor demand in the United States, often secured by contractual agreements, and declining during downturns, at times through mandated repatriation programs. Immigration became particularly noticeable prior to the Mexican Revolution (1910-1921), and accelerated after its outbreak. Nearly 10% of Mexico's population fled the nation between 1900 and 1930 (Cross & Sandos, 1981). Workers were frequently recruited to work in the United States in construction or railroads in such places as Chicago or Kansas City and by the 1920s had became the backbone of the work force in agriculture, meat packing, brickyards, and canneries in many parts of the United States (Hoffman, 1974). However, after the stock market crash of 1929, national and local policies shifted to denying further entry to new Mexican immigrants and repatriating those already here. Between 1929 and 1937, over 458,000 Mexicans were repatriated (Hoffman, 1974).

The situation was reversed during World War II when a severe labor shortage once again made labor recruitment appealing. The Bracero Program (1942-1964) operated as a contract labor program intended to relieve the shortage in agriculture; after the war, and as the economy continued to expand, many workers found illegal employment in manufacturing. The resulting rise of undocumented workers came to a temporary halt when the United States entered a recession after the Korean War (1950-1953). In a repatriation drive labeled Operation Wetback, some 1,075,168 Mexicans were deported in 1954, and 242,608 in 1955 (Acuna, 1984; Kiser & Kiser, 1979).

Termination of the Bracero Program marks the beginning of the second period of immigration. The earlier program was replaced by the Border Industrialization Program in Mexico (1965 to present), which was intended to direct displaced braceros and undocumented workers into export platform industries called *maquiladoras*. Instead, the legacy of fluctuating immigration laid the groundwork for using immigrant labor as an economic buffer in the United States to be easily accessed during times of economic stress (Morales, 1983; Morales & Tamayo, 1992). Since the mid-sixties, growing unemployment in Mexico coupled with the prospect of employment in the United States precipitated a high and steady flow of immigration, to a large extent comprised of undocumented persons attracted to declining industries and low-wage jobs (Cornelius, 1992).

Puerto Ricans: Among Puerto Ricans, migration reflects the dependent relationship of the island, first as a United States possession in 1898, and eventually as a semiautonomous commonwealth in 1952. This status resulted in second-class citizenship for residents, who maintain no national representation in the U.S. Congress and cannot vote for the presidency, but are linked by a common currency and the unrestricted access of U.S. capital into Puerto Rico and of Puerto Rican residents into the United States.

Initial migration from Puerto Rico was small, but a strong, circular migration developed and accelerated after World War II with the economic expansion of the United States followed by failed efforts of rapid industrialization in Puerto Rico (Bean & Tienda, 1987; F. Bonilla,

1992). Despite implementation of Operation Bootstrap (1948-1965), a program designed to modernize the plantation economy, attainable levels of industrial growth failed to materially reduce unemployment among the growing population. This policy and its aftermath precipitated a migratory flow that grew from an annual average of 18,700 between 1940 and 1950, to 41,200 between 1950 and 1960, and then dropped to 15,000 between 1960 and 1970 (Centro de Estudios Puertorriqueños, 1979).

The postwar migrants were attracted to the main industrial centers of the eastern seaboard, especially New York, where they entered blue-collar jobs in the textile and garment industries. Following the recent industrial restructuring on the island as well as in the United States, those lacking transferable skills and complementary training were left in poverty, permanently displaced, and with few options beyond migration from Puerto Rico to the U.S. mainland (Meléndez, 1987). The outcome has been the worst indices of unemployment, labor force participation, and poverty among Latinos, and little recourse for influencing national policies regarding relocation assistance, social welfare, or economic development.

Cubans. Cuban immigration has been dominated by waves of political refugees, beginning with a massive influx after the 1959 revolution. Cubans in the United States grew from 34,000 persons in 1950 to 79,000 in 1960, and again to more than 500,000 in 1970. Cuba imposed restrictions on persons seeking asylum in the United States during the 1970s, so the number of Cubans in the United States (approximately 831,000 in 1980) grew thereafter largely due to natural increase. Shortly after the census enumeration in 1980, a second major wave of over 125,000 refugees was released during the Mariel incident.

With each successive group, the composition of immigrants became poorer and less skilled. Whereas the prerevolution and early postrevolution immigrants consisted of business and intellectual elites with their wealth intact, those arriving after the Bay of Pigs invasion were economically dispossessed, less educated, and more likely to consist of women, children, and students. In contrast to other Latino groups, Cubans were recipients of government resettlement assistance. Aid included job training, job placement, professional recertification, research and teaching programs, and local school reimbursement policies (Rogg, 1974). A Cuban Resettlement program was instituted in 1967 to prevent urban concentration, but although over 60% of the population dispersed, most (66%) had returned to Miami or the New York metropolitan area by 1970.

The complex composition of Cuban immigration has resulted in multiple forms of incorporation into U.S. society. Prerevolution immigrants experienced downward occupational standing, despite their greater wealth base (Massey, 1983). In contrast, early postrevolution refugees, who saw their stay as temporary, developed tight-knit communities of ethnically segregated enclaves. Within the enclave, job mobility and remuneration were more sheltered than in the nation's peripheral industries. The enclave allowed residents to build on their entrepreneurial and professional talents to a larger extent than has been evident among other Latino groups. It also provided a base for building on the communities' wealth (Portes & Bach, 1985). More recent immigrants have suffered to a greater extent due to job losses created by the restructuring.

Other Latinos. In recent years, economic refugees from the Caribbean, political refugees from Central America, and immigrants from the remainder of Latin America have increased in number. U.S. military involvement in Central America has led to a sharp rise of immigration from this area, consisting of persons with a wide range of backgrounds. At least two immigrant streams have surfaced: one group consisting of the poor and dispossessed, and another of political refugees. Many immigrants from the Caribbean are the product of repressive regimes and disarticulated low-wage service and light-industrial employment. In a repeat of previous history, the economically displaced immigrants appear to be following in the footsteps of Puerto Ricans and Mexicans. In some cases they are becoming the newest wave of low-wage urban labor. But certain elites, benefiting from refugee status, have followed the Cuban mode of incorporation, even replicating the creation of immigrant enclaves.

Repeated patterns of migration and immigration, especially among Puerto Ricans and Mexicans, reveal the nature of the adjustment mechanism immigrants have historically supplied to the economy. Unlike notions of labor absorption into a "melting pot" during periods of economic expansion and of immigrant succession, the role here was initially one of cushioning the economy during periodic fluctuations. This function then changed to one of assisting in the transition of the restructured economy, which required removal of the cushion and a more universal downward pressure on labor. With the transformation, a process of adjustment that was once peripheral to the workings of the labor market has now become a more central concern.

INTERPRETING THE TRENDS

The increasingly obvious economic weakness threatens the most vulnerable segments of society. Despite employment growth, the GNP growth rate was lower in the 1980s than during any decade since the 1930s, and productivity grew at only one third the rate it had reached in the 1960s. Factory usage, or capacity utilization, has been on the decline since the 1960s, pointing to deteriorating economic performance. Reinvestment in productive capacity and social infrastructure needed to restore competitive strengths has not occurred. In the absence of policies aimed at industrial investment or technological innovation to guide balanced growth, firms have responded by seeking to lower the cost of labor, and governments have responded by providing complementary legislative mechanisms, each with the objective of increasing productivity.

Productivity is measured as the value of output per unit of input, such as labor or technology. Productivity growth is hardly a static concept and requires constant investment to raise quality, improve efficiency, or lower the market response time. It is also the primary determinant of national per capita income, and hence, the standard of living. In the words of the economist Michael Porter:

> The productivity of human resources determines their wages, while the productivity with which capital is employed determines the return it earns for its holders. High productivity . . . supports high levels of income. It also creates the national income that is taxed to pay for public services which again boosts the standard of living. The capacity to be highly productive also allows a nation's firms to meet stringent social standards which improve the standard of living, such as in health and safety, equal opportunity, and environmental impact. (1990, p. 6)

Low-cost labor, declining social infrastructure, deregulation, environmental degradation, and a "favorable" exchange rate have all contributed to an aura of growth without a sustainable base. The problem is that as long as cheap labor and other cost-cutting measures that lead to economically disenfranchised communities are the driving mechanisms to economic expansion, lasting productivity cannot be achieved.

In this context, Latinos have historically constituted a perversely appropriated stock of low-cost, easily expendable labor (Sassen, 1988). This function was not predicated on citizenship or language, as some of the most impoverished were citizens and English speakers. Rather it was an issue of redefining the workings of the labor market to make it more responsive to the competitive climate at the expense of Latino and other low-wage labor. Though this economic strategy was, in fact, fed by high rates of immigration, and by high numbers of new Latino entrants into the labor force, it was reinforced by national policies designed to encourage unfettered market competition through notions of labor market flexibility. This concept of flexibility, which could be applied selectively prior to the most recent restructuring, is universal today.

TOWARD A THEORETICAL UNDERSTANDING OF THE NEW INEQUALITY

Labor market flexibility refers to the breakdown of rigidities in an economy that hinder adjustments in wages, hours, and work relations. According to Harrison and Bluestone (1987), a flexible workplace is one where "the ability to exercise greater control over the conditions of work (including wages) [exist] so as to restore private profits in an increasingly competitive world" (p. 2). The observation of Guy Standing of the International Labour Organisation is that flexibility is "little more than a euphemism for labour *insecurity*" (p. 6). Flexibility can be expressed through wage setting, numerical determinations, functional definitions, and time worked (Rosenberg, 1989). Breaking up the so-called rigidities of a given society has generally entailed destruction of conventions that protected certain segments of society. The economist Samuel Rosenberg (1989) notes, "Behind *flexibility* lies the more serious question of the relative balance of power between different groups in society. Those critical of the whole notion of flexibility argue . . . that it really calls for increasing the autonomy and freedom of action of the most powerful groups in society, weakening the welfare state, and 'placing the burden of adjustment on the shoulders of the weakest'"(p. 8).

Manipulation of the labor force, whether directly through immigration policies, or indirectly through benign neglect of the level of the minimum wage relative to rising costs of living, or more recently through relaxed environmental standards, has historically required state intervention. In the last two decades this has taken the form of deregulating the labor market to eliminate "rigidities" and approximate a purely competitive labor market. This occurred through redefinition of the minimum wage, employment benefits, and immigration law. Placed in the contradictory role of trying to preserve its productive base while simultaneously weakening access to power created by the welfare state, the United States adopted policies that effectively shifted the burden of adjustment onto such groups as immigrants, women, and minorities (Offe, 1984). The resulting growing social inequality, second-class citizenship, and poverty traps were dimensions of "flexibility" of the restructured economy that depended on low-wage labor.

The insecurity that permeated employment filtered out to the larger society. Those who were hardest hit were the destitute and isolated persons without social anchorage that William J. Wilson designated the "underclass" (W. J. Wilson, 1987). The underclass formulation originally set out to define a social-structural phenomenon. According to Wilson:

> Discussions of inner-city social dislocations are often severed from the struggles and structural changes in the larger society, economy, and polity that in fact determine them, resulting in undue emphasis on the individual attributes of ghetto residents and on the alleged grip of the so-called culture of poverty. . . . Our central argument is that the interrelated set of phenomena captured by the term "underclass" is primarily social-structural and that the inner city is experiencing a crisis because the dramatic growth in joblessness and economic exclusion associated with the ongoing spatial and industrial restructuring of American capitalism has triggered a process of hyperghettoization. (Wacquant & W. J. Wilson, 1989, p. 8)

Emphasis on the African-American experience and on the dysfunctional community has distanced the underclass literature from the larger structural foundations of class fragmentation, isolation, and economic dissolution affecting racial groups. Among Latinos, Puerto Ricans are seen as most convergent with the black experience. However, when understood as part of an economic process, the creation of an underclass has broader implications. After asking the question "Is there an Hispanic underclass?" the sociologist Joan Moore (1989) continues:

> Does Wilson's analysis of the black underclass apply to Hispanics? A review of the literature suggests that economic restructuring operates similarly in the Rust Belt, but with much more complexity in the Sun Belt, because of specialized subcommunities. At the neighborhood level, there is no new exodus of middle-class Hispanics, and with the exception of schools, local institutions (family, churches, and businesses) appear to be

reasonably effective. Street problems are encapsulated in many communities. To apply to Hispanics, the theory needs amplification and specifica-
tion. (p. 265)

Although this analysis is true of the social basis for production and
reproduction of a disattached segment of society, other economic forces
are still at play that have the effect of disenfranchising certain groups.
It is appropriate to expand the underclass concept to include communities in which the mechanisms for wealth creation—especially the development and use of human resources—as well as the articulation of
political voices have been disrupted, as seen among Puerto Rican
migrants and Mexican immigrants. We thus see the issue as one that
extends beyond narrowly empirical and pathological social concepts of
underclass to one that is more systemic and fundamental to the structure
of the economy and the labor market.

One of the outcomes of greater global interaction is an awareness of
labor market distinctions in different market economies. As opposed to
other factors of production, labor is able to accumulate skills, organize,
and establish conventions dictating its usage. For the most part, labor
is less mobile or interchangeable than other factors. It is also a political
commodity that expresses the core of a society's structure.

A market for labor is defined by the means used to allocate and supply
labor and is conditioned by the means of entry into employment and the
nature of mobility (Morales, 1991). One model of labor utilization evolved
from the laissez-faire tradition and depends upon creation of a mobile
market of autonomous individuals with undeterred access to employment.
This is the legacy of the British and the U.S. political economy. Comparative international studies suggest that Japanese and German labor markets, among others, developed along lines that explicitly inhibited labor
mobility and access to employment. These amount to distinctions in the
internal (within firm) and external (interfirm) labor markets. For example,
in the United States the external labor market is highly mobile and the
internal labor market is relatively inflexible, whereas in Japan and to some
extent Germany, just the opposite is the case (Morales, 1991).

Consequently, workers in the United States can hypothetically enter
into any position, and thereby expand the labor pool in any segment of
the labor market. Such is not the case in the other instances. These
differences reflect the way risk is allocated within society. During
periods of economic stress, market uncertainties are externalized into
the labor market in the United States. They are expressed as changes in

occupational patterns or in the recourse to socially disattached labor, such as guest workers. In the United States this creates direct pressures to reduce welfare claims and to pursue policies of labor cheapening, but these strategies are less apparent in counterpart economies. Distinctions regarding rights associated with work are more clearly drawn around citizenship and placement in society in Japan and Germany than in the United States. From the U.S. perspective this may be seen as not socially desirable; nonetheless, a certain clarity of social purpose is achieved. The government and private sector *can* join forces to avoid disruptive or excessive competition, and distribute risk throughout the labor force (Tyson & Zysman, 1989). For Latinos in the U.S. economy, who have all too frequently absorbed the brunt of economic risks and provided flexibility in the labor market, it is important to recognize and reflect upon alternatives of this kind. The instances in this volume illustrate both ways in which market and state forces combine to systematically deny accommodation to some while easing the incorporation for others when the political will is present.

OVERVIEW AND SUMMARY

The chapters that follow document the effect of recent structural changes on Latinos in the United States. The argument is that the predicament confronting Latinos stems from the confluence of structural factors and racial and ethnic barriers, as well as deficits in human capital that are produced and reproduced in urban areas and have become exacerbated in the course of the restructuring. The problem is acute, and we further argue that it is not temporary, but symptomatic of deeper issues requiring fundamental changes in order to rectify the growing income disparity.

To address these issues, we begin at the national level and trace the trends toward inequality over time. As shown in Chapter 2, the recent surge in inequality has produced (a) a widening gap between minority male and white male incomes as minority male incomes fell more rapidly, (b) a widening between minority female and white female incomes despite trends toward a closing of the gender income gap, and (c) a more rapidly widening income gap within Latino and African-American populations than among whites. The principal dynamics driving increased wage inequality since the mid-1970s are: (a) a widening gap between higher- and lower-income wage earners and a declining share of middle-income earners, (b) a widening gap between a white concentration in upper-income groups and a disproportionate minority concentration in lower-income groups, (c) a widening gap between immigrant and nonimmigrant incomes, (d) widening gaps between high and low educational achievement, and (e) renewed or increased ethnoracial wage discrimination. From this aggregate analysis, the significance of direct racism, or differences in earnings not accounted for by age, education, or experience, is shown to be less important in explaining why Latinos are doing poorly in the U.S. labor market than are structural and human capital variables.

A finer level of detail is found in the regional studies of Los Angeles, New York, Chicago, Miami, and San Antonio. The situation in Los Angeles illustrates the centrality of new immigrants in revitalizing the downtown area and in contributing to a growing economic underclass comprised of the working poor. It also demonstrates the lack of significant progress realized by Mexican Americans as a whole, despite gains in the region. The New York story captures the situation of Puerto Ricans, a group that increasingly displays both economic and social dysfunction. Chicago provides an example of repeated community disruption, which in turn has prevented a stable economic and political Latino voice to emerge in proportion to its contribution. Miami, to the contrary, shows how stable community formation can lead to the successful integration of an immigrant group into the United States. And finally, San Antonio reveals the mirage behind the promise of high-tech development for significantly improving the economic well-being of Latinos.

Complementing the national and regional studies are theoretical essays that focus on the meaning of Latino employment in world-competitive metropolitan areas, and on the environmental paradox created by Latino employment. These chapters situate the phenomena previously identified within the context of global trends, yet with a broader understanding of domestic trade-offs. A neglected dimension of the new inequality as it bears on Latinos, that is, exposure to environmental hazards on the job and in their home communities, stands out in this connection. Together the chapters seek to convey a new reality to which all U.S. social scientists need to be attentive—there are no significant national issues that can be treated adequately in abstraction from the Latino presence, especially in our largest cities.

Drawing on this material, in the final chapter we examine potential policies for addressing the most pressing problems identified. We seek to demonstrate that policies aimed at elimination of the underlying instability in the labor market must be complemented with policies directed at strengthening the developmental objectives of metropolitan areas if issues of Latino impoverishment and growing inequality are to find resolution.

NOTES

1. Data for 1969 and 1989 are used because both years approximate similar points in the business cycle, thereby eliminating cyclical distortions. Data for the 2 years are based on different industrial classifications, and are thus not completely compatible, though at broad levels of aggregation, discrepancies are expected to be minor.

2. Poverty level wages in 1979 were $6 per hour using 1988 dollars, or $12,000 per year of full-time work for a family of four. Three times the poverty level was $18 per hour, or $36,000 per year.

2

The Changing Economic Position of Latinos in the U.S. Labor Market Since 1939

Martin Carnoy
Hugh M. Daley
Raul Hinojosa Ojeda

INTRODUCTION

The U.S. economy has gone through major changes in the past half century, and with it, so have the economic and social conditions of the Latino population. The 1940s, 1950s, and 1960s saw Latinos move out of rural society into factories and clerical jobs. By 1970, only a small proportion worked in the fields. With the same constraints on foreign immigration that had prevailed since the early 1920s, they, along with African Americans, played the role of a new industrial labor force, as young whites shifted into rapidly expanding professional, sales, and administrative work. But when this expansionist, "Fordist"[1] manufacturing stage ground to a halt by the mid-1970s, much of Latinos' economic progress did too. Increased competition in the world economy ended U.S. international dominance and the postwar boom. Pushed by increased foreign competition, U.S. business deindustrialized, perhaps faster than it might have if it had been willing to modernize predepression manufacturing plants (Bluestone & Harrison, 1982).

There was a rapid shift in employment from manufacturing into services, mainly high-value-added business, health, and educational services, but also low-value-added custodial, protective, and restaurant work.[2] Changing product markets and new technologies forced manufacturing and services to reorganize and automate. This required new skills for those employees who now had to work with more sophisticated, computerized machines. At the same time, Third World-style sweatshop industries grew up in places such as Los Angeles and Miami, based on the availability of immigrant labor.

Latinos are a more integral part of this "restructuring" phase than they were of the previous manufacturing expansion. Changes in immigration law in 1965 brought large numbers of them to the West and South. Many continued North. Latinos were only 2.5% of the labor force in 1960; by 1990, they were almost 8%, and this growth is expected to continue into the next century.[3]

Both earlier New Deal expansion and later restructuring had a profound effect on Latino income. In the 1940s, 1950s, and 1960s, Latinos began to make solid headway in improving their economic position. Their wages rose rapidly in absolute terms and relative to those of white males and females (see, for example, Borjas & Tienda, 1985; Tienda & Borjas, 1986). Poverty rates among Latino families fell sharply (U.S. Bureau of the Census, Current Population Survey, 1988a). But the period after 1969 is marked by an overall relative decline (Figures 2.1a and 2.1b). As Figure 2.2 shows, this decline applies to all three major Latino groups—Mexican-origin Latinos (MOLs), Puerto Rican-origin Latinos (PROLs), and Cuban-origin Latinos (COLs).

Why did Latinos do so well in the earlier period and fare so poorly in the post-1973 restructuring? Was there something about the nature of restructuring—especially deindustrialization—that left them behind? Did their educational progress slow down? Was this an immigration phenomenon? Or was it something else, such as increased discrimination or changing family patterns?

Our objective in this chapter is to explain the sources of both the relative increase of Latino incomes in the earlier period and the sharp turnaround in Latino male economic position *even relative to declining white male real income* during the past 15 years. We also attempt to explain the relative decline in this same period of Latina incomes relative to (rising) white female incomes.

The analysis focuses on four main reasons for change: the kind of work Latinos do, their relative education, the wages they are paid for the same characteristics as whites, and their immigration status.

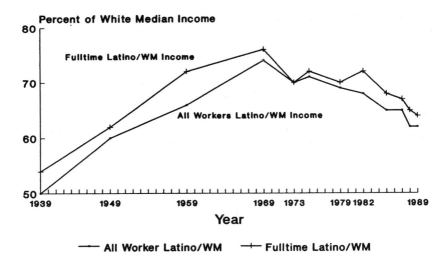

Figure 2.1a. Latino-White Male Median Income Ratios, 1939-1989
SOURCE: U.S. Census and CPS Data.

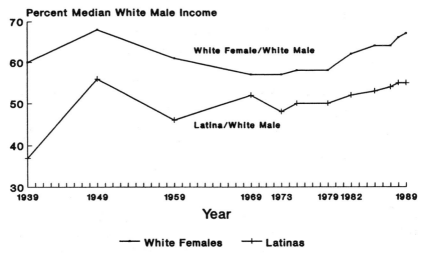

Figure 2.1b. Female-White Male Median Income Ratios, Full-Time Workers, 1939-1989
SOURCE: U.S. Census and CPS Data.

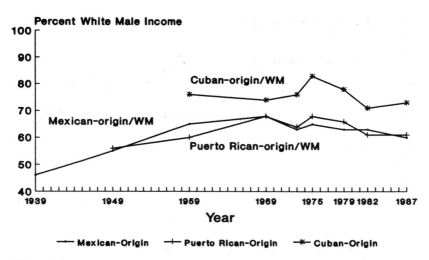

Figure 2.2. Latino-White Male Median Income Ratios, by Latino Group, 1939-1987
SOURCE: U.S. Census and CPS Data, All Workers.

Previous researchers have argued that structural and technological changes in the economy are crucial to understanding *changes in the relative wages* of discriminated-against minorities and women. Historical shifts from an agriculture- to a manufacturing-based economy, and more recently from traditional manufacturing to restructured manufacturing and services due to increased world economic competition, have in this discussion had an important effect on the relative economic position of various groups in the economy. In particular, these changes, combined with U.S. business reaction to them and the discrimination built into the system, have produced greater inequality (Bluestone & Harrison, 1982; Levy, 1988; Wilson, 1987).

A second argument claims that structural constraints are less important than the amount of human capital brought to the labor market by minority groups. This suggests that increased education is the key to increasing minorities' relative wages (for example, Freeman, 1976; Hanushek, 1981; McCarthy & Burciaga Valdez, 1985; J. Smith & Welch, 1986, 1989). Smith and Welch also show that shifts out of agriculture and from the South to the North were significant in raising black male relative incomes in the period before 1960, but that the civil rights movement and affirmative action had only a small impact on black male relative incomes after the Civil Rights Act of 1965. McCarthy and Burciaga Valdez argue that a key variable explaining (primarily Mexican-origin) Latinos' lower relative income is their lower rate of attending and completing college—and that college completion, unlike many other variables, does not increase appreciably as Latinos move two and three generations away from initial immigration.

A third set of studies (for example, Barrera, 1979; Bergmann, 1986; Hartmann, 1981; Myrdal, 1944; M. Reich, 1981) focuses on the larger issue of explaining wage discrimination against minorities of color and women in the U.S. labor market. Although they discuss *changes* in relative wages, the importance of their analyses lies more in their explanation of discrimination (the persistence of wage differences) and its impact on the U.S. labor market. The essence of their argument is that the nature, or structure, of the U.S. economy and society keeps minorities and women in low-income jobs and pays them less for similar work. In different degrees, the analysis contends that discrimination serves the system (even though it may be contradictory to the system's avowed ideology), so it is maintained.

Drawing on these previous studies, we have developed a set of independent variables and a simulation methodology that analyzes Latinos' relative income from 1939-1987. The simulation analysis is carried out at different points in time and allows us to "track" the influence of changes in key variables (sectoral employment structure, human capital, wage discrimination) on incomes (see Appendix 2.1 for an explanation of the simulation model).

SECTORAL EMPLOYMENT STRUCTURE

The industries in which Americans worked changed drastically between 1940 and the late 1980s, and the change was greater for Latinos than for whites. In 1940, 35% of Latino males worked in agriculture, far more than the 14% of whites. By 1960, these percentages had become much more equal as Latinos moved out of agriculture, and by 1970, agricultural work had ceased to be an important occupation for any ethnic group. Simultaneously, Latino males were rapidly incorporated into manufacturing, nearly reaching proportional parity with white males in 1960, and then moving higher as the white percentage steadily declined. After 1970, however, Latinos rapidly lost manufacturing employment so that they equalized with whites at about 20% of total jobs in 1988.

Changes in the sectoral composition of the labor force seem to be important in explaining Latino males' economic problems in the 1980s. Latinos were moved out of manufacturing jobs in the 1970s, but on average were not able to get into high-end services to nearly the same degree as whites. Instead, they tended to find work in low-paying sectors such as agriculture, retail trade, and construction, and in personal and restaurant services.

We can estimate the impact of these shifts on Latinos' income relative to whites by simulating what Latino incomes would have been in each year if they had the same sectoral distribution of jobs as white males. The simulation gives us two pieces of information: (a) It tells us how many percentage points of relative income Latinos could gain (or lose) on average in a given year if they worked in the same industries as white males, assuming that they were paid the same as white males in each industry; and (b) it tells us how much the effect on Latino incomes of changing sectoral composition of employment increased or decreased over time.

Figure 2.3 presents the simulation results. They suggest that in the great U.S. wartime and postwar expansion, the shift into urban jobs was a major reason that Latinos drew closer to white incomes. In the next section, we show that this job shift was accompanied by a rapid increase in minority education. It is not easy to separate out which was "causal": Did more education lead to industrial employment, or did industrial employment in urban areas raise education levels? Probably both. What about in the post-1973 economic restructuring? Did sectoral shifts hurt Latino incomes more than white incomes? Figure 2.3 suggests that they did. Changing sectoral employment had a negative effect on Latino incomes, much smaller than the earlier positive impact, but still a significant fraction of the increasing total Latino income gap. As Latino employment after 1969 shifted out of manufacturing and was increasingly absorbed in relatively low paying construction, restaurant and custodial services, and retail trade, the income gap explained by sectoral employment shifts increased from 3 to 8 percentage points for males and from 0 to 4 percentage points for females. The effects are smaller for full-time Latino workers and negligible for Latinas, but in the same direction.

Because the decline in total measured relative income for Latino males was not enormous in the 1970s and 1980s,[4] these increases in the sectoral income gap show that whatever happened to Latinos with regard to income in the 1970s and 1980s was explained significantly by

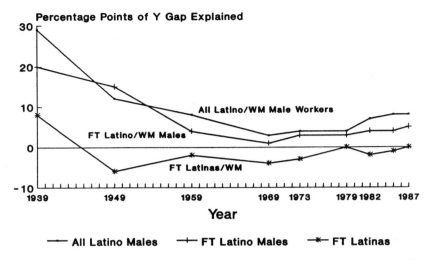

Figure 2.3. Latino-White Male Y Gap Explained by Differences in Sectoral Employment, 1939-1987
SOURCE: Simulations from U.S. Census and CPS Data.

sectoral shifts, and as the "all worker"/full-time comparison suggests, the employment shift hit hardest the less than full-time Latinos and Latinas—these were falling farthest behind whites educationally and were more likely to be foreign-born.

The sectoral composition of jobs was not the only aspect of the job market that changed after 1973. "Good" managerial, white-collar, and technical jobs continued to expand as a proportion of total jobs, but "bad," low-paying, service jobs made a comeback after many decades of decline. And, mainly because of deindustrialization, the "middle" continued to disappear. Yet, it was not until the 1980s that this change in the job market affected Latino males differently from whites. Unlike the situation in the 1970s, when the middle also declined, Latino job mobility in the 1980s was adversely affected. As far as jobs were concerned, Latino and white males went in opposite directions.

The figures in Table 2.1 show what happened to minority males and females compared to whites in the three decades since 1960. We estimated the percentages in the table by constructing a matrix with 14 industrial sectors, ranked by employees' average annual income, along

Table 2.1 Employment Shares by Industry/Occupation and Ethnic/Gender Group, All Workers, 1960-1988

Job Level/Group	1960	1970	Year 1980	1986	1988
Total Employed					
I (high)	24.6	25.5	28.2	30.9	32.4
II (middle)	40.2	39.6	38.2	34.5	34.2
III (low)	35.1	35.0	33.6	34.5	33.4
White Males					
I	28.4	29.4	32.3	35.6	37.2
II	41.2	38.9	36.5	32.3	32.1
III	30.4	31.8	31.3	32.1	30.7
Latino Males					
I	10.5	13.9	16.2	15.5	16.9
II	37.8	40.2	37.8	34.8	33.7
III	51.6	45.8	46.0	49.6	49.4
White Females					
I	19.2	20.2	24.6	28.6	30.5
II	47.5	46.0	43.7	40.2	39.4
III	33.2	33.8	31.7	31.2	30.4
Latina Females					
I	5.2	11.5	13.6	15.6	17.3
II	50.0	52.3	46.1	44.8	42.5
III	44.9	36.2	40.3	39.7	40.3

SOURCE: U.S. Bureau of the Census, 1/1000 Public Use Sample [PUMS] (1960, 1970, 1980), Current Population Survey (1986, 1988).

one axis, and 10 occupational categories, also ranked by average income, along the other axis. The cells in this matrix were divided into three groupings called high-paying jobs, middle-paying jobs, and low-paying jobs. The groupings were somewhat different for men and women, but in general, professionals and managers were in high-paid jobs; craftspeople, operatives, and clerical and sales workers were in middle-paid jobs; and low-end service workers and laborers were in low-paid jobs.

Between 1970 and 1988, and especially after 1980, the proportion of U.S. workers in middle-paying jobs declined, mainly because of the decline in manufacturing. The proportion of higher-paying jobs increased, mainly because employment in information-based services increased. And the proportion of lower-paying jobs stayed about the same.

Table 2.2 Native-Born Mexican-Origin 25-34-Year-Old Males by Level of
Education, 1960, 1970, 1980 (in percent)

Level of Schooling	1960	1970	1980
Less than 12 years	78.1	45.8	31.0
HS Complete	12.8	35.2	33.8
Some College	3.8	12.3	22.9
College Comp.	2.8	2.5	5.8
Grad School	2.4	4.2	6.4

SOURCE: U.S. Bureau of the Census, PUMS (1960, 1970, and 1980). All Worker Sample.

But the Latino experience of these changes was very different from
whites' experience. Latino males moved up rapidly into high-paying
jobs in the 1960s and 1970s, but this movement all but stopped in the
1980s. Latinas continued to move into these better jobs, mainly because
of new opportunities in retail trade. When we separate out the largest
single group of Latinos, those of Mexican origin (MOLs), the figures
are even sharper. After a rapid increase in the 1970s, the percentage of
males in higher-paying jobs declined in the 1980s from 14.4% of all
MOLs employed to 13.6%.[5]

THE EDUCATION EFFECT

In 1940, only about 6% of Latinos (primarily of Mexican origin) had
completed 12 or more years of schooling. This compared with about
40% of young white Americans who had attained that level. In 1965,
65% of whites and 52% of Latinos in this age group had graduated high
school. By 1987, 86% of whites and 60% of Latinos had done so.[6]

These data suggest that after making large gains in 1940-1965, Latinos
fell behind whites educationally in the 1970s and 1980s. This results
mainly because most younger Latinos in the new wave of post-1965
immigration had low levels of schooling to begin with or only stayed in
U.S. schools a few years until old enough to work. When U.S.-born Latinos
are separated out, the educational picture changes somewhat. The percentage of 25-34-year-old Mexican Americans in the census sample who had
completed high school or went on to college increased rapidly in 1960 to
1970 (the 1950s school generation of Mexicano-Latinos), and continued
to rise in the 1970s but more slowly (see Table 2.2).

In 1976, the percentage of *all* high school graduates 18-24 years old who were enrolled in college was about the same, 33% for Latinos and whites.[7] A year later, the percentage of *recently graduated* high school seniors also reached parity between Latinos and whites at about 50% (National Center for Educational Statistics, 1988, Table 273; see also Jaynes & Williams, 1989, Figure 7-6). Yet this was the historical high point for the proportion of minorities entering college, and as such, it signaled a distinct change in the nature of Latino educational progress. The proportion of young Latinos enrolled in college fell in the late 1970s, as it did for whites. But white enrollment rates recovered in the 1980s and Latino rates did not. Whites' rates are now far above those of the mid-1970s, whereas Latinos' continue to drop, or at best stayed even depending on whether all 18- to 24-year-olds or just recent graduates are used as the reference group. A much higher fraction of Latinos (about 55% in 1976-1988) also continued to attend 2-year institutions compared to whites (35%).

Declining enrollment rates also imply declining growth in the percentage of the young Latino labor force with 4-year-college degrees. The most disturbing statistic is the relatively slow growth in the number awarded to Latinos despite the rapid increase in the Latino population.[8]

What makes this slow growth of college enrollment and graduation so mysterious is that the payoff to college graduation rose for Latinos relative to white males in the 1980s and stayed high for Latinas relative to white females. The private rate of return to college graduation (4 years of college) over high school completion was 33% for Latino males employed full-time in 1959, 35% in 1979, and 49% in 1987. This compared to 41% in 1959 for full-time white males, 38% in 1979, and 44% in 1987. For full-time Latinas, the rate fluctuated, but was about 40% in both 1979 and 1987, compared to a rate rising for white females from 31% to 43%. This translates into a relatively high income payoff for Latinos from investment in college education, at least as high as for whites—but the two groups responded very differently in the 1980s to these parallel opportunities (Carnoy, Daley, & Hinojosa Ojeda, 1990a).

Income Differences and the Education Gap

How did the large relative gains in Latino education up to 1970 and the slowdown of the past 20 years influence Latino relative incomes? Turning again to our simulation model, we can estimate the contribution of educational differences to Latino-white income differences over time (see Figure 2.4).

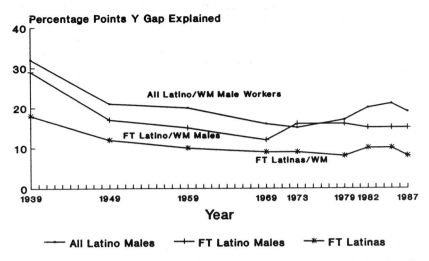

Figure 2.4. Latino-White Male Y Gap Explained by Differences in Educational Attainment, 1939-1987
SOURCE: Simulations from U.S. Census and CPS Data.

Moving through the years, the potential percentage point increase in income that could be achieved by equalizing educational attainment between Latinos and white males tends to decrease. What we call the education gap—the income difference attributable to education differences[9]—declines. Because educational attainment itself becomes more equal in each decade, the effect of education differences on income differences generally becomes smaller. At the same time, differences in income themselves become smaller, in part because educational differences decline. For example, by 1949 (in the all worker sample), equalizing Latino education to white males' would have increased Latino income by 21 percentage points, or about 10-11 points less than in 1939. In 1949, Latino median income was 60% of white males'. Thus, the education gap decreased more rapidly than the income gap but still explained about half the total income gap at the end of the 1940s. One of the difficulties of attributing these gains to education is that—as we showed above—there were also continuing large shifts of Latino workers from agriculture to manufacturing in both the 1940s and 1950s. Changes in relative Latino income in this period seem more related to such sectoral shifts than to the simultaneous educational gains. Thus, sectoral shifts in the 1940s and

Table 2.3 Education Gap as Proportion of Income Gap, Latino Males, 1939-1987 (in percent)

Year	All Workers	Full-Time Workers
1939	64	63
1949	52	45
1959	59	54
1969	62	50
1973	50	53
1979	55	53
1982	62	53
1985	60	47
1987	54	46

SOURCE: Figure 2.4 data divided by income gap data (see Figure 2.1a).

1950s seemed to have an even more powerful impact on Latinos' relative economic position than relative education gains.

In the 1960s, the education gap began getting smaller again, implying a further income catching up that was related to Latino education gains, and the gap tended to get larger after 1969, especially for Latino males who did not work full-time. That, in turn, explains an important part of Latinos' *lack* of economic progress in the last decade. About 15-17 percentage points, half the difference between Latino and white males' income, could now be eliminated if education were equalized (Table 2.3). The education gap explains a similar percentage of the income difference between Latina and white female full-time workers. In the late 1980s, about 9 percentage points of the Latina-white female income difference, about 55% of the total, would be eliminated if education were equalized.

Why did the education gap stop shrinking, and even in the mid-1980s tend (for Latino males) to grow larger? There are still large differences in the percentage of whites and Latinos—even native-born Latinos—in the labor force that drops out of high school, but this difference is slowly closing. More and more minorities are, one way or another, finishing high school.

Important as dropout differences are (especially for Latino males) the answer to the 1980s education gap lies mainly somewhere else. That somewhere else is at the college level. The reasons are fairly simple. First, incomes to college graduates, regardless of ethnicity, race, or gender, rose much more rapidly in the 1980s than to high school graduates. This made college education relatively more valuable—gave

Table 2.4 Latino/White Male Median Income Ratios, 25-34-Year-Old Full-Time Workers by Level of Schooling, 1975-1987 (proportion of white male median income)

Year	Latino HSDs	Latino HSGrad	Latino ColGrad
1975	0.79	0.86	0.99
1979	0.78	0.89	0.88
1982	0.82	0.88	0.90
1985	0.76	0.80	0.95
1987	0.78	0.81	0.88

SOURCE: U.S. Bureau of the Census, PUMS (1980), Current Population Survey (1976, 1983, 1986, 1988).

it a greater "weight" in assessing the overall average value of an ethnic group's education. Second, it was just in the 1980s that Latinos drastically slowed their surge into the nation's colleges. They did not respond to the "new" structure of incomes. Even though they are increasing their educational attainment, they are doing it mainly by increasing their high school completion rate. Whites, to the contrary, are increasing their average education by continuing on and raising the percentage that has completed college. As the real income of the college-educated held steady and income of high-school-educated fell in the 1980s, the income-weighted gap in years of schooling increased between Latinos and whites.

THE INCOME GAP AND WAGE DISCRIMINATION

A first approximation of wage discrimination is the relative income that Latinos earn with the same education and age as white males. Table 2.4 shows that college, and especially high school completers, 25-34-year-old Latinos, employed full-time, have lost some income ground to their white counterparts since 1975. This suggests that Latinos could, indeed, be facing increasing wage discrimination. The table also suggests that Latinos get paid only 80%-90% of white income for the same education and age, implying a 10%-20% discrimination rate in the 1980s. Data presented in this way are not corrected for other factors, however, such as regional disparities, civil status differences, sectoral employment differences, foreign birth, or time worked (even among full-time workers, time worked varies).

Now suppose that Latino workers had the same education and work experience as white males, were distributed across economic sectors

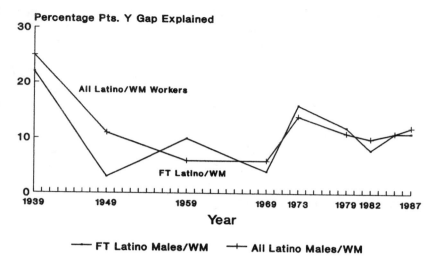

Figure 2.5. Latino-White Male Income Gap Explained by Wage Discrimination, 1939-1987

SOURCE: Simulations of U.S. Census, CPS.

and regions of the country in the same way, had the same marital status, and worked the same number of hours and weeks per year, but were paid a Latino "price" for each of those attributes. Simulating that situation, we estimated what Latinos would earn if they were "like" white workers, but paid like Latino workers. The result is an approximation of the lower "price" that Latinos get for their work even if they are like white workers in a number of important ways. We call this price difference income or wage discrimination. There are problems with equating a residual of this kind with discrimination. Some unknown variables, such as the quality of schooling, and others important to explaining employability or the capacity to produce have probably been left out. But we feel that this is a reasonable approximation for understanding whether Latinos are facing greater or less wage discrimination in the labor market.

Figure 2.5 shows how wage discrimination, measured in percentage points of income difference between Latino and white males, has behaved in the past 50 years.[10] Although there are some differences between the full-time and all worker samples, the general trends are the same. Wage discrimination fell sharply in the 1940s for Latinos and stayed at a very low level until the new immigration that began in the late 1960s and reached high levels in the 1970s and 1980s.

These simulations are necessarily dominated by Mexican-origin Latinos because they are by far the largest group in the sample. Second, the increase in the 1970s in what we call wage discrimination was influenced by the new immigration and a much higher proportion of young Latinos in the labor market who were foreign-born, spoke poor English, and faced much more limited employment opportunities. But the increase in wage discrimination between Latinos and whites, especially in the 1980s, also reflects the shift of Latino labor into the lower paying parts of the manufacturing and service sectors. "Third World" manufacturing in the Southwest—garment sweatshops and low-wage assembly plants—have thrived because of the availability of Latino workers willing to work for low wages.

This raises two issues: (a) Was the increased "discrimination" we observe in the 1980s the result of declining school performance of Latino students? and (b) Was the increased "discrimination" mainly the result of an increased proportion of foreign-born workers with low English-language ability and limited access to better paying jobs?

Latino School Performance

Latino pupils have scored much lower than whites on standardized school achievement tests as long as test score results have been recorded by ethnic group. There is no doubt that lower reading and math abilities at every level of schooling are both a reflection of and have contributed to minority economic and social problems. But differences in Latino and white scores declined between the late 1960s and the late 1980s even as white student attainment remained unchanged. The Latino gains may have been larger were it not for the influx of "language-handicapped" Latino immigrants after 1965.[11] In any case, the Latino-white gap did close (see Table 2.5). The gains are not limited to reading scores. Latinos significantly reduced the difference between their math and science scores and those of whites in this same 20-year period. The reduction in the math gap was about 33%-45%.

What makes the reduction of the achievement gap all the more impressive is that it occurred during (a) a period of increases in the percentage of Latinos who were completing high school and (b) a time of "crisis" in U.S. schools—a time when, for example, whites' reading scores stayed almost constant. The 1980s were also a period of increas-

Table 2.5 National Assessment of Educational Progress Reading Scores for African-American, Latino, and White Students by Birth Cohort and Age Test Taken

Birth Cohort	Ethnic Group	9	Age Test Taken 13	17
1954	White			291*
	Latino			—
1958	White		261*	293
	Latino		—	252
1962	White	214*	262	293**
	Latino	—	232	261
1966	White	217	264**	296
	Latino	183	237	268
1971	White	221	263	295
	Latino	190	240	271
1975	White	218	261	
	Latino	187	240	
1979	White	218		
	Latino	194		

SOURCE: Mullis and Jenkins (1990). See also M. Smith and O'Day (1991, Table II). Data from five assessments are reported—1971, 1975, 1980, 1984, and 1988. The scores are the reading proficiency scale scores. The standard deviation for the age 9 scores is about 40 points; for the age 13 scores, about 35 points; and for the age 17 scores, about 40 points.
*"White" scores for the 1971 assessment (1962 cohort of 9-year-olds, etc.) included Latinos.
**The 17-year-old scores assigned to the 1962 birth cohort are from the 1980 NAEP and so should be for a 1963 birth cohort. The 13-year-old scores assigned to the 1966 birth cohort are also from the 1980 NAEP, so should be for a 1967 birth cohort.

ing poverty in the Latino communities. Yet, it was precisely "disadvantaged" students who were making gains relative to the advantaged (as measured by parents' education) (Mullis & Jenkins, 1990; M. Smith & O'Day, in press, pp. 24-26).

These data suggest that increased "discrimination" in the 1980s, the way we measured it, is not the result of an increased school achievement gap between Latinos and whites. That gap closed in the 1980s. The relative quality of Latino high school graduates therefore did not fall during the decade although the discrimination residual rose.

Latino Immigration and Discrimination

If we separate foreign- from native-born Mexican-origin Latino (MOL) males—MOLs are the largest group in our Latino sample—we can get

Table 2.6 Relative Income and "Wage Discrimination" Residual, Foreign- and Native-Born Mexican-Origin Males, 1959-1979 (percentage points of income)

Year	Foreign-Born MOLs		Native-Born MOLs	
	Relative Income	Wage Discrimination	Relative Income	Wage Discrimination
1959	58	27	69	3
1969	68	14	73	3
1979	61	14	69	6

SOURCE: U.S. Bureau of the Census, PUMS (1960, 1970, 1980).

some idea of what the discrimination residual was for each in 1959-1979 (foreign-birth is not available in the U.S. Bureau of the Census, Current Population Survey, so we are limited to census year data). The data in Table 2.6 support the notion that wage discrimination as such is low for Latinos and that much of the increase in discrimination residual is due to the increase of foreign-born in the Latino labor force. Native-born MOLs had only a 3%-6% residual in this period, suggesting some but relatively little wage discrimination. Their wages relative to white males did fall in the 1970s, but mainly because native-born MOLs in the labor force became much younger during the decade. Foreign-born MOLs, to the contrary, showed a sharp decline in their residual over this period from 27% in 1960 to 14% in 1970-1980. Their relative wages also fell in the 1970s, but mainly because of a drop in average education. A good argument could be made that much of the higher "wage discrimination" for foreign-born MOLs is rooted in limited English-language capability.

GENDER AND LATINA INCOME

In the past, Latinas were much more likely to work in manufacturing than were white women. These were the Mexican cannery workers and the Puerto Rican women who labored in New York factories. They were also domestics, waitresses, and kitchen workers, but by the 1960s, this was the atypical Latina worker (only 11% were employed in low-end services). Latinas—particularly Mexicanas—have historically had less education than white women; yet with the same level of education, they earned about the same pay. So Latinas have not faced pay discrimination as Latinas, but rather as women.

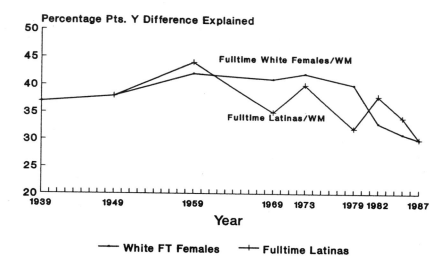

Figure 2.6. Latina-White Male Income Gap Explained by Wage Discrimination, 1939-1987

SOURCE: U.S. Census, Full-Time Sample.

The simulation residual, or "wage discrimination" effect for white women and Latinas working full-time when they are made to "look like white men" but are paid like women (Figure 2.6) and the simulation residual when Latinas are compared to white women (Figure 2.7) tell the same story. If we ignore the gyrations of the Latina graph, due mainly to the relatively small Latina sample, we see that the difference in earnings between them and white females was and is due to differences in attributes (mainly education), not wage discrimination.

But when we deal with women's income, we also must recognize that economic differentiation among women still occurs through marriage. Because society chooses to pay women considerably less for their labor, their economic well-being depends much more on other income earners and sources of wealth than does men's. It is here that white women gain much of their advantage over their Latina counterparts. They marry higher earning men than do Latinas. They tend to have children later in life, giving themselves time to invest in education, to develop labor market skills, and to earn income. And compared to women of Puerto Rican origin, when they do have children, they (and Mexicanas and

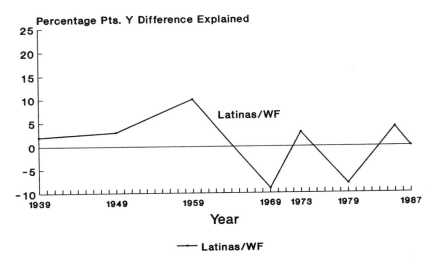

Figure 2.7. Latina-White Female Income Gap Explained by Wage Discrimination, 1939-1987
SOURCE: Log Income Simulations.

Cubanas) are much more likely to be married and living in a household with a man present.

Young Mexican-origin women are also much more likely than whites to have children early in life; they are also highly likely to *marry* young. Assuming that family formation early in life has a negative effect on young adults' educational investment, the overall impact on Latina and Latino economic performance of early childbearing would also be negative. In this case the poverty rate is associated with the traditional nuclear family rather than a female-headed family, because—compared to, for example, women of Puerto Rican origin—a much higher fraction of these young, less-educated Mexican-origin Latinas are married (to young Latino males).

The combination of youthful family formation and wage discrimination makes the Latino family doubly disadvantaged, and with the absence of male income earners in many families of Puerto Rican origin, makes them triply disadvantaged: (a) Should the higher wage earning male be the single provider, his lower human capital and lower than white income even for *the same education and other attributes* (about

12% for all Latinos together but only 6% for native-born MOLs in today's labor market) usually leaves the family with significantly fewer resources than a single-earner, male-headed, white family; (b) should the Latina spouse in a male-headed household choose to work, she also has lower human capital, on average, than her white counterpart; (c) women of Puerto Rican origin are much more likely to be single heads of households than white women. This disadvantage is the most onerous because the single income earned by minority women is low on three counts: minority women are less educated than white women and so get lower paying work; because they are less educated, they are less likely to get full-time work; and as women they suffer, on average, a 35%-40% wage penalty even with the same human capital as men.

These differences are summarized in Table 2.7. Married Latinas living with their husbands have access to significantly lower income than white women, but do even worse when they are female single heads of household. Latina heads of household are younger and less educated than their white counterparts, and are less likely, as single heads of households, to work full-time, so they earn a lot less. But the worst of it is, women of Puerto Rican origin are much more likely to fall into this low-income, female-head-of-household category and to be raising children in what are almost *necessarily* conditions of poverty. A high fraction of this category of family is below the poverty level (55% of Latinas as compared with a "relatively low" 29% of whites). The end result of the much lower proportion of Puerto Ricans in married-couple families (83% of white families are married-couple families compared with 74% of Mexican-origin Latinos, and only 52% of Latinos of Puerto Rican origin)[12] is the low median income of the average Puerto Rican family ($15,000 in 1987 compared to $20,000 for the median MOL family). This despite the relatively (compared to Mexican-origin Latinos, for example) higher average income of married-couple Puerto Rican families.

WHAT EXPLAINS DECLINING LATINO INCOME IN TODAY'S LABOR MARKET?

Our analysis suggests that Latino males' income rose relatively to white males' in 1940-1970 for two main reasons: their shift in sectoral employment from agriculture to manufacturing and their simultaneous increased education. It is difficult to separate these two effects. After a

Table 2.7 Median Female Incomes by Family Status and Ethnicity, 1987 (in dollars and percent of income)

Family Status	White	Race/Ethnicity Latino	MOL
Married-couple families	36,883	24,677	22,908
Female head-of-household, no husband present	18,685	9,805	11,384
Female, no family, living alone	13,548	7,786	7,946

SOURCE: U. S. Bureau of the Census (1988c, Table 4).

sharp drop in wage discrimination against Latinos in the 1940s, declines in discrimination were a smaller factor in explaining Latino advance in the 1950s and 1960s than sectoral employment shifts or increases in education. Latinas' income relative to white females' rose sharply in the 1940s from employment shifts, in the 1950s and 1960s because of educational increases, and in the 1960s also due to a reduction in wage discrimination.

Since 1970, sectoral employment shifts and education were also foremost in shaping the decline in Latino relative incomes for both males and females. Although it appears that wage discrimination increased sharply in the 1970s and 1980s, this effect was probably mostly the result of the rising proportion of new immigrants in the Latino labor force. When we divide MOL males into native- and foreign-born, our residual measure of wage discrimination is much higher for the foreign-born, and only rose slightly in the 1970s for the native-born. The higher residual for foreign-born, we argue, could well be a "limited English" effect rather than wage discrimination per se.

This points to three key conclusions regarding the present situation for Latinos:

1. Because Latinos are so crucial to the low-wage expansion of at least part of U.S. manufacturing and of the expansion of low-wage services in the new "restructuring" phase of U.S. economic growth after 1973, it is logical that Latino labor would have been overwhelmingly incorporated into such jobs. Latinos' overall economic position in the past 20 years has therefore been shaped in a significant way by the polarization of the job market in this period (the "disappearing middle" in Bluestone and Harrison's [1988] terminology).

2. At the same time, Latinos have fallen behind whites in amount of education. The education gap continues to explain about one half of the

total income gap between Latino and white males even as the income gap grows. Much of the educational effect in the 1980s resulted from the low proportion of Latinos with college education in the face of rapidly rising payoffs to completing college for whites and Latinos, males and females. Because jobs and education are closely related, it is hard to say whether the expansion of low-wage jobs has "enticed" even native-born, young Latinos to leave high school before completion or to end their educational investment at high school graduation, or whether barriers to college attendance (such as the shrinking pool of grants-in-aid for college education) have forced young Latinos to take low-income jobs. But the fact is that by not completing college in rapidly increasing numbers, MOLs and PROLs remain among the least schooled groups in U.S. society, and this is true not just because of the growing proportion of low-schooled immigrants. Native-born Latinos are also much less likely to go to college than Asian Americans, whites, or blacks. This keeps them out of higher paying jobs. What makes the issue more perplexing is the improving performance in the 1980s of Latinos compared to whites on high school national tests of reading, math, and science.

3. Measured wage discrimination has not been as important a factor in explaining why Latinos and Latinas earn much lower income than whites, nor a major explainer in the decline of Latino relative income in the 1970s and 1980s. This suggests that racism is not as crucial to understanding why Latinos are faring increasingly poorly in the U.S. labor market in the 1980s as the persistence of the education gap and the growth of the sectoral employment gap, and it implies that a "class" rather than a "race" analysis is more relevant for understanding the Latino economic position in the 1980s and 1990s.

A class position points toward strategies that improve educational quality and opportunities, "upgrade" U.S. production to more technologically intensive goods, reduce unemployment, and equalize income distribution—in other words, policies that would benefit low-skilled, less-schooled labor whether Latino or not. The educational improvement strategy is, we believe, especially relevant for Latinos, as there exists such a large and persistent schooling gap between Latinos and whites. Ultimately, Latinos themselves have to address politically the reduction of this gap. At the community and state levels, as they have already begun to do in Texas, Latinos can focus on lack of educational resources available to Latino children. The problem is not just bilingualism; it is the low quality of primary and secondary schooling for Latinos in *both* Spanish and English. Expectations are also low in the schools, and parents are often not knowledgeable enough to demand higher standards for their children, or if knowledgeable, not taken seriously by school administrators and teachers. A high percentage of Latino children also come from low-income homes with little preparation for schooling when they enter kindergarten. They would benefit from the expansion of greatly underfunded Head Start programs and hardly existent after-school programs.

Most of those young Latinos who finish high school will need financial help in attending college—this help is currently much less available than it was 10 years ago and needs to be substantially increased if Latinos are to attend and complete college in significantly greater numbers. But it is not just financial aid that stands in the way of Latino educational progress at the college level. Latino politics and political leaders have to make Latino educational achievement a linchpin of the community's ideology. They have to help create an increased awareness among parents and Latino youth that higher education is a major key to Latino advancement—one way to swim against the tide of a polarizing economy.

APPENDIX 2.1: SIMULATION RATIOS

Three ratios are obtained from the regression simulation, each a comparison with white male earnings.

$$R_k = \frac{V_k Q_k}{V_\mathrm{w} Q_\mathrm{w}} = \left[\left(\frac{\sum\limits_{i=1}^{n} \mu + \sum\limits_{j=1}^{m} b_{jk} x_{ijk}}{n} \right) - \left(\frac{\sum\limits_{i=1}^{n} \mu + \sum\limits_{j=1}^{m} b_j \mathrm{w} x_{ij} \mathrm{w}}{n} \right) \right]$$

$$P_k = \frac{V_k Q_\mathrm{w}}{V_\mathrm{w} Q_\mathrm{w}} = \left[\left(\frac{\sum\limits_{i=1}^{n} \mu + \sum\limits_{j=1}^{m} b_{jk} x_{ij} \mathrm{w}}{n} \right) - \left(\frac{\sum\limits_{i=1}^{n} \mu + \sum\limits_{j=1}^{m} b_j \mathrm{w} x_{ij} \mathrm{w}}{n} \right) \right]$$

$$C_k = \frac{V_\mathrm{w} Q_k}{V_\mathrm{w} Q_\mathrm{w}} = \left[\left(\frac{\sum\limits_{i=1}^{n} \mu + \sum\limits_{j=1}^{m} b_j \mathrm{w} x_{ijk}}{n} \right) - \left(\frac{\sum\limits_{i=1}^{n} \mu + \sum\limits_{j=1}^{m} b_j \mathrm{w} x_{ij} \mathrm{w}}{n} \right) \right]$$

Where:

R_k = the ratio of the estimate of group k's log income and the estimate of White male log income,

P_k = the Price Effect for group k,

C_k = the Attribute Effect for group k,

b_{jk} is the estimated regression coefficient for the jth variable in the estimated regression equation for group k; and x_{ijk} is the value of variable j for individual i in group k.

Our analyses were based on a postulated earnings function in which annual income depends on industry and location of work, personal characteristics, and human capital factors, such that,

$$\ln E = \mu + G\alpha + I\beta + P\gamma + R\delta + M\varepsilon + L\zeta + IM\eta + S\theta + AT\iota + \ln W\kappa + \ln H\lambda + \xi$$

where:

E = annual wage and self-employment earnings,

G = a vector of mutually exclusive dummy variables indicating group gender/ethnicity,

I = a vector of mutually exclusive dummy variables indicating industrial sector,

P = a binary variable indicating private versus public sector employment,

R = a vector of mutually exclusive dummy variables indicating geographic region of residence,

M = a vector of mutually exclusive dummy variables indicating marital status

L = a vector of mutually exclusive dummy variables indicating labor market experience,

IM = a binary variable indicating immigrant status,[1]

S = a vector of mutually exclusive dummy variables indicating level of schooling,

AT = a binary variable indicating whether the individual is still attending school,[2]

W = the number of weeks employed during the previous year,

H = an estimate of the number of hours per week employed during the previous year.

μ is the baseline log earnings intercept, $\alpha, \ldots, \lambda$ represents associated coefficients or vectors of coefficients, and ξ represents random error. Five distinct models were established for our Type I regression runs, each drawing on the full earnings function in equation 1. These include:

1. A human capital equation in which log earnings is regressed against labor market experience and education.

$$\ln E = \mu + L\zeta + IM\eta + S\theta + AT\iota + \xi$$

2. The human capital equation with time worked included.

$$\ln E = \mu + L\zeta + IM\eta + S\theta + AT\iota + \ln W\kappa + \ln H\lambda + \xi$$

3. A structural equation in which log earnings is regressed against industrial sector, public employment, marital status, and region.

$$\ln E = \mu + I\beta + P\gamma + R\delta + M\varepsilon + \xi$$

4. The structural equation with time worked included.

$$\ln E = \mu + I\beta + P\gamma + R\delta + M\varepsilon + \ln W\kappa + \ln H\lambda + \xi$$

5. A combined factors equation where log earnings was regressed against human capital and structural factors, including time worked.

$$\ln E = \mu + I\beta + P\gamma + R\delta + M\varepsilon + L\zeta + IM\eta + S\theta + AT\iota$$
$$+ \ln W\kappa + \ln H\lambda + \xi$$

APPENDIX NOTES

1. Not available in CPS data.
2. Not available in CPS data.

CHAPTER NOTES

1. For an analysis of mass, assembly-line production and why it became obsolete, see Piore and Sable (1984).

2. In the discussion in this chapter, high-value-added services are defined to include the financial, insurance, and real estate sector, business services, health services (public and private), and educational services (public and private). Public sector is included, although we did include the labor force in the public sector as a separate variable to measure its separate effect. Low-value-added services includes personal services, custodial services, protective services, and restaurants and bars.

3. See Hudson Institute, *Workforce 2000* (Johnston, 1987). The composition of the Latino population also changed significantly. Those counted in the labor force by the 1940 census were 93% of Mexican origin (MOLs); in 1960, 71% were MOLs and 25% of Puerto Rican origin (PROLs); and by 1988, the MOLs had dropped to 61%, PROLs fell to 10%, those of Cuban origin had risen to 8%, and 21% were from other Latin U.S. and Caribbean countries.

4.. The total income gap increased 9 percentage points for Latinos in 1969-1987 (for both the all worker and full-time samples), and only 4 percentage points of that in the 1980s (3 for full-time Latinos).

5. The figures for Mexican-origin males and females are as follows:

	1960	*1970*	*1980*	*1986*
Males				
I	11.7	9.4	14.4	13.6
II	29.4	39.5	32.6	30.6
III	58.5	50.7	53.1	55.8
Females				
I	10.0	12.5	16.1	19.3
II	36.0	44.2	39.3	38.4
III	54.0	43.3	44.6	42.4

See Carnoy, Daley, and Hinojosa Ojeda (1990b, Appendix E).

6. These data are comparable with those for blacks and whites reported in Jaynes and Williams (1989, pp. 335-336).

7. But the percentage of all 18-24-year-olds enrolled was 27% for whites, 23% for blacks and 20% for Latinos. See National Center for Educational Statistics (1991, Table 171) and Jaynes and Williams (1989, Figure 7-6).

8. An indicator of this slowdown is that the number of Latinos enrolled in 4-year colleges increased by 43,000 in 1976-1980 and only 29,000 in 1980-1984. In 1984-1988 the rate of increase rose again to 50,000 but on a much larger potential base than in the 1970s (see National Center for Educational Statistics, 1991, Table 194). By 1991, the percentage of 25- to 29-year-old high school graduates who had completed four or more years of college had risen for whites from the levels of the mid-1970s to 29.7%, whereas the percent had fallen for blacks to 13.6% and stayed even for Latinos at 16.4% (see National Center for Educational Statistics, *The Condition of Education, 1992*. U.S. Department of Education, Office of Educational Research and Improvement, 1992 [NCES 92-096], Table 22-23).

9. The education gap shown in Figure 2.4 is based on regression estimates where education, work experience, and foreign birth are the independent variables and log of income is the dependent variable. This is known as the human capital model. Other variables, such as sector worked in, region worked in, and civil status are not controlled for.

10. We call the difference "wage discrimination" because in the figure, time worked per year is taken account for. The residual therefore measures the difference in pay *rates* to the different groups.

11. The California State Department of Education estimates that the number of limited English proficiency (LEP) students in California schools shot up in the early and mid-1970s, from 168,000 in 1972 to 290,000 in 1976. By 1990, the number had increased to 860,000. A high fraction of these are Latino. (See California State Department of Education, Office of Bilingual Education, Language Survey Report, Sacramento, CA, Fall, 1991.)

12. The corresponding figures for Cuban-origin Latinos (77%) and those of Central and South U.S. (69%) are close to the Mexican average. Puerto Ricans are therefore a prominent outlier.

3

The Illusion of Progress:
Latinos in Los Angeles

Rebecca Morales
Paul M. Ong

OVERVIEW

After decades of steady growth, Los Angeles has become yet another symbol of economic decline. The end of the cold war closed or scaled back many defense-related industries. An estimated 200,000 defense-related jobs are projected to be lost in California between 1990 and 1997, the majority from the Southern California region (Vartabedian, 1992). This loss comes on the heels of a transformation of the industrial base from manufacturing to services that changed the sectoral composition and led to a bifurcation of the remaining manufacturing into high- and low-technology extremes. The loss of high-technology jobs adds unemployment to a problem of growing inequality. The result has been a widening of the cleavage between those benefiting from the change and the many who have not.

Among those most seriously affected have been the city's largest minority—Latinos. Approximately one in six of the nation's Latinos lives in Los Angeles County. According to census reports:

Los Angeles' estimated 894,000 Hispanic population increase between 1980 and 1985 [was] greater than the total 1985 Hispanic population in any

other metropolitan area except New York. . . . Moreover, the estimated
international migration component for Los Angeles of 463,000 for 1980-85
[was] in itself larger than the total 1985 Hispanic population in all but six
other metropolitan areas. (Word, 1989, p. 65)

Growth of the Latino population coincident with economic restructuring and job loss has resulted in a segment of society that is both
extremely impoverished and isolated from avenues of change.

As the separate effects of demographic growth and economic con-
traction and change interact with each other, the divisions of the local
economy have deepened along racial lines. Stratification of workers by
race and occupation, with immigrants employed in declining manufacturing sectors, blue-collar occupations, and low-wage services and
U.S.-born Chicanos occupying a lower economic rung relative to Anglos, now appear as hardened positions as the ladders for mobility are
progressively removed. This racial and economic inequality is produced
and further reproduced through institutional means, persistent discrimination, and restrictive public policies.

In this chapter we examine the process underlying growing inequality
in Los Angeles and its effect on the Latino population. We will study
how the problem has been defined, perpetuated, and reinforced over
time. The purpose is to weigh the theoretical positions that provide
partial explanations for the situation. Toward this end, we begin with a
theoretical overview and proceed to an analysis of restructuring, income inequality, the process of labor absorption, and community formation in the region. This is augmented by measures of economic
welfare. Our findings indicate a pattern of obstacles in the process of
labor absorption that contribute to the current economic disparity. The
outcome is a group of working poor and a population increasingly
disenfranchised but vital to the continued competitiveness of low-wage
industries and an unstable economy.

THEORETICAL CONSIDERATIONS

The current literature on persistent poverty and growing misery tends
to fall into three schools of thought. One position holds that in freely
operating labor markets, economic well-being is a function of personal
attributes. This line of reasoning is premised on free market principles
and reflects the ideas on which U.S. labor markets are structured. Based

on concepts of individual choice and unencumbered market clearing procedures, it is argued that those entering the labor market receive returns commensurate with their skills or experience. According to this position, Latinos who do poorly are not well equipped to meet the needs demanded in the market. This argument carries much validity when markets are freely functioning, but it loses explanatory powers when markets are restricted or less than perfect.

Thus, a second argument centers on market barriers. This can happen in several ways. One market impediment is racism. Markets tend to operate according to a mixture of economic and social preferences. Irrational market behavior based on racist preferences therefore results in a less than efficient outcome. Another form of restriction comes from institutional barriers, such as biases in the legal system, educational processes, investment procedures, and the like. If discrimination is argued to be the situation, market imperfections and market barriers contribute to the poor performance of Latinos, calling for intervention through public policies to ameliorate the problem.

A third argument is predicated on structural factors that create de facto obstacles to economic mobility. Such are argued to have occurred with the recent restructuring, resulting in diminished sectoral and occupational opportunities, the intrametropolitan geographical displacement of jobs, and a breakdown of the social compact that previously provided certain assurances, protections, and stability in employment, income, and social welfare. From this line of reasoning, Latino poverty and inequality can be attributed to the loss of good jobs, their relocation, and an eroding social safety net.

The position put forth here is that although Latinos are often deficient in the attributes that should give them better returns, this alone is insufficient to explain the economic standing of Latinos in Los Angeles. Rather, wage discrimination and such institutional impediments as unequal access to education and a history of disrupted community formation have combined with structural factors to severely disadvantage this segment of society. Further, among recent Mexican immigrants, yet another dynamic is at work, instrumental in the recent reindustrialization of certain low-wage industries.

This argument requires an understanding of the competitive nature of the labor market. In an economy organized to capture short-term profits through cost minimization and output maximization, labor markets are designed to assure competitive behavior among autonomous decision makers. But national labor markets also require control from external influences if they are to avoid excessive competition. Here the

Table 3.1 United States and Los Angeles Employment Patterns

	1973	1989	1973	1989	Percent Increase
United States Total	76,790	108,581	100.0	100.0	41.4
Mining	642	722	0.8	0.7	12.5
Construction	4,097	5,300	5.3	4.9	29.4
Durable Mfg	11,891	11,536	15.5	10.6	-3.0
NonDur Mfg	8,262	8,076	10.8	7.4	-2.3
TPU	4,656	5,705	6.1	5.3	22.5
W/S Retail	16,606	25,809	21.6	23.8	55.4
FIRE	4,046	6,814	5.3	6.3	68.4
Service	12,857	26,892	16.7	24.8	109.2
Government	13,732	17,727	17.9	16.3	29.1
Los Angeles Total	3,029.6	4,222.9	100.0	100.0	39.4
Mining	10.5	9.2	0.3	0.2	-12.4
Construction	107.8	153.7	3.6	3.6	42.6
Durable Mfg	556.9	577.0	18.4	13.7	3.6
NonDur Mfg	264.1	314.7	8.7	7.5	19.2
TPU	177.3	212.1	5.9	5.0	19.6
W/S Retail	681.0	964.5	22.5	22.8	41.6
FIRE	184.1	291.9	6.1	6.9	58.6
Service	605.8	1,176.7	20.0	27.9	94.2
Government	442.1	523.1	14.6	12.4	18.3

SOURCE: Bureau of Labor Statistics, *Employment and Earnings*, various years, California Employment Development Department.

critical issue concerns the point at which economic uncertainty is translated into undesirable downward pressure on wages and employment security, thereby creating excessive competition. Chicanos, and most particularly recent Mexican immigrants, have been caught in the situation of buffering excessive competition. The following examination of Los Angeles provides insight into this problem.

THE LOS ANGELES ECONOMY

In keeping with nationwide economic transformation, Los Angeles changed in its sectoral composition during the 1970s and 1980s. Between 1973 and 1989 nongovernmental services increased from 49% to 58% of all jobs, representing a growth of 65% (Table 3.1). Much of this consisted of services to manufacture (Cohen & Zysman, 1987; Noyelle,

1987; Noyelle & Stanback, 1983). According to one report, jobs attributed to producer services in Los Angeles grew by 30% between 1977 and 1981, and made up one quarter of all net new jobs (Sassen, 1988). Although much smaller, the contribution made by manufacturing was also significant. When the nation grew by approximately 1 million manufacturing jobs between 1970 and 1980, nearly one fourth (over 225,000) were located in the Los Angeles region. From 1969 to 1987, the absolute number of manufacturing jobs increased from 880,000 to 906,000. At the same time other major metropolitan areas experienced a decrease: Detroit lost 134,000 manufacturing jobs during this period; Philadelphia lost 207,000; Chicago lost 422,000; and for New York the loss was 460,000. As a result, Los Angeles emerged from the 1980s as the largest manufacturing center in the United States, and one of the largest in the world.

However, manufacturing employment had become highly polarized (Table 3.2).[1] Traditional durable goods industries, such as rubber tires, steel, and automobiles, that had provided middle-income jobs were lost and replaced by very high and very low tech employment. The extremes consisted of aerospace, communications equipment, and electronics on the one hand—industries that were dependent upon defense contracts; and textiles, furniture, and apparel on the other—industries that were declining elsewhere in the nation. During 1987, employment in aerospace industries, including aircraft parts and guided missiles, was 148,700. The Southern California high-technology complex comprised the largest agglomeration of scientific, engineering, and technical workers in the world. At the other end of the employment spectrum was an equally significant cluster of operative and manual workers engaged in export-competitive production.

These seemingly disparate industrial clusters shared a common characteristic of being extremely market sensitive and prone to employment fluctuations. This was evident in the amount of part-time, part-year jobs.[2] Thirty-nine percent of male workers and 61% of female workers fell into this category in 1970. By 1980 the figures were 61% and 66%, respectively. To protect themselves against market fluctuations, employers increased not only the amount of part-time, part-year work, but also the extent of subcontracting, often to smaller, less stable establishments. Between 1969 and 1988, the number of large manufacturing firms, or those employing 500 or more persons, dropped by 18%, even as the number of small firms, defined as those with 1 to 49 employees, increased by 15%.[3] In some cases, subcontracting relationships, especially

60 LATINOS IN A CHANGING U.S. ECONOMY

Table 3.2 Manufacturing Employment in Los Angeles

	1973	1987	Change	Growth
L.A. Manufacturing	821.0	906.4	85.4	10.4%
Nondurables	264.1	307.1	43.0	16.3%
Durables	556.9	599.3	42.4	7.6%
Two-Digit Industries				
Food Processing	49.9	48.6	−1.3	−2.6%
Textile	10.7	10.6	−0.1	−0.9%
Apparel	64.9	92.3	27.4	42.2%
Paper	16.5	18.7	2.2	13.3%
Printing	43.3	59.8	16.5	38.1%
Chemicals	28.5	28.2	−0.3	−1.1%
Petroleum	13.5	10.6	−2.9	−21.5%
Rubber/Plastics	30.9	33.1	2.2	7.1%
Leather	6.0	5.2	−0.8	−13.3%
Lumber Goods	11.5	12.7	1.2	10.4%
Furniture	33.2	38.7	5.5	16.6%
Stone/Clay/Glass	25.0	17.8	−7.2	−28.8%
Primary Metal	26.2	20.8	−5.4	−20.6%
Fab. Metal	74.5	68.0	−6.5	−8.7%
Machinery	79.9	65.2	−14.7	−18.4%
Elect. Equip.	107.5	155.3	47.8	44.5%
Transp. Equip.	153.3	172.2	18.9	12.3%
Instruments	25.0	28.3	3.3	13.2%
Misc. Mfg.	20.8	20.3	−0.5	−2.4%
Major Three-Digit Ind.				
Women's Outerwear	38.2	65.4	27.2	71.2%
Misc. Plastic	19.7	27.1	7.4	37.6%
Communications	53.6	91.2	37.6	70.1%
Elect. Components	16.2	26.2	10.0	61.7%
Aircraft & Parts	106.0	129.0	23.0	21.7%
Total	233.7	338.9	105.2	45.0%

SOURCE: California Employment Development Department, 1988.

among high-technology firms, resulted in new suburban industrial agglomerations, although this trend was also apparent within the central city among low-wage manufacturers in the garment district (Scott & Paul, 1988; Soja, Morales, & Wolff, 1983.)

With the decline in firm size, rise of unstable employment, and sectoral shifts within manufacturing, labor organizing became more difficult, and union membership dropped. From 1970 to 1983, the percent of all manufacturing employees who were unionized in Los

Angeles fell from 32% to 21% (California Department of Industrial Relations, various years). Jointly, the increase in part-time employment and subcontracting, and declining union protection depressed average wages for production workers. Between 1967 and 1982, real average hourly wages for production workers in Los Angeles fell by 8%, while the national average rose by three percent.

As the economy became more polarized, certain high-skill occupations, such as managerial, combined with certain low-skill occupations, such as those related to services, enjoyed robust growth. In contrast, craft jobs, which had previously afforded manufacturing workers avenues for upward mobility, grew at a rate well below that of the local economy as a whole. Within manufacturing, a bifurcated labor force also emerged, exemplified as growth at the high and low ends of the skills scale and a decline at the center. The decline in manufacturing wages negatively affected skilled workers, but most particularly unskilled workers. During the late sixties, the average wage for unskilled workers in Los Angeles was higher than for all other metropolitan areas, but by the eighties, it was 10 to 15 percentage points lower (U.S. Bureau of Labor Statistics, "Wage Differences," various years). Similarly, job creation reflected a growing division in the work force between those with preferred skills and job attachment and those without such benefits. With the restructuring, new entrants into the labor force confronted an economy marked by increased employment uncertainty and lower remuneration. For immigrants and others such as minorities with few job skills, this carried the implication of fewer opportunities for advancement in mainstream society and a growing division based on race and class.

The employment and wage polarity visible nationwide was particularly acute in Los Angeles. Despite a higher average per capita income in Los Angeles compared to the nation (the 1986 per capita income in Los Angeles was $16,988 in contrast to $14,639 for the nation), income was more unevenly distributed. The GINI index, a measure of income inequality based on income distribution, indicates that income inequality among Los Angeles families became particularly pronounced in the 1970s and remained high throughout the 1980s (Research Group on the Los Angeles Economy, 1989). Further, from 1969 to 1987, the level of inequality was continuously higher in Los Angeles than nationwide.[4] Examination of poverty data substantiates the existence of this trend, with poverty being 1 percentage point lower than for the rest of the nation in 1969 and over 2 percentage points higher in 1987 as poverty itself experienced a secular increase.[5] Seen as a whole, the income and poverty data indicate that the effect of restructuring was not only more extensive in Los Angeles than in the nation, but also resulted in an inequality that preceded that of the nation in occurrence.

OVERVIEW OF MEXICAN LABOR
IN LOS ANGELES

The transformation of the Los Angeles economy led to a recomposition of the labor force by race, gender, and immigrant status. Already an ethnically varied society, Los Angeles became even more so. From 71% non-Hispanic (NH) white and 15% Latino in 1970, the metropolitan area changed to 53% NH white and 27% Latino in 1980, and to 41% NH white and 36% Latino in 1990. In the decade from 1980 to 1990, Latinos increased by 71% in the city of Los Angeles. In the county, Latinos increased by 62%. Along with an ethnic recomposition, the labor force also changed in its gender composition due to a dramatic increase in the number of female workers. The number of male workers grew by 15% in the seventies, while the number of female workers grew by 35%. Growth among Mexican and Asian women essentially tripled (Ong & Morales, 1988).

The growth of the Latino labor force is one of the major sources of new labor in Los Angeles, with Mexican immigrants playing a key role. In 1970, 55% of all new entrants were youths, 33% were domestic migrants, and only 12% were immigrants.[6] By 1980, immigrants had risen to 26%, youths declined to 52%, and domestic migrants had dropped to 22%. Overall, the cohort of recent immigrants was 169% larger in 1980 than in 1970. Greatest gains were made by Mexicans, who made up 43% of the new immigrant entrants in 1980, in contrast to 28% in 1970. According to the U.S. Bureau of the Census, approximately 65.5% of all Mexican immigrants into Los Angeles between 1975 and 1980 were undocumented (Passel & Woodrow, 1984). From 1980 to 1985, one half of the Mexican immigrant population in the United States was estimated to be undocumented, with an even larger proportion residing in Los Angeles (Word, 1989, p. 65). Of growing significance in recent years have been Central Americans, but as their numbers, as well as those for Caribbeans or South Americans, are much smaller in comparison to Mexicans, they have been difficult to trace using aggregate statistics. The massive influx of Mexican immigrants has made Los Angeles uniquely relative to other metropolitan areas in the United States.

Although immigration dominated the growth of the Mexican labor force during this period, the number of young Chicano (Mexican origin citizens) new entrants was also significant. Over one quarter of net new growth came from Chicanos, or U.S.-born Mexicans. During the seventies, the number of working age Chicanos increased by 50%, from 292,000 to 437,000. Further, at the beginning of the decade, the number of Chicanos between the ages of 6 and 15 (the next group of new workers) was approximately 40% higher than the number of Chicanos between the ages of 16 and 25 (the existing group of new workers).

In general, the Mexican immigrant and Mexican origin labor force is predominately male, younger than NH white counterparts, and less educated. From 1970 to 1988, approximately 64% of the combined Mexican labor force was male. In 1980, 77% of all Mexican males between the ages of 16 and 64 were in the labor market, compared to 75% of NH whites. The difference is more pronounced after controlling for variations in age structure. If Anglo males had the same age structure as all Mexican males, the labor force participation rate of the former would have been only 71%. Mexican immigrant and Mexican origin women, however, had a lower participation rate than Anglo females in 1980 (48% vs. 54%), even after adjusting for age structure (48% vs. 53%).

These aggregate figures mask important distinctions and trends within the combined Mexican female population. Immigrant women are less likely to be economically active than U.S.-born women of Mexican descent (Chicanas). Chicanas, however, realized a significant increase in the labor force participation rate during the seventies, reaching close to parity with Anglo females in the mid-eighties. Their increase in labor market activity caused the Chicana labor force to grow more rapidly than the Chicano (male) labor force. During the seventies, the number of Chicana workers increased by 79%, which was 33 percentage points higher than for Chicano workers.

Compared to Anglos, Mexican workers on the whole are younger. In 1980, Chicano workers were on average 4 to 5 years younger than Anglo workers, and Mexican immigrant workers were about 7 years younger. The age difference held for both males and females. Three factors contributed to the age gap. First, immigration has been dominated by younger workers. Of the newly arrived who are of working age (16-64), over half are under the age of 24. Second, U.S.-born Mexicans have a younger age pyramid. Approximately one third of working age Chicanos in 1980 were under the age of 24, but the same was true for only

Table 3.3 Characteristics of the Los Angeles Labor Force, 1980

	Anglo All	Chicanos	Mexican Immigrants Established	Recent
Mean Years of Schooling				
Males	13.7	11.3	7.9	6.8
Females	13.1	11.3	8.3	6.8
Percent Without High School Degree				
Males	14.2	40.6	70.5	83.9
Females	12.3	36.3	64.5	83.8
Percent With College Education				
Males	30.0	6.8	2.6	1.7
Females	19.4	4.8	2.0	1.7

SOURCE: U.S. Bureau of the Census, PUMS (1980, 1% data set).
NOTE: Established immigrants entered prior to 1970; recent immigrants entered in 1970 or later.

one fifth of NH whites. Third, Mexicans overall are more likely to enter the labor market at an earlier age, a pattern that is evident in the labor force participation rates of young adults (16-23). The 1980 labor force participation rate for all Mexican males was 13 percentage points higher than that for NH white males (55% vs. 42%).

Despite their active participation in the labor force, the overall educational achievement of Mexican workers is relatively low. Table 3.3 provides a statistical profile of educational attainment for NH whites and three groups of Mexican workers (Chicanos, pre-1970 immigrants, and immigrants who entered between 1970 and 1980). On average, NH whites had 2 years more schooling than Chicanos, a disparity also apparent among those without a high school education. Although less than 1 in 7 NH whites did not finish high school, approximately 4 in 10 Chicanos did not. Similarly, although Chicanas are about as active in the labor market as Anglo females, the former had a lower rate of school attendance. At the other end of the educational spectrum, NH whites were five times more likely to have a college education than Chicanos.

The educational gap is even greater between NH whites and immigrants. On average, NH whites had 5 years more schooling than earlier cohorts of immigrants, and 6 to 7 years more than recent immigrants. Recent immigrants were six times more likely to not have a high school degree as NH whites, and only one tenth as likely to have had a college

Table 3.4 Los Angeles Employment Statistics, 1979-1980

	Anglo All	Chicanos	Mexican Immigrants Established	Recent
1980 Unemployment Rates				
Males	4.7%	8.9%	5.7%	8.6%
Females	4.6%	8.8%	9.4%	11.4%
Weeks Unemployed, 1979				
Males				
0 weeks	84.1%	79.1%	83.0%	77.1%
4 or more weeks	12.9%	18.0%	12.3%	17.9%
Females				
0 weeks	82.7%	80.1%	79.2%	76.3%
4 or more weeks	12.4%	15.2%	16.7%	19.0%
Wages and Earnings, 1979				
Males				
Means				
Hourly pay	$12.15	$8.36	$7.46	$5.32
Annual earnings	$22,840	$13,830	$12,460	$8,180
Distributions				
$4 or less per hr	12.5%	21.5%	23.0%	50.8%
Less than $8K/year	16.1%	27.6%	25.8%	53.9%
Females				
Means				
Hourly pay	$7.27	$5.88	$5.52	$4.90
Annual earnings	$10,330	$7,700	$6,640	$5,540
Distributions				
$4 or less per hr	26.8%	43.4%	52.0%	74.3%
Less than $8K/year	43.3%	55.4%	64.0%	82.8%

SOURCE: U.S. Bureau of the Census, PUMS (1980, 1% data set).
NOTE: Established immigrants entered prior to 1970; recent immigrants entered in 1970 or later.

education. Along with low educational attainment, two thirds of recent immigrants possess limited English-language skills. The situation is improved for more established immigrants, but even among this group, 4 of 10 have poor English-language skills.

The combination of low human capital and decline in stable, full-time middle-income jobs resulted in Mexican labor being unevenly integrated into the L.A. economy. On the whole, Mexican workers have been more likely to experience greater instability of employment. Table 3.4 shows two measures of unemployment: the unemployment rate for the first week of April 1980, the reference week for the 1980 census, and the number of weeks workers were unemployed in 1979. Both indices show that Mexican workers were more likely to be unemployed in a given week, and that over 1 year's time, they were less likely to have escaped unemployment (zero weeks of unemployment), and more likely to have suffered 4 or more weeks of unemployment. The one exception is pre-1970 male Mexican immigrants, who experienced proportionately less unemployment. Although the unemployment rate of Mexicans is relatively high, it actually hides the fact that most are employed in jobs with high turnover rates, seasonal or cyclical fluctuations, and extensive part-time work.

Mexicans are also low-wage workers. The disparity in hourly wages can also be seen in Table 3.4. Compared to Anglo males, Chicanos, in the aggregate, received 31% less in wages, established immigrants earned 39% less, and recent immigrants 56% less. The proportion of the labor force that earned $4 or less per hour, or low-wage workers, varied across groups. Although only one in eight Anglo males fell into this category, the same was true for half of the recent Mexican immigrants. The gaps in annual earnings followed a similar pattern, but were larger because Mexican workers had fewer hours and weeks of employment. Recent immigrants earned only 36% of that of NH whites, which translated into a short-fall of over $14,000. A sample of the 1988 Current Population Survey for Los Angeles revealed that the unemployment rate for Mexicans was more than one and one half times as high as that for NH whites (4.1 vs. 6.6%).[7] Although over half of Mexican workers earned less than $8,000 (in 1979 dollars) the previous year, this was true for only one quarter of Anglo workers.

There are also systematic differences among female workers, but the gaps are smaller because of a wage compression endemic to females. As shown in Table 3.4, Chicanas received only 81% of the wages of Anglo females on an hourly basis. Among recent immigrants, the predominant characteristic was low wages (74%), as shown by those earning $4 or less per hour.

Further, Mexicans displayed a stratification of the labor force based on nativity and time of entry into the United States. The vast majority of immigrant and new-entrant Chicanos (e.g. youths new to the labor force) are trapped within the secondary sector, in contrast to established Chicano workers.

The profound problems faced by Mexican immigrants and Chicanos have changed the face of poverty in Los Angeles. With each recession, there were fundamental shifts in income distribution that pushed a disproportionately greater number of Latinos into poverty (Ong, 1988).[8]

Table 3.5 Distribution by Industry and Occupation, Los Angeles, 1980

	Anglo All	Chicanos	Mexican Immigrants Established	Recent
Males				
Durable Mfg	20.2%	25.4%	34.3%	33.0%
Nondurable Mfg	6.7%	11.1%	14.4%	17.3%
Craft Occupations	20.2%	24.7%	24.9%	18.8%
Operatives/Laborer	14.5%	34.9%	45.7%	51.2%
Observations	9,685	1,357	763	1,411
Females				
Durable Mfg	11.0%	17.7%	20.1%	24.8%
Nondurable Mfg	5.5%	11.0%	23.7%	39.2%
Craft Occupations	2.5%	5.3%	7.0%	7.7%
Operatives/Laborer	5.4%	19.7%	37.5%	59.9%
Observations	7,015	983	413	674

SOURCE: U.S. Bureau of the Census, PUMS (1980, 1% data set).
NOTE: Established immigrants entered prior to 1970; recent immigrants entered in 1970 or later.

As a result, by the mid-1980s, Latinos comprised nearly 60% of those living below the poverty line.

INDUSTRIAL EMPLOYMENT AND MEXICAN IMMIGRANTS

To a large extent, Mexican workers have been drawn into industrial production. They are employed in both durable and nondurable industries, although overrepresentation is greater in nondurable goods (Table 3.5). Recent immigrants are also most concentrated in this sector. Approximately one half of male immigrants and over two thirds of female immigrants worked in manufacturing. Concentration in manufacturing is reflected in the occupational patterns: A large majority of all Mexican males were in blue-collar occupations, as were nearly half of the females. Immigrants were more likely to fall into these categories than Chicanos. Concentration in manufacturing is coupled with employment instability and low wages, which has contributed to low incomes. Throughout the eighties, Mexican workers were nearly twice as likely to be in manufacturing than Anglo workers (39% vs. 17%) (U.S. Bureau of the Census, CPS, 1988).

Further, Mexican immigrants were more likely to be concentrated in the industrial sector than recent European immigrants, who are used here as a comparison group. Mexicans arriving in the late sixties and late seventies held a one in two chance of being employed in manufacturing; their European counterparts not only had a lower probability of working in manufacturing but also a significantly declining probability over time. Mexican and European immigrants were essentially following different employment paths. Europeans moved away from industrial work, paralleling the overall trend for Los Angeles, but Mexicans continued to be located in manufacturing. Further examination of Mexican immigrants shows a gender difference. In absolute terms, the largest number of males were employed in furniture, fabricated metals, machinery, electrical equipment, and apparel. In those sectors, they accounted for a significant amount of the net new growth of male employment. The largest number of females were employed in apparel, with electrical equipment as a distant second. As one might expect, Mexican immigrants were concentrated in blue-collar occupations. Only 30% of recent male immigrants from Europe in 1980 held craft, operative, or laborer occupations, though this was true for 65% of Mexican males. Alternatively, only 8% of recent female immigrants from Europe were employed in blue-collar occupations, in contrast with 62% of Mexican female immigrants (Morales, Ong, & Payne, 1990).

Immigrants, and Mexican immigrant workers in particular, have been a major source of new labor in both durable and nondurable sectors of manufacturing. The number of new immigrants exceeded the total addition of jobs by 59%, suggesting that they actually replaced existing workers in these sectors. Among new male entrants in durable goods manufacturing, immigrants made four times their contribution, and provided nearly all the new employment in nondurable goods manufacturing. Female immigrants experienced similar, if less dramatic gains. Female immigrants contributed 49% of the share of female new entrants in durable goods manufacturing, and 59% in nondurable goods manufacturing. Although men were more likely to be employed in durable goods manufacture, women were more likely to be employed in nondurable goods manufacture. Within the male-dominated durable goods industries, women also entered into gender-specific occupations, reflecting a persistent gender division of labor (Morales & Ong, 1991). Overall, women's employment was also less secure and paid lower wages than that of men (Morales & Ong, 1991).

Despite enactment of the Immigration and Control Act of 1986 (IRCA), the high rate of absorption of new Mexican immigrants into the industrial sector has continued since the early eighties, and Mexican immigrants remain in an economically disadvantaged position. Their extreme sectoral concentration, and the fact that these sectors are highly competitive, creates pressures on wages and earnings. Half of the recent Mexican immigrant population earned poverty level wages in 1980, in contrast to 20% of the total work force (Morales et al., 1990). This, coupled with the fact that 58% of Mexican male and 75% of Mexican female immigrants were part-time workers, led to extremely low annual earnings. Lower earnings also reflect low educational attainment, limited employment experience, and limited English-language abilities, but these factors provide only a partial explanation.

Historically, immigrants start at entry level positions, and make their way upward through a process of economic assimilation. In contemporary Los Angeles, however, recent Mexican immigrants face distinct limitations. The downward pressure on manufacturing wages has had a substantial adverse impact on entry level jobs for Mexicans. Recent cohorts of Mexican immigrants have suffered a deterioration in their economic position relative to both European immigrants and earlier cohorts of Mexican immigrants. Regression analysis reveals substantial gaps in earnings between Europeans and Mexicans even after accounting for education and potential years of labor market experience (see Appendix 3.1 for discussion of the regression model). In 1970, Mexican males earned about 40% less than European males, ceteris paribus, and Mexican females earned about 30% less than their European counterparts. The gaps became even larger in 1980, increasing to 56% among males and 49% among females.[9]

Further analysis of the data shows that newly arrived Mexican males faced declining employment opportunities. An examination of differences across time within individual ethnic groups yields information that is independent of intergroup variations such as English-language ability. Although in 1980 recent European immigrants performed as well as their predecessors did in 1970, this was not true for Mexican males—recent immigrants in 1980 earned 12% less than their predecessors, ceteris paribus.

The results for females are ambiguous but nonetheless revealing. European females showed the same pattern as European males in that there was no difference between recent immigrants in 1970 and those arriving in 1980. The data do not suggest a systematic decline for Mexican females, yet the results are completely at variance with those for other female and male groups. Earnings among Mexican females were not correlated with either educational attainment or potential years of labor market experience. In other words, older Mexican females and better educated Mexican females are not likely to fare better than younger and less educated Mexican females. The fact that wages of Mexican immigrant females are compressed suggests that they confront an unyielding wage floor (Morales et al., 1990).

The decline in real wages for recent Mexican immigrants, their concentration in industrial sectors most open to international competition, and their critical role in sustaining the manufacturing base in Los Angeles are interconnected phenomena. Due to limited English-language ability, they are often employed by firms where informal employer-employee relations based on ethnic and kinship ties prevail and where formal protection of workers, provided either by the state or by organized labor, is absent. Concentration of labor has the effect of pushing wages downward, a process similar to the concept of labor "crowding" (Bergmann, 1974). For females, the outcome is perpetuation of a wage floor that restricts opportunities for an increase in earnings. In turn, low wages have the effect of stimulating overall growth at the industry level. Low wages not only make existing firms more competitive within a global economy, but also provide the incentive for further capital investments, thus expanding local employment.[10]

Low economic status is a product of characteristics of the workers such as low educational attainment and limited English-language ability, combined with structural conditions. Although human capital factors clearly play a role in determining wages, workers do not enter a competitive labor market where wages are set at the value of the marginal productivity of labor. Segmentation creates barriers that prevent the equalization of wages across ethnic groups and in various locations. By way of illustration, Mexican female immigrants are commonly found in unskilled and semiskilled jobs in integrated circuit board manufacturing throughout greater Southern California (Fernandez-Kelly & Garcia, 1986). In New York City, immigrant workers predominate in low-wage jobs that "require low skill levels, minimal language proficiency, and often include undesirable night or weekend shifts" (Sassen, 1988, p. 157). Within the New York service sector, where 16.7% of jobs were low wage (varying from 10.8% of jobs in finance, insurance, and real estate to 23.9% in business services and 18.9% in remaining services), the employment of immigrants was common (Sassen, 1988, p. 158). Thus certain new immigrants, such as Mexicans, are crowded into the lower end of the job structure in both services and manufacturing employment in selective locations nation-wide, and within these regions, this function is reinforced in their communities.

THE FORMATION OF IMPOVERISHED BARRIOS

Historically, stable communities have led to the creation of wealth and the ability for residents to invest in themselves. In Los Angeles, the central business district (CBD) and nearby East Los Angeles, which have traditionally been sites for Latino immigrant communities, have not performed this role. Despite the sense of identity and potential for garnering means offered by these barrios, they rarely provided the resources for developing abundance. Latinos were excluded from other communities through restrictive deeds during the interwar years, and consistently limited in their financial ability to move (R. Romo, 1983). Periodic acts of repatriation further weakened the community structure, and with it the people's economic and political base (Hoffman, 1974; Morales & Tamayo, 1991). As a consequence, though these communities were often sites of choice for Latinos, they also became places for pooling low-wage labor critical to the economy of the region. One historian traces the relationship between development of the barrio and growth of the regional economy accordingly:

> From 1910 to 1920 Los Angeles attracted thousands of new immigrants, principally Mexican, while the influx of immigrant labor slowed in other American cities. . . . By 1920 Los Angeles' industries had formed a close association, perhaps even a dependent relationship, with the local Mexican labor force. . . . From 1910 to 1930 the principal Mexican enclaves of Los Angeles, located in the inner city and formerly inhabited by poor natives, European newcomers, and Asian immigrants, lost their heterogenous characteristics and instead of becoming segregated by socioeconomic criteria became segregated racially. (R. Romo, 1983, pp. 6-10)

Another scholar wrote that by the 1930s, "The fragmented society of the white majority complemented the isolated communities of the ethnic minorities and, along with the dispersal and decentralization of the metropolis, emerged as integral features of twentieth-century Los Angeles" (Fogelson, 1967, p. 204). This legacy of racial separation and economic interdependence has continued to the present.

Table 3.6 Characteristics of Barrio Residents by Neighborhood Type, 1980

Poverty Rates	Below 20%	20-39%	30-39%	40%+
Foreign-Born	30%	44%	49%	53%
Non-English-Speaking	17%	27%	34%	38%
Lived Abroad in 1975	7%	13%	17%	22%
Adults w/o High School Degree	63%	73%	79%	85%
Employment Ratio				
Males	78%	78%	77%	74%
Females	49%	46%	47%	44%
Blue-Collar Workers	42%	44%	45%	48%

SOURCE: U.S. Bureau of the Census, 1980 Census, SFT3 Files.
NOTE: Blue-collar workers based on all residents.

The role of Mexican immigrants as low-wage labor perpetuates impoverished barrios, especially in the CBD and nearby communities. Latino neighborhoods with a relatively high number of immigrants also experience high levels of poverty (Table 3.6).[11] Approximately half of the residents in poor neighborhoods are foreign-born, and about one third do not speak English.[12] One fifth of the residents in the two poorest categories of neighborhoods have been in the United States for less than 5 years. Examination of IRCA applicants indicates that undocumented aliens are heavily concentrated in these neighborhoods (U. S. Immigration and Naturalization Service, unpublished data). Poor, immigrant barrios tend to be located within and around the central business district.

The abundant supply of immigrant labor is revitalizing and reindustrializing the inner city of Los Angeles around low-wage jobs. An analysis of building activities in the City of Los Angeles during the 1980s shows that Latino areas received approximately their share of office and commercial development and more than their share of industrial and warehousing development. The parity index for poverty barrios (neighborhoods with a poverty level of at least 40%) was 1.52 for industrial uses and warehousing, and 1.01 for office and commercial developments. Poor barrios (neighborhoods with a poverty level in the 30% to 39% range) fared better, with respective parity indices of 2.24 and 1.27. Investments in industrial and warehousing activities are taking place in the city center where they can take advantage of low-wage Latino labor and enjoy proximity to related industries. There has also been extensive conversion of existing structures and retailing space. Many older low-rise buildings in the southeastern part of the CBD have been subdivided to house sewing shops and retail outlets that cater to Mexicans and other Latinos. With this new vibrancy, inner-city development has taken a dualistic character. Employment in downtown and adjacent areas consists of a mixture of highly paid professionals engaged in financial and corporate activities combined with a substantial number of low-wage workers employed mainly in manufacturing.

This form of economic development has left immigrant communities with a relatively high jobs-to-workers ratio. Data from the 1985 American Housing Survey reveal that areas with a Latino majority contained 12.8% of the region's adult population, 11.7% of its workers, and 18.4% of its jobs. Consequently, recent immigrants have not suffered from the employment spatial mismatch evident elsewhere in the nation and among other segments of society in Los Angeles, such as African Americans or Chicanos. Forty-two percent of Mexican immigrant workers live in barrios located around the CBD, and a substantial proportion work in nearby areas.

The resulting poverty neighborhoods are unlike those documented in the literature on the black underclass (W. J. Wilson, 1987). Poverty in African-American communities is due to joblessness, but in barrios it is related to the quality of employment. Partial evidence is provided in labor force participation rates across neighborhoods. In 1980, the labor force participation (LFP) rate for Latino males in poverty barrios was 83%—which was comparable to the LFP rates for Latino males in other areas (85% in both poor and poverty Latino neighborhoods). LFP rates for Latinas were lower, though they also did not vary significantly across neighborhoods (50% in poverty barrio neighborhoods, 52% in poor barrios, and 53% in nonpoor barrios). At the same time, unemployment rates varied substantially, with Latino workers in poverty areas experiencing the highest rates. Yet even these rates —10.6% for males and 12.7% for females—were much lower than those for black workers in poverty ghetto areas. The revitalization of the central city around low-wage Latino labor promoted a type of economic development that has eluded other major urban areas. Despite low levels of educational attainment in immigrant barrios, employment ratios are high, with a large percentage of the workers employed in blue-collar jobs. That poverty remains high reflects the extent to which Latinos comprise a growing segment of the working poor.

CHICANOS: INTERGENERATIONAL MOBILITY OR PERSISTENT INEQUALITY?

Persistent racial inequality also appears to compound the employment obstacles created by a restructured economy. Evidence of this is particularly strong among Chicanos, who continue to earn less than U.S.-born NH whites. Wage discrimination is defined as the difference in the rewards to labor based on race. This difference can be estimated through multiple regressions in which the influence of human capital variables is controlled. To test for wage discrimination, a standard human capital model was employed using two approaches (see Appendix 3.2). The first was based on the assumption that returns to schooling and labor market experience are identical for both Chicanos and U.S.-born NH whites, making the cost of being Chicano an independent factor. The second allowed for an additional racial effect through differences in the monetary returns to schooling and labor market experience.

The results from both approaches showed a sizable degree of racial discrimination when Chicano males are compared to NH white males. The first model yielded estimates in line with other studies of earnings (Chiswick, 1978; Reimers, 1985). For each year of education, earnings increased by 7%-8%. Earnings also increased with years of experience, although at a declining rate. As shown in the estimated parameter for the Chicano variable, Chicano workers earn 13% less than Anglo workers, ceteris paribus, according to the first model. Results from the second approach were similar. As expected, Chicanos received lower rewards for schooling and years of labor market experience, indicating that Chicanos faced a different and lower structure of rewards than NH whites. In total, Chicano workers earned 12% less because of racial differences, a figure nearly identical to the estimate based on the first approach. Moreover, the lower returns to education detected in the second approach indicated that the earnings gap between a highly educated Chicano and highly educated Anglo is greater than that between a minimally educated Chicano and minimally educated Anglo. Thus, higher education does not make Chicanos immune to wage discrimination.

Wage discrimination is just one mechanism that lowers the economic status of Chicano workers. Others include barriers to factors that could improve mobility, specifically barriers to acquiring human capital. According to human capital theory, training that contributes to a worker's productivity garners higher remuneration. Mexican workers in total have less schooling, a crucial form of prelabor market human capital. Systematic variations in education between NH whites and persons of Mexican origin, and among subgroups within the Mexican labor force, affect their hourly wages and annual earnings. As predicted by human capital theory, the group with the least schooling, or recent immigrants, have fared worst, and the group with the most schooling have fared best.

The educational gap between NH whites and Chicanos is also a product of racial disparities in educational opportunities. Mexicans on the whole in Los Angeles have encountered a history of racial segregation and low-quality education. In the early part of this century, the Los Angeles School District maintained separate schools for Mexicans, and adopted an objective of "Americanizing" Mexicans rather than providing an education for upward mobility (R. Romo, 1983). This pattern has continued into the present. In the early seventies, two thirds of Mexican pupils were consigned to predominantly Mexican schools (Caughey, 1973, p. 11). In a study of Mexican students in Los Angeles schools, segregation was identified as "a substantial depressant of motivation to learn" (Caughey, 1973, p. 76). The adverse impact of segregation has been reinforced in recent years by severe overcrowding in elementary schools having a predominantly Mexican student population. Poor facilities and few resources contribute to substandard academic performance and a high dropout rate. In the last two decades, there has been literally no improvement: The reading scores for high schools in the Eastside, which contains most Mexican students, have consistently ranked at the bottom quarter of the nation, and dropout rates have averaged over 40%.[13] Access to higher education has been equally dismal. In 1967, there were only 70 Chicano students at UCLA, the major university in the region (Acuna, 1984, p. 142). Since then the number of Chicanos at UCLA has increased, however enrollment remains disproportionately low relative to their population.[14]

Racial barriers to the acquisition of human capital within the labor market can be understood as unequal access to on-the-job training (OJT). One measure of the acquisition of OJT is the rate at which earnings increase with years of experience in the labor market. The group with greater access to OJT should show a larger increase in earnings, whereas the group with less access to OJT should show a smaller increase. Table 3.7 lists the average earnings in constant dollars of NH whites and Chicanos in 1970 and 1980, with each group disaggregated by decades

Table 3.7 Earnings Gap Between Anglo and Chicano Workers, 1970-1980

Cohorts by Different Years of Experience	Mean Earnings		Percent
	Anglos	Chicanos	
1970.A (1-10 yrs)	$13,400	$10,900	−18
1970.B (11-20 yrs)	$23,100	$15,700	−32
1970.C (21-30 yrs)	$26,000	$16,500	−36
1970.D (31-plus yrs)	$21,900	$14,800	−33
1980.A (1-10 yrs)	$14,700	$10,600	−28
1980.B (11-20 yrs)	$25,500	$16,100	−37
1980.C (21-30 yrs)	$30,400	$17,200	−43
1980.D (31-plus yrs)	$25,600	$15,200	−41
Percent Growth			
1980.B/1970.A	90%	48%	NA
1980.C/1970.B	32%	10%	NA
1980.D/1970.C	−1%	−8%	NA
Growth in Gap			
1970.A-1980.B	NA	NA	19
1970.B-1980.C	NA	NA	11
1970.C-1980.D	NA	NA	5

NOTE: Percentage gap is defined as (Avg. Chicano − Avg. Anglo)/(Avg. Anglo).
SOURCE: 1980 Census, SFT3 Files.

of experience. The careers of cohorts can be approximated by comparing average earnings of one cohort in 1970 with that of a more experienced cohort a decade later (e.g., Chicanos with 1-10 years of experience in 1970 compared to Chicanos with 11-20 years of experience in 1980). The data reveal that earnings in real terms grew more rapidly for NH whites than for Chicanos, with a difference ranging from 34 percentage points to 53 percentage points. This suggests that Chicanos have had limited access to the type of OJT that translates into better pay.

Barriers to internal promotions are a related concern. Numerous reports suggest that Mexican employees as a group in the public sector, particularly in local government, experience limited upward mobility. In the county government, Mexicans receive less than an equitable share of jobs, and those who are employed are less likely to move up in rank (Larson, 1990; Los Angeles County, 1988). Such Mexican underrepresentation in upper-level jobs is suggestive of on-the-job discrimination.

Together, wage discrimination, inadequate education, lack of on-the-job training, and barriers to internal promotion exacerbate problems of low returns that are heightened through the increase of low-wage jobs.

RACIAL INEQUALITY IN PERSPECTIVE

As the proportion of the L.A. work force classified as low-wage workers is approximately the same as that for the nation as a whole, the growth of low-wage work locally and throughout the United States indicates that the process in Los Angeles is driven by external forces. The pressures of increased competition forced employers to improve their cost structures. This resulted in more unstable working conditions, lower wages, and increased subcontracting. The industrial landscape was shaped by growth of small firms; decline of unionization; rise of services, especially services to manufacturing; and in some cases, a geographic shift of manufacturing to what were previously peripheral sites. Within Los Angeles, the restructuring further redefined the local economy along ethnic lines. For recent immigrants who already start at a lower level than others, the ceiling for upward mobility has been lowered. Among Chicanos, restructuring of the Los Angeles economy has restricted their mobility by eliminating blue-collar jobs with decent wages.

Educational, training, and language programs have also systematically failed to prepare Chicanos and immigrants to be productive and competitive workers. The failures on these fronts are not the product of explicit discrimination, but an unwillingness by society to ensure fairness. Because the allocation of funds and resources is predicated on financial ability rather than principles of social justice, Mexicans, who are politically and economically weak, have fallen through the cracks. Racial inequality is then produced and reproduced through inherently unequal institutions. For those fortunate enough to acquire the prerequisite training and education for better jobs, finding meaningful employment is still problematic. Apparent unfair hiring and promotional practices have lowered Chicano earnings relative to that of Anglo counterparts with equivalent education and years of work experience. Such practices result in low rewards to education and work, and send a negative signal to Mexican youths. It discourages them from pursuing additional schooling and further alienates them from the work force.

Racial discrimination and economic restructuring interact to form a more pernicious social injustice. Racial discrimination is strengthened because economic cleavages are overlaid on top of racial lines. In turn, the economic polarization generated by restructuring is less subject to political challenge because the allocation of workers into different sectors is based in large part on race. If all groups were equally exposed to the risk of being marginalized, then the potential for governmental intervention would be greater. However, these economic risks are placed more heavily on Latinos and minorities—groups that are politically weak and isolated.[15]

CONCLUSION

As illustrated in Los Angeles, the effects of inequality lie largely at the metropolitan level. Yet the means for addressing the problem are often beyond local reach. Local governments have only limited legislative and initiative authority. They are particularly weak when it comes to harnessing resources for generating and distributing wealth (Goldsmith & Blakely, 1991.) However, in the absence of clear national directives that would encourage competition based on long-run productivity, the economy will continue to move toward a cheaper labor force. Thus, cities such as Los Angeles that are most responsive to international markets will continue to depend on low-cost labor to retain economic advantage. This course of action lays the groundwork for many negative consequences in the long run. The lack of avenues for upward mobility are sure to create prospects that run counter to our national welfare. Yet until the problem of excessive competition is addressed nationwide, Los Angeles will continue to face problems of Latino poverty and growing inequality.

APPENDIX 3.1

Regression Analysis of Immigrant Earnings

The following two regressions were used to analyze the relative position of immigrants across ethnic groups but within a given year:

$$(1)\ LnWg70 = a + HG + EXP + EXP2 + TOPW + DmOTHER\ WHITE + DmMexican + DmAsian + e$$

$$(2)\ LnWg80 = a + HG + EXP + EXP2 + TOPW + DmOTHER\ WHITE + DmMEXICAN + DmASIAN + e$$

The first equation models the 1969 annual earnings of immigrants entering the Los Angeles labor market in 1965-1969, and the second

examined the 1979 annual earnings of those entering in 1975-1979.
Both regressions were estimated separately for males and females.

The independent variables include the number of completed years of
education (HG), and years of labor force experience (EXP). A second
squared experience variable was included (EXP2) to approximate the
quadratic effect of experience on wages. Becker (1975), among others,
has shown that the returns to experience increase at a decreasing rate.
A fourth independent variable (TOPW) was used to overcome the
inconsistency between coding of the wage variable in the 1970 and 1980
Census. The upper limit cutoff for annual earnings of the two censuses
differ ($50,000 in 1970 and $75,000 in 1980). When earnings from the
1970 Census are adjusted to 1979 dollars, the upper cutoff exceeds
$75,000. In lieu of more accurate estimates of upper limit earnings, the
dummy variable for top wages (earnings of $75,000 or more in each
cohort group) was included to reduce the distortion caused by the cutoff.

The relative earnings position of races was established by using
dummy variables with European immigrants being the category excluded from the group. Relative to the earnings of European immigrants,
three races were examined: Mexicans, Asians, and Other Whites. The
European group includes Canadians, Australians, and New Zealanders,
as well as Western Europeans. The Other White category consists of
immigrants from Eastern Europe and the Middle East, but not Latin
America. Immigrants have changed significantly across cohorts. In
1965-1969, more than 70% of the "white" immigrants were European,
but in the second period, a larger percent came from Eastern Europe and
the Middle East. Because the dependent variable is expressed in natural
log terms, the coefficient for the dummy variables can be read as the
percent difference from Anglo (European) earnings.

We use the following regression to analyze the relative position of
immigrants across time but within individual ethnic groups:

(1) $LnWg = a + HG + EXP + EXP2 + TOPW + Dm1979 + e$.

The model uses a pooled sample of workers from both years (1969 and
1979). All incomes are converted to constant dollars, and a common
upper limit is used regardless of year. The first four independent variables are described above. This model includes a dummy variable for
1979 observations, which should capture any differences across time,
after controlling for educational level and potential years of labor
market experience. All regressions used persons who worked full-time

and year round to eliminate the influence of variations in the amount of employment.

Los Angeles SMSA, Earnings for Full-Time Male Immigrant Workers

Equations (1) and (2) All Male Immigrants	1965-1969 Cohort	1975-1979 Cohort
CONSTANT	4.1885**	4.3589**
HG	0.0430**	0.0365**
EXP	0.0357**	0.0285**
EXP2	−0.0006**	−0.0005**
TOPW	NA	1.6397**
DmOTHERWT	−0.1374*	−0.2450**
DmMEXICAN	−0.4023**	−0.5567**
DmASIAN	−0.4738**	−0.2856*
R-SQUARED	0.2685**	0.3078**

Equation (3) Combined 1969+1979	European Males	Mexican Males	Asian Males
CONSTANT	4.1715**	3.9186**	3.7769**
HG	0.0437**	0.0334**	0.0383**
EXP	0.0374**	0.0287**	0.0439**
EXP2	−0.0006**	−0.0004**	−0.0010**
TOPW	1.3394**	2.2402**	1.6048**
Dm1979	−0.0392	−0.1220**	0.1656**
R-SQUARED	0.1447**	0.0854**	0.1059**

SOURCE: U.S. Bureau of the Census, PUMS (1970, combined 5% and 15% data sets; 1980 A Sample). * = significance at 0.05 level or less; ** = significance at 0.01 level or less; otherwise, coefficients are not significant.

Los Angeles SMSA, Earnings for Full-Time Female Immigrant Workers

Equations (1) and (2) All Female Immigrants	1965-1969 Cohort	1975-1979 Cohort
CONSTANT	4.1520*	4.3526
HG	0.0416**	0.0228**
EXP	0.0038**	0.0122**
EXP2	−0.0001**	−0.0003**
TOPW	NA	NA
DmOTHERWT	−0.1632	−0.1838**
DmMEXICAN	−0.2991**	−0.4921**
DmASIAN	−0.0282	−0.2239*
ADJ. R-SQUARED	−0.3279	−0.2231**

Equation (3)

Combined 1969+1979	European Females	Mexican Females	Asian Females
CONSTANT	4.1949**	4.1134**	4.0399**
HG	0.0304**	0.0021	0.0413**
EXP	0.0323**	0.0052	0.0178*
EXP2	−0.0010*	−0.0001	−0.0004**
TOPW	NA	NA	NA
Dm1979	−0.0112	−0.0697	−0.2278*
ADJ. R-SQUARED	0.1056	−0.0024	0.0922

SOURCE: U.S. Bureau of the Census, PUMS (1970, combined 5% and 15% data sets; 1980 A Sample).
* = significance at 0.05 level or less; ** = significance at 0.01 level or less; otherwise, coefficients are not significant.

Los Angeles SMSA, Earnings for All Female Immigrant Workers

Equations (1) and (2)
All Female Immigrants

	1965-1969 Cohort	1975-1979 Cohort
CONSTANT	3.9562**	3.6965**
HG	0.0216*	0.0244**
EXP	0.0067	0.0267**
EXP2	−0.0001	−0.0005**
TOPW	NA	NA
DmOTHERWT	−0.2302*	−0.1531*
DmMEXICAN	−0.4004**	−0.3007**
DmASIAN	−0.2034*	−0.1193*
R-SQUARED	0.0875**	0.0765**

Equation (3)

Combined 1969+1979	European Females	Mexican Females	Asian Females
CONSTANT	3.8374**	3.5904**	3.3422**
HG	0.0227*	0.0064	0.0423**
EXP	0.0256**	0.0128*	0.0299**
EXP2	−0.0006**	−0.0002*	−0.0007**
TOPW	NA	NA	NA
Dm1980	−0.0843	−0.0243	−0.0129
R-SQUARED	0.0379**	0.0033**	0.0582**

SOURCE: U.S. Bureau of the Census, PUMS (1970, combined 5% and 15% data sets; 1980 A Sample).
* = significance at 0.05 level or less; ** = significance at 0.01 level or less; otherwise, coefficients are not significant.

APPENDIX 3.2

Regression Analysis of 1979 Earnings

Dependent Variable: Log of Annual Earnings

| | Estimated Coefficients | | | |
| | Total | | Anglos | Chicanos |
	(1)	(2)	(3)	(4)
Ind. Variables				
Constant	1.637	7.725	1.498	2.383
Years of Education	0.077	0.090	0.081	0.055
Years of Experience	0.057	0.070	0.059	0.040
Experience Squared	−0.093	−0.115	−0.094	−0.068
Log of Total Hours	0.846	—	0.855	0.793
Limited English	−0.058*	—	−0.222*	−0.087*
Chicano	−0.133	−0.169	—	—
Observations	6,897	6,897	5,902	995
Adj. R-Sq.	.362	.134	.368	.250
F-ratio	625.39	268.47	685.73	67.36

* Coefficient is not significant at .05 level. All other coefficients significant at the .01 or lower level. Coefficients for years of experience squared is scaled by 100. Chow-test for homogeneity of Anglos and Chicanos yield an F-ratio of 8.62 and $p < .001$.
Equations 1 and 2 (represented by columns 1 and 2) together constitute the estimated parameters to approach 1. Equations 3 and 4 (represented by columns 3 and 4) together constitute the estimated parameters to approach 2.

NOTES

1. The year 1987 was used as the end date because data for 1989 are not compatible with 1973 data at the two- and three-digit SIC level.

2. Part-time, part-year workers were employed less than 36 hours per week, or less than 50 weeks per year.

3. Calculations are based on data from the U.S. Bureau of Census series, *County Business Patterns*. The number of firms with 50 to 499 employees increased by 20%.

4. The GINI coefficient is equal to twice the difference between the observed distribution of family income measured by the Lorenz curve and the projected curve if income were equally distributed. Values range from 0 to 1 with 0 indicating complete equality, and 1 total inequality. The GINI coefficient in Los Angeles was as follows: 1969—.368; 1979—.401; 1987—.397. For the nation, it was as follows: 1969—.349; 1979—.365; 1987—.392 (Research Group on the Los Angeles Economy, 1989: 15).

5. The poverty rate measured as the percent below poverty for Los Angeles was as follows: 1969—11.0; 1979—13.4; 1987—15.6. Comparable rates for the nation were:

1969—12.1; 1979—11.7; 1987—13.5 (Research Group on the Los Angeles Economy, 1989: 15).

6. A new entrant refers to a person who had been in Los Angeles for 5 years or less at the time of the survey, or had been out of school for 5 years or less.

7. The unemployment rates were calculated for those individuals who stated that they were either at work, not at work but employed, or actively seeking employment. The statistics on earnings were based on those who earned at least $1,000 and were between the ages of 18 and 64. Relaxing these restrictions increases the percentage of workers who earned less than $8,000 for both groups, but the relative difference between persons of Mexican origin and Anglos persists. These Mexicans were about twice as likely to fall into this low-earnings category.

8. According to Ong (1988), "Recessions in Los Angeles pushed proportionately more people into poverty. The U.S. poverty rate increased by about a half of a percentage point for a percentage point increase in the national unemployment rate, while the L.A. poverty rate increased by about one and a third percentage points for a percentage point increase in the local unemployment rate" (p. 8). Further, within Los Angeles, Latinos were more negatively affected than Anglos. "For every one percentage point increase in the local unemployment rate, Hispanic poverty increased by over two percentage points, but Anglo poverty increased by less than a point" (p. 10).

9. The regressions also show that the gap between Asian and European males closed during the seventies, but was still substantial in 1980. The gap between Asian and European females increased. The decline in economic status is not merely an artifact, although the model could not control for English-language ability. Although the 1980 Census collected language data, the 1970 Census did not. Consequently, the model variables may be absorbing some of the effects of the pervasiveness of limited English-language ability among Mexican immigrants. But this bias should not account for the majority of increase in the earnings gap unless there was a systematic and substantial decrease in the average English-language ability of Mexican immigrants relative to the English-language ability of European immigrants.

10. The supply of low-wage labor is necessary but certainly not the only crucial factor. If the wage level is the determining factor, then we should see an exodus of firms and capital south of the border where labor is even cheaper. However, this is not the case. When asked about the choice of Southern California, one manager replied quite candidly: "The area offers virtually the same type of labor we found across the border, but here we don't have to deal with the Mexican red-tape and we are closer to our preferred markets" (Fernandez-Kelly & Garcia, 1986, p. 25). In general, employers sought an underemployed labor force at low-cost locations, yet with good access to the Los Angeles consumer market, as well as the region's infrastructure for distribution of goods and associated financial and administrative services.

11. Census tract level data are available only for all Latinos, but it is assumed the patterns are similar for Mexicans as a whole. A census tract is defined as being predominantly Latino if at least half of the population was Latino.

12. Available statistics on nativity, English-language ability, and place of residence in 1975 are for all residents and not just for Chicanos and Latinos. It is likely the statistics understate the influence of the foreign-born population within the Chicano/Latino community as those who were not Chicano or Latino were also less likely to be immigrants.

13. Estimates for high schools in East Los Angeles come from Woo (1988). Approximately one third of all U.S.-born Latino youths do not finish high school, a proportion that remained constant for nearly two decades (Ong & Morales, 1988). Nationally, about 40% of all Latino youths (immigrants and U.S.-born) drop out of high school, in contrast to 17% of all black students and 14% of whites (Koretz, 1989).

14. As contained in an unpublished report prepared by UCLA's Student Affirmative Action Office in 1988.

15. Lack of a political voice is beginning to change. In 1986 the Mexican American Legal Defense and Education Fund (MALDEF) successfully sued the Los Angeles City Council over redistricting and the need for more Latino representation. MALDEF, along with the ACLU and the Department of Justice, also won a redistricting suit in Los Angeles County in early 1991. The suit charged that the supervisoral districts illegally divided the largely Latino communities, thereby depriving them of representation. Despite the large Latino population in the county, there had not been a Latino supervisor elected into office in 138 years.

4

Decline Within Decline:
The New York Perspective

Andres Torres
Frank Bonilla

REGIONAL ECONOMIC CHANGE
AND INEQUALITY

The conditions of poverty and disadvantage faced by Latinos and other New Yorkers are inextricably connected to broader forces shaping economic opportunity within the metropolitan area and the nation as a whole. Regional economic decline, industrial restructuring, renewed immigration, labor market discrimination, changing social support infrastructures, and the local impacts of federal and state legislation are among the forces constraining the life chances of the metropolitan work force. Puerto Ricans, the principal Latino population in the region since the 1950s, have been especially hard hit by a recent, negative confluence of such factors. That experience has brought into the open the continuing vulnerability of Puerto Ricans among many other workers during periods of both economic expansion and decline. Both earlier and subsequent migration flows—African Americans in the 1930s and 1940s as well as Cubans in the 1960s and Dominicans since 1970—exemplify related but distinctive patterns of incorporation into the local work force, shaped in each instance by the timing, magnitude, and composition of migration flows. Today, the evolution of the three principal Latino groups in the region speaks to the diversity of Latino experiences here and around the United States as a whole. It is the effects of such forces that place a particular stamp on each of these trajectories, at the same time casting fresh light on the nature of ongoing social transformations in the U.S. and global economy.

None of the restructuring scenarios that have been advanced fully encompasses the New York case, especially from a Latino perspective, though each offers insights that help shape a depiction of the local process. Our reading of the New York instance is informed by several divergent characterizations that seek to capture the essentials of economic realignments in the region. As will be seen, the "bottom-up" view from within the Latino community, attempted here, both challenges and reinforces elements of each approach.

Few analysts question that something is afoot on a global scale that reaches into life everywhere, especially in cities like New York. Some affirm that a new mode of production, which they call *flex tech,* is in the making (Piore & Sabel, 1984; Scott & Storper, 1986). Characterizations of the flex-tech economy point to a reassertion of regionalism along with the decentralization and out-sourcing of production, innovations in management, dehierarchization, and worker participation. They point as well to the siting of firms in locales in which the work force has modest wage expectations and lacks a tradition or experience of union organization and where the costs of social reproduction weigh lightly on the private sector. Evidence of flex-tech presences abound in the region, though New York City clearly only partially fills this bill.

The city manifestly also does not quite square with rival notions about the emergence of a new *regime of accumulation.* (Heilbroner, 1989a). The regime change idea includes many of the components of technological and managerial innovation associated with flex tech. There is more emphasis, however, on ideological and value changes, especially in class relations, that are implicit in ongoing restructuring. In this view, an alleged breakdown of a preexisting "Fordist," mass production regime, tying worker gains to enhanced productivity, set in motion a process through which the business class has been institutionalized as the *universal class.* Leading working-class organizations have, in this scenario, opted to protect their status and pass on the downward pressures on earnings and the social wage to less secure workers—minorities, immigrants, women, and young entrants into the labor market. The accumulation regime perspective also emphasizes the detachment of the economy from its traditional political and spatial moorings. Capital with no enduring commitments to localities or sets of workers comes to operate in political spaces in which state power also shies away from guaranteeing social infrastructures for the whole population (Heilbroner, 1988).

A third, primarily sociological slant on the current crisis/transition hails the emergence of a so-called postindustrial society. These analyses focus on the changing structure of employment and social relations as various mixes of services become the commanding sectors of a growing number of national economies. The postindustrial trajectories of nations and their regions, however, are quite distinctive (Rein, Anderson, & Rainwater, 1987). The paths into the postindustrial age differ in the mix of services (especially the role of the public sector), the impacts on labor supply and demand, the consequences for social stratification and class contention, and the efficacy of state responses to the dislocations in employment and income affecting different groups.

A fourth, "global city" perspective draws selectively from many sources but emphasizes a world system focus in accounting for the changing condition of a few "megacities" as a function of their specialized niches in the world economy (Friedmann & Salguero, 1988; Rodríguez & Feagin, 1986; Sassen, 1988). The special virtue of this approach is in seeing cities like New York not as First World spaces invaded by backward peoples and cultures but as the most advanced capitalist formations working through their increasingly contradictory potential for drawing the most varied human contingents into the joint creation and destruction of economic resources, political institutions, and new cultural formations.

It is important to recognize that much analysis of economic trends proceeds in complacent disregard or direct rejection of the questions about the restructuring of relations between the economy and political institutions that are highlighted in this volume (Baumol, 1989). Internationalization of the economy means for these observers only a redeployment of some manufacturing and a few services. Research and development, communications, and currency markets remain, in their view, tightly reined within national or international bodies controlled by the more powerful nations. Foreign investment in the United States and its major cities is still modest and perhaps only transitorily essential. Questions of U.S. competitiveness and reassertion need to be addressed, but there are also opportunities and imperatives for international cooperation crying for attention (L. Smith, 1988).

Whatever the long-term implications for the world and national economies of lasting changes in the structure of labor demand and supply, New York and its environs provide a unique setting in which to observe the interplay of forces acting locally and at a distance to shape the contemporary use and misuse of human resources. More than ever, in growing numbers and diversity, Latinos and their conditions bring into view problematic aspects—positive as well as negative—of the emergent economy.

Declining Vitality and Competitive Position of the Region

Key trends—in job growth, unemployment rates, and relative wages— point to a long-term decline in the economic vitality of New York and its environs. A sustained slippage in the region's performance relative to the national economy signals the waning vigor of local development. Since 1972 its share of national output, population expansion, job generation, and personal income has dropped steadily. Between 1972 and 1982, for example, the Gross Regional Product fell as a proportion of Gross National Product from 12.3% to 10.9%. There was a parallel erosion of shares in total employment (from 9.7% to 8.6%) and aggregate personal income (from 12.5% to 10.0%). These lackluster showings are projected to continue through the 1990s (Regional Plan Association, 1986).

Within the tristate region that includes the southeastern counties of New York State (Long Island, New York City, Westchester, and others), northern New Jersey, and southern Connecticut, New York City's share of employment has fallen from 57% in 1969 to 48% in 1987 (Port Authority of New York and New Jersey [Port Authority], 1987, p. 59). Between 1976 and 1986, New York City's share of local job growth was only 28%, considerably below its portion of total jobs in 1976, which was almost 50% (S. M. Ehrenhalt, 1987, p. 36).

After decades during which unemployment rates in the city exceeded the national average, this differential began to close in 1979, primarily because of rising national unemployment. By the time of the recession of 1981-1982, the rates in New York City and the region were surpassed by national levels of unemployment (Port Authority, 1984, p. 13, 1987, p. 59). Although this change was widely read as an improvement in the relative condition of the local economy, it was to some extent nullified by falling labor participation rates and declining employment-population ratios. The continued drop in unemployment rates during the 1980s nevertheless indicated that the local economy was participating in the post-1982 economic expansion.

Of course, in tracking local labor market conditions, shifts in employment levels must be closely coupled with trends in relative wages. To the extent that labor costs are lower here than elsewhere in the United States, the city's attractiveness to business is presumably enhanced. The mid-1970s marked a turning point in this regard. Between 1960 and 1971 local wage increases approximated those at the national level. Over the course of the decade, manufacturing wages at both levels rose at an average annual rate of about 5% (Federal Reserve Bank Quarterly, 1981). By the early 1970s this pattern was reversed. Throughout the decade manufacturing workers in the city consistently received lower wage increases than workers in the nation as a whole. It is possible that the large influx of immigrant labor during this period contributed to the slower pace of wage increases in New York's manufacturing sector.[1]

Between 1980 and 1985, however, manufacturing earnings in New York City surpassed the national average. This pattern, combined with a rising local inflation rate, has concerned officials worried that New York may once again be losing its competitive edge (S. M. Ehrenhalt, 1987, p. 17). Currently, the economy seems dangerously adrift in a hard-to-read transition as the boom of the 1980s has lost momentum. The stock market crash of 1987 stifled job growth in the financial services sector, and traditional manufacturing resumed its long-term slide (Noyelle, 1989). Fears of an extended recession combined with a fiscal crisis that may rival that of the mid-1970s presage a troubled final decade as the century draws to a close (Rohatyn, 1990).

Economic Restructuring: Industry and Occupational Shifts

In 1950 the New York City economy was characterized by a fairly diversified industrial base. Manufacturing, comprising 1,040,000 jobs, or 29.8% of the total, led all sectors. Services, including financial, insurance, real estate, and other, accounted for 24%, and the trade sectors represented 21.5%. By 1983, the manufacturing share of employment had fallen by half to 15% and that of services almost doubled to 44% (Bienstock, 1977; Port Authority, 1980, 1984).

The continued evaporation of manufacturing jobs during the 1980s was especially worrisome. From 1980 to 1986, New York City lost manufacturing jobs at nearly three times the national rate. This pace was twice as great as that of the rest of the metropolitan region, which includes suburban New York City and northeastern New Jersey. The contrast is even starker when the city is compared with its immediate

suburban ring, where manufacturing jobs grew moderately during the
period (S. M. Ehrenhalt, 1987, p. 32).

The erosion of the manufacturing sector also contributed to a significant transformation in the occupational distribution of the locally
employed. This was most evident in the reduction of blue-collar workers from 37.5% in 1950 to 24.4% in 1980. Decomposition of occupational shifts by race/ethnic group indicates that these changes affected
the various groups differently. By 1980 a substantial proportion of
Puerto Rican workers (38.1% vs. 22.9% for the total population) still
toiled as blue-collar workers. African-American workers were increasingly concentrated in clerical (from 19.1% in 1960 to 27.7% in 1980).
A sizable proportion, close to a fourth, were also to be found in
blue-collar occupations in 1980 (Center for Puerto Rican Studies, 1986,
Table 9-NYC; U.S. Bureau of Labor Statistics, 1968, Table 9).

Immigration and Resident Minority Labor

Despite the backdrop of a gradual regional slump and a services-
oriented industrial restructuring, the local economy has absorbed significant numbers of immigrant workers during the last two decades.
Explanations for this seeming paradox take two forms. In one view the
advancing internationalization of the city's economy and expansion of
its higher wage tiers has offset the labor-displacing effects of industrial
restructuring by generating the base for new activities drawing on
low-wage labor (Sassen, 1988). New economic niches have come into
being for unskilled workers in both low-paying services as well as a
"downgraded" manufacturing sector. At the same time, a "loosening of
worker-employer ties" has opened up new entry points for unskilled
immigrants, further weakening institutional arrangements that formerly
provided security and shelter to resident unskilled labor (Freedman,
1983).

A supply-side view stresses demographic changes in the native or
established work force, especially the shrinking pool of those willing
to accept jobs in the secondary labor market among immigrant offspring
(Waldinger, 1986). It is this labor "shortage" that is said to provide an
effective "pull" for the new immigration, though most researchers still
argue against the idea that recent immigrants are a significant substitute
for those already in place (Borjas, 1990; Simon, 1989). Nevertheless,
there is some evidence that resident minorities may be having less
success than newcomers in finding a place within the restructured

economy. In 1980, participation and unemployment rates for "Other Hispanics," which includes many new immigrants, indicates greater incorporation into the work force of these contingents than for African Americans and Puerto Ricans. Joblessness is greater for African Americans (11.2%) and Puerto Ricans (11.9) than for Other Hispanics (10.2%). Conversely, labor force participation rates for the former groups are lower than for the latter. Comparisons of Asian Americans with recent Asian immigrants show similar patterns (Glazer, 1988).

As discussed below, other research on New York points toward a correlation between a rising presence of Dominicans and Asians in manufacturing and a partial displacement of Puerto Ricans. The mechanisms by which these repositionings of segments of the labor force are accomplished appear to be more intricate than those readily captured by econometric tests for labor substitution. Substitution and wage effects aside, it is just as reasonable to argue that new immigrants, rather than competing directly with resident minority workers, constitute a convenient condition for the reorganization of firms by employers seeking ways to circumvent the prevailing costs of unskilled and semi-skilled labor.

Discrimination

The persistence of discriminatory patterns in hiring, pay, and promotion practices of key industries reinforces the negative effects of the interplay of labor demand and supply conditions that have been described. Three sectors in which the share of minority employment manifests serious lags are construction, financial services, and government.

Construction was one of the fastest growing sectors during the 1980s. An industry in which formal education is less important, it would have been an ideal source of expanded job opportunities for minorities. Yet reports show that African-American employment in the region's construction firms actually declined during the period, as did representation in registered apprenticeship programs. Anecdotal evidence concerning Latinos suggests they have fared only slightly better. These outcomes have been traced to the failure of municipal and state officials to enforce affirmative action provisions, allowing free play to the racism still manifest among industry employers and unions (Bailey, 1990).

Despite a sizable increase in financial sector jobs between 1975 and 1982 (from 322,800 to 389,100), the share of these jobs held by African Americans and Latinos rose only modestly from 22.3% to 26.1%. By far the greatest source of added jobs was in office and clerical occupations, where the minority portion reached 36.8% (Schaller, 1983). More recent studies focusing on the 1980s show that even these gains were short lived, as growth of the sector slackened and concern with affirmative action cooled (Bailey, 1990; Stafford, 1990). The reach of discriminatory practices extends as well to the system of private job placement agencies, many of which sideline minorities when recruiting for employers.[2]

Black and Latino representation in New York's public sector, though steadily increasing during the 1980s, is similarly still disproportionately concentrated in poorly paid clerical and service occupations (Stafford, 1985). New evidence also demonstrates that implementation in the city of the Immigration Reform and Control Act of 1986 (IRCA) has resulted in widespread discrimination against immigrants and persons perceived as aliens (City of New York Commission on Human Rights, 1989).

Empirical studies of wage inequality in the local labor market further illustrate continuing disparities linked to race. Varying applications of labor market segmentation analysis provide evidence of wage discrimination against African Americans and Latinos (Meléndez, 1988; Torres, 1988). After taking into account educational, demographic, and occupation/industrial characteristics of workers, this research indicates that in 1980 discrimination accounted for one third to one half of the wage differentials between Hispanic and non-Hispanic white males. One fifth to one half of Hispanic women's wage differentials were attributable to similar unequal treatment (Meléndez, 1988). In each decennial year between 1960 and 1980, blacks and Puerto Ricans were subject to wage discrimination in at least one labor segment. In 1970, there was measurable wage discrimination in both primary and secondary labor markets (Torres, 1988).

POPULATION, LABOR FORCE, AND RELATIVE EARNINGS

General Population

One of the most significant demographic trends in the postwar period has been the rising proportion of African Americans and Puerto Ricans in the city's population, with their combined share almost tripling between 1950 (12.6%) and 1980 (32.5%) (Brecher & Tobier, 1977, pp. 65, 85, 88; New York City Department of City Planning, 1985, p. 6;

Tobier, 1984, p. 104). Latino groups in the aggregate comprised 19.9% of the city's population by 1980, increasing their share from 16.2% in 1970. The share of total population held by all minority groups, including Asians, amounted to 48.2% in 1980 (New York City Department of City Planning, 1985, p. 2, Table 2). By 1990, this share had risen to 56.8% (*New York Times,* April 17, 1990). Such significant shifts, occurring during a period of zero growth in the total population, highlight a profound change in the racial and ethnic composition of the city's population.

Although a presence in New York since the turn of the century, Puerto Ricans arrived en masse immediately after World War II. Through the 1970s and 1980s the principal component of population increase among Puerto Ricans has been natural growth, as the initial migrants were succeeded by second-generation children (F. Bonilla & Campos, 1981). During the 1980s a new migration of about 40,000 persons arrived in the United States from Puerto Rico (Regional Plan Association, 1988). This post-1970 migration includes a higher proportion of educated and skilled labor, reflecting rising educational levels on the island, but remains chiefly a movement of low-skilled labor rather than anything approximating a "brain drain" (Ortiz, 1986; Rivera-Batiz, 1987). How many of these newcomers have prior experience of life in the United States is an open question.

Other Latinos began to arrive in large numbers during the 1960s, first Cubans and later Dominicans and Colombians. After initial settlement within the city, Cubans began in the 1970s to relocate to the suburban ring, especially northern New Jersey, as well as to Florida.

During the 1970s and 1980s, the principal component of population increase for other Latinos continued to be immigration, although it is expected that the share of the second generation will increase significantly among Dominicans and Colombians throughout the 1990s. The considerable number of undocumented persons of Latino origin, put at anywhere from 25% (Waldinger, 1990) to 50% (Bogen, 1987) above the documented population, complicates these estimates.[3] The growth rate of non-Puerto Rican Latinos continues to exceed that of Puerto Ricans, so that the share of Puerto Ricans among all Latinos should continue to decline.

Labor Force Population and Status

Demographic changes are reflected in the labor force as well. In 1987, blacks, Latinos, and Asians constituted 49.3% of the New York City labor force (U.S. Bureau of Labor Statistics, 1987).

Despite a rising share in the overall population and labor force, Puerto Ricans have faced declining participation and rising unemployment over time. In 1950, Puerto Ricans—and African Americans—had higher labor force participation rates than the citywide average. But this relative position was reversed by 1980, as labor force entry and job retention failed to keep pace with population growth. The one exception was for African-American women, who maintained a fairly stable participation rate, staying within close range of 50% from 1950 to 1985. By 1985, the rate for Puerto Ricans had declined to only 40%, less than that for black workers (Center for Puerto Rican Studies, 1986, Table 8-NYC; Community Service Society, 1987, pp. 17, 27; U.S. Department of Labor, 1975, pp. 62-63).

Data on unemployment rates offer further signs of persistent gaps in labor market access. Comparisons of 1960 to 1980 indicate a deterioration in unemployment ratios between the total and minority labor force, including by gender. For example, the ratio of black male to total male unemployment rose from 1.55 to 2.33; the ratio of Puerto Rican male to total male unemployment rose from 2.11 to 2.16. Similar patterns prevailed among females. For women, the ratio of black to total unemployment rose from 1.27 to 1.69, and the ratio of Puerto Rican to total increased from 2.08 to 2.14 (Center for Puerto Rican Studies, 1986, Table 8; U.S. Department of Labor, 1975, p. 71).

Relative Earnings

Figure 4.1 summarizes relative earnings data for the decennial years 1950-1980.[4] Comparisons with white male earners show that since 1950, only Cuban males, African-American females, and Puerto Rican males achieved sustained improvement in relative earnings. Even for these groups the reduction in inequality was very modest over the 30 years: twelve percentage points for Cuban males, 7 percentage points for African-American females, 5 percentage points for Puerto Rican males. Available data on Dominicans, based however on very small samples for 1950 and 1960, show large increases for males and decreases for females.

Data for the 1970-1980 interval further illustrate the enduring pattern of earnings inequality. In 1970 the hierarchy of earnings stood in the following order: white males, Cuban males, African-American males, Puerto Rican males, Dominican males, white females, African-American females, Cuban females, Puerto Rican females, and Dominican females.

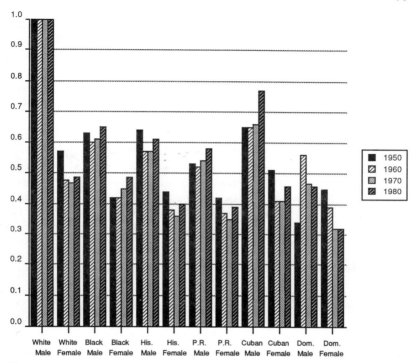

Figure 4.1. Relative Earnings Ratios: Other to White Male

By 1980, white females and African-American females (who by now shared the same level of earnings) attained higher earnings than Dominican males. Between 1970 and 1980, the earnings gap between white males and all other groups was reduced only slightly. Except for Cuban males, no group increased its ratio of relative earnings by more than 4 percentage points. Closest to white males were Cuban males (77% of white male earnings) and African-American males, whose ratio increased from 61% to 65%. Dominicans registered no change.

Separate data on educational attainment reveal a variety of patterns with regard to the relationship between education and improvement in relative earnings between 1970 and 1980. For white females this improvement was fairly evenly distributed across all educational cohorts. African Americans experienced their largest earnings increases in non-college categories. For Puerto Rican males the most significant improvement took place at the two extremes of the educational attainment distribution, and for Puerto Rican females progress was greatest at the higher education levels (F. Bonilla & Torres, 1989).

WORK AND INEQUALITY

Given the expansion in regional employment between 1970 and 1980, what can we say regarding broad processes leading to growth or decline in the labor force presence of racial/ethnic groups? Shift-share analysis was used to track three influences on employment change: overall regional growth, industry shifts, and racial/ethnic distribution within the labor force.[5] A second approach applies a quintile analysis to trace the distribution of earnings within each racial/ethnic group.

Components of Racial/Ethnic Employment Change

Despite patterns of aging and emigration that would tend to reduce their share in the regional labor force, white workers were able to take advantage of the job expansion stimulated by the growth of services industries. At the same time, they appeared to be sheltered from the damaging effects of the decline in manufacturing, as they essentially retained their share of employment in this sector. Growth in the public sector was also important for them.

African Americans benefited primarily from overall employment expansion in the region and somewhat less from rising share in the labor force. The principal source of employment growth was the services industries. Blacks also increased their representation in the public sector.

For Asian Americans, rising share in the labor force was the main source of employment growth, especially in the fastest growing industries. It appears that for them, increasing employment followed a dual pattern, experiencing greater representation at the upper (high-end services) and lower (traditional manufacturing and retail trade) ends of the industry distribution.

Puerto Ricans were the only group to suffer an absolute decline in employment in the region between 1970 and 1980. Although overall regional employment growth protected them from even greater declines, the shift from manufacturing to services had a particularly detrimental impact on Puerto Rican workers. Dwindling shares were manifested across a number of industry sectors: traditional manufacturing, retail trade, transportation, and high-end services. Compared to other minority groups, Puerto Rican share declined along a broader range of industries. Unlike white workers, Puerto Rican employment did not benefit enough from regional growth to offset a falling representation.

For Dominican workers, the most prominent influence on employment growth was a marked increase in share, reflecting significant immigration to the region in this period. Of secondary importance was the impact of overall regional growth. The main areas in which Dominicans increased share were traditional manufacturing (responsible for half of the greater share), low-end services, and retail trade. The fact that the shares of Asian Americans and Dominicans in traditional manufacturing and retail trade increased, even as these shares declined for Puerto Ricans, lends credence to the notion that the former groups, however indirectly, have been substituted for the latter in these industries.

Changes in the Earnings Distribution

Table 4.1 reports the earnings quintile distributions for each race/ethnic group.[6] Within-group distributions mirror patterns of internal stratification, as they indicate the share of total earnings received by each quintile. For example, in 1970, the poorest 40% of Dominican workers received 77.2% (16.9% + 60.3%) of the earnings of all Dominican workers, whereas the top 40% received only 6% of total labor market income. From this perspective we see that Dominican workers in 1970 were overwhelmingly low-wage workers.

There is evidence of increased internal polarization for Puerto Ricans and Dominicans between 1970 and 1980: Each group experienced a large decline in the second quintile (−12.7% for Puerto Ricans, −17.2% for Dominicans) accompanied by increases in the lowest and upper quintiles. By contrast, African-American and white earnings show fewer signs of polarization, although a decline (−11.0%) in the second quintile among African Americans points to a slackening of mobility gains.

Data for earlier years show that for Puerto Ricans, mobility was greater during the 1960s than 1970s (Table 4.2). Between 1960 and 1970 the share of earnings held by the top 60% of workers rose from 30.7% to 40.1%, a rise of 30.6%. During 1960-1970 this share rose 24% (9.8 percentage points).

For Dominican labor the 1960s represented upward mobility from the lowest to the second quintile, with minor change in the top 60%. Puerto Ricans also evidenced greater gains in the 1960s than in the 1970s. In

Table 4.1 Summary Tables of Within-Group Earnings Quintile Distribution, 1970-1980

	White	AA	H	PR	Dom
1970					
1.	20.1	20.9	19.3	19.1	16.9
2.	18.6	32.7	40.4	40.8	60.3
3.	16.6	25.2	22.9	24.6	16.9
4.	21.0	15.6	13.2	12.6	5.2
5.	23.7	5.6	4.2	2.9	0.8
1980					
1.	19.8	21.4	20.7	22.0	23.9
2.	18.3	21.7	29.9	28.1	43.1
3.	19.4	29.2	28.7	30.5	23.8
4.	20.7	19.2	14.5	14.3	7.1
5.	21.8	8.4	6.3	5.0	2.0
Change in Quintile Distribution: 1970-1980					
1.	−0.3	+0.5	+1.4	+2.9	+7.0
2.	−0.3	−11.0	−10.5	−12.7	−17.2
3.	+2.8	+4.0	+5.8	+6.0	+6.9
4.	−3.0	+3.6	+1.3	+1.8	+1.9
5.	−1.9	+2.8	+2.1	+2.0	+4.2

SOURCE: U.S. Bureau of the Census, PUMS (1970, 1980).
NOTE: AA—African-American; H—Hispanic; PR—Puerto Rican; Dom—Dominican.

the 1970s we observe the apparent impact of low-wage immigrant labor among Dominicans, as the share going to the lowest quintile rises (from 16.9% to 23.9%). Nevertheless, substantial movement into middle quintiles is also evident for this group.

LATINO LABOR IN POSTWAR NEW YORK

Puerto Ricans: Opportunities Foreclosed

Glancing retrospectively upon the early postwar period (the 1940s and 1950s) it would seem to have been reasonable to expect that over time Puerto Ricans would be absorbed fairly successfully into the local economy (Glazer, 1988, p. 68). The aging of the white population created a vacuum in the labor market that was expected to be filled by the growing African-American and Puerto Rican population. Assuming continued

Table 4.2 Quintile Earnings Distribution, 1960-1980 (in percent)

	AA	*PR*	*Dom*	*Cuban*
1960				
1.	27.0	25.0	30.8	25.8
2.	32.9	44.2	44.6	35.5
3.	26.6	22.8	18.5	22.0
4.	10.5	6.0	4.6	10.8
5.	3.0	1.9	1.5	5.9
1970				
1.	20.9	19.2	16.9	17.6
2.	32.7	40.8	60.3	32.1
3.	25.2	24.6	16.9	24.4
4.	15.6	12.6	5.2	19.4
5.	5.6	2.9	0.8	6.5
1980				
1.	21.4	22.0	23.9	18.3
2.	21.7	28.1	43.1	23.0
3.	29.2	30.5	23.8	28.7
4.	19.2	14.3	7.1	19.2
5.	8.4	5.0	2.0	10.8

SOURCE: U.S. Bureau of the Census, PUMS (1970, 1980).
NOTE: AA—African-American; H—Hispanic; PR—Puerto Rican; Dom—Dominican.

regional vitality and an effective educational system, there was no a priori reason to doubt the likelihood of successful incorporation of these groups into the economic mainstream.

But well before the mid-1970s ushered in the radical restructuring of the city's economy, an earlier phase of economic stagnation began to undercut opportunities for Puerto Ricans. The late 1950s to mid-1970s were characterized by a dual problem of secular decline in the region's economic strength and a shift within the employment structure toward high-skilled occupations connected to the growing high-tech corporate services sectors. These trends imposed severe constraints on Puerto Rican labor, which by the 1960s was just beginning to establish a more stable and diversified foothold in the local economy. For Puerto Ricans the principal outcome of this period was labor force displacement, manifested in a sharp decline in labor force participation and a rise in unemployment from 1960 to 1970.

Following these developments came a second phase of restructuring (mid-1970s to late 1980s) that set in motion additional processes detrimental to subsequent development of the Puerto Rican community. These may be termed "foreclosing" processes in the sense that they obstructed common paths of incorporation and upward mobility that some earlier groups of labor experienced in New York. Puerto Ricans, as well as African Americans, share the common circumstance of having been subject to these structural hindrances on a very large scale. Two such processes were particularly damaging: (a) the erosion of stable jobs and (b) the reorganization of light manufacturing based on immigrant labor.

Job Erosion. The erosion of stable jobs, incipient during the late 1960s to mid-1970s, became magnified in the second wave of restructuring and appeared in two important areas: among large corporations and in the public sector. The complex of jobs associated with the former offered the potential of long-term employment opportunities for resident minorities who were increasing their share of the local labor force. The presence in the earlier phase of large corporations characterized by internal labor markets, along with a political climate generally open to affirmative action policies, made this a potentially significant sector for Puerto Ricans and African Americans.

But leading up to early 1970s many of these large corporations—for a number of which the city served as a base for headquarters operations—relocated to other regions. These firms were gradually replaced by service industries (e.g., finance, communications, and information processing) largely tied to national and international commerce. These enterprises established a new profile of occupations and labor processes, much less accessible and rewarding for African Americans and Puerto Ricans. The new jobs often relied on contingent, nonunion labor, which supplanted the stable employment paths of earlier large corporate structures. Many new employers imported alternate sources of labor, including college-trained whites from other states (Alba, 1984), or turned to commuter labor in the suburban ring.

Throughout the postwar period public sector employment has been an important source of stable jobs for New Yorkers. Until the mid-1970s, municipal and state workers benefited from greater job security in comparison to private sector workers. Wages and fringe benefits were comparable to those in the private sector (Bienstock, 1977). During the 1960s, municipal employment expanded considerably, absorbing rising numbers of African American and Puerto Rican workers. Between 1950 and 1975, the share of all jobs held by the public sector rose from 10.6% to 17.5% (Bienstock, 1977; Port Authority, 1980; 1984).

The fiscal crisis of 1975-1976 precluded further expansion of this sector for almost a decade, and by 1983 this share had fallen to 15.5%. For two reasons, Puerto Ricans particularly were subject to the damaging effects of curtailed public employment. First, they were the most recent group to enter the municipal labor force and were therefore more susceptible to layoffs instituted by the city. Second, compared to African Americans, they appeared less able to exercise the political power necessary to establish and preserve a sizable niche within the public sector (Torres, 1991).

A gradual resumption of minority increases took place in the mid-1980s, but this proved to be a temporary reprieve. In the face of a new fiscal crisis, as the 1990s decade opened, the city administration proposed a reduction of 25,000 jobs (including 15,000 layoffs) for the 1991 and 1992 fiscal years (*New York Times*, January 6, 1991). As in the past, civil service protections will be suspended. In 1975, 25,000 unionized municipal employees were fired as part of an agreement staving off bankruptcy for city government (Shefter, 1985, p. 135).

Reorganization of Light Manufacturing. In the 1970s a new set of light manufacturing firms filled the vacuum created by capital flight in the 1960s and early 1970s. The labor force attached to the earlier manufacturing complex, which had been displaced to a significant extent, was not redeployed into the newly evolving sector. The growth of the new sector was dependent on a lower cost of labor, a condition met by the use of new sources of immigrant labor. This cost reduction was partially due to the characteristics of immigrant enterprises in which workers were willing to forego wage demands in exchange for the opportunity to work in the host country. Here family and ethnic ties functioned to cushion potential class conflicts within the immigrant enterprise. The lower wages and inferior working conditions that are significant features in this reorganized manufacturing sector (garments, novelties, furniture, consumer electronics, etc.) restricted labor participation by resident minority labor (Sassen, 1988; Waldinger, 1986). As a group with an historically high representation in light manufacturing, Puerto Ricans were particularly hurt by this restructuring.

Other important processes reinforced these exclusionary mechanisms. The decline of class-based politics, persistence of discrimination, and resurgence of interethnic rivalries was a natural outcome of the new political context that emerged in the wake of the city's fiscal crisis. Overall, minorities emerged as the principal losers, as attested to by the continued rise in racial poverty and persistence of racial differentials in unemployment through the mid-1980s. Within minority-dominated spheres, Puerto Ricans appeared to be the greatest losers in the competition for scarce resources and job opportunities. The growing lag in recent years in the socioeconomic status of Puerto Ricans as against African Americans points to this uneven deterioration (Community Service Society, 1989).

Finally, the social decomposition and disarray so visible within the Puerto Rican community and family continue to hamper labor force participation and upward mobility.[7] The rise in working-class poverty, the polarization of earnings within the labor force, and the decline in opportunities for long-term, stable employment generate a perception among potential entrants to the labor market that participation is not worth the sacrifice involved in taking low-paying, dead-end jobs.[8] As successive age cohorts are released from the educational system, the gap increases between the skill requirements of the occupational structure and the skill levels of those new to the labor force.

This far-reaching crisis suggests that the principal dynamics and processes affecting Puerto Rican conditions have shifted from the domain of the formal economy and state to the neighborhood and household. Neither the labor market nor the social support apparatus serves as a reliable avenue for community mobility. Traditional ideals of orderly social ascent through assimilation or racial integration are contradicted by the contemporary turmoil and discontinuity in the "ethnic queue."

Dominicans: Tentative Incorporation

In 1980, Puerto Ricans and Dominicans comprised roughly 70% of the New York Latino population. Cubans, Colombians, and Ecuadorians accounted for the next largest contingents.[9] A comparative perspective on the Puerto Rican and Dominican experience accents important parallels and differences.

The occupational distribution of the Dominican labor force in 1980 is similar to that of Puerto Ricans in 1960. The proportions of blue-collar and manufacturing-based occupations are roughly equivalent, suggesting that Dominicans are experiencing a similar initial incorporation into the New York economy. Despite important changes in the industrial structure, another Caribbean labor pool has been allocated into the same industrial sectors (Hernández, 1989). It is a considerably revamped manufacturing sector, dependent on lower labor costs, that has largely absorbed Dominican labor. But since the mid-1980s, the garment industry has suffered a new period of decline (S. M. Ehrenhalt, 1987, p. 17). This trend, along with the arrival of the 1990-1991 recession, threatens the initial inroads achieved by Dominican labor.[10] These difficulties add to the problematic experience of the 1980s, during which Dominicans saw a polarization of labor earnings, rising inequality, and greater poverty among the employed.[11]

Recent studies call attention to the entrepreneurial activity of the Dominican community (Grasmuck, 1984; Waldinger, 1986). This is visible in areas such as restaurants, bodegas (grocery stores), and light manufacturing. Although reliable comparative data are not available, this appears to be an area of contrast with the Puerto Rican community. Puerto Rican neighborhoods no longer abound with the small businesses (bodegas, barber shops, beauty salons, travel agencies, etc.) that thrived in the barrios during the 1950s and 1960s. Many were driven out by the expansion of full-service chain stores and supermarkets; others closed down as the original owners retired and relocated to Puerto Rico.

In several areas, Dominican small businesses have filled the vacuum, but the markets for these activities are still limited to economically depressed ethnic enclaves. Competition from supermarkets and fast-food outlets, the practice of many owners who repatriate revenues to the Dominican Republic, and the narrow consumer market to which these businesses appeal limit the potential reach of this ethnic-based strategy. Short of some dramatic turnaround in the conditions underlying these enclaves, these small enterprises are not likely to expand vigorously or to spur reinvestment of capital in the local neighborhood. It remains to be seen whether the Dominican neighborhood-based small businesses will flourish beyond the initial immigrant cohort, distinguishing them from the Puerto Rican experience.

The New York Dominican community has also entered an important phase of political activity at the local level. (Georges, 1984; Gutierrez, 1988; Linares, 1989). This process will enable more effective action in the public sector, as has been the case historically for African Americans and more recently for Puerto Ricans. But the prospects for employment expansion in this sector are limited by the city's fiscal condition. The push toward reducing the size of city government will likely diminish employment opportunities for Dominicans and other recent immigrants.

As this larger context continues to be dominated by politics of austerity and restricted state functions, the pressures sustaining competitive rather than coalitional interethnic relations will continue to operate. The government's role as employer and supplier of services will be increasingly strained as it seeks to manage the conflicting claims made upon it by the poorer racial/ethnic communities. In this competition, the more recent immigrant groups such as Dominicans will probably fare less well than even the resident minorities.

Finally, one notes very disturbing signs of extreme poverty and social stress within the Dominican community. Problems of housing, education, and health are surfacing in alarming degrees. Washington Heights, the area of greatest Dominican concentration, is consistently identified as one of the most depressed areas within the city and nation. In 1980 close to a quarter of families in the area lived below the poverty line; between 1980 and 1984, the percentage of households receiving welfare assistance increased from 19.1% to 24% (Torres-Saillant, 1989). Other symptoms of poverty plague this area: one of the highest rates of lead poisoning, a dangerous lack of prenatal care (28.5% of all births), more overcrowding than in any other New York City school district, and the highest homicide rate in the city (Gutierrez, 1988).

In 20 years (1965-1985) the community has traversed a path toward relative deprivation similar to that lived by Puerto Ricans. Other factors may serve to further impede Dominican social mobility. Unlike Puerto Ricans, Dominicans do not arrive as U.S. citizens, making them less eligible early on for certain types of jobs and social supports. Although numerically significant in a growing number of districts, their ability to convert residential concentration into voting power is subject to the time lag required by the naturalization process.[12] A people with a greater African heritage than Puerto Ricans, Dominicans may find their racial composition used as an additional barrier against them. The confluence of these factors may subject this community to even greater difficulties than those faced by Puerto Ricans.

SOCIAL INFRASTRUCTURE

In the increasingly volatile economic environment that has been described, New York has been bracing itself for additional shocks. Clearly, the city's public and private support systems for the unemployed and working poor, all under severe strain, face intensified demands. The specific ways in which this institutional infrastructure intermeshes with and responds to the successive dislocations driven by recent restructurings and downturns of the local economy play an integral part in cushioning or accentuating the polarizing trends that have been observed, giving them a distinctive regional cast.

In November 1990, a summit conference of big-city mayors convened by New York's David Dinkins brought into graphic focus key dimensions of a growing disarticulation of state and market institutions that now threatens cities large and small across the nation. The preamble to the conference program pinpointed the impact of federal pullbacks on local capacity to fill these gaps:

> The local struggle to maintain and extend the systems necessary to compensate for vast dislocations has been set back by national economic, social and political policies. This has been especially true in the last decade. For example, a general revenue-sharing program that distributed $4.5 billion in 1981 has since disappeared. Housing programs . . . were cut from $30 billion a year to $7 billion per annum. These cuts would have been devastating under any circumstances, but were particularly debilitating in a decade of unprecedented immigration into metropolitan areas. (Urban Summit, 1990, p. 2)

In New York City, federal aid as a percent of local revenue dropped to 9% in 1990 from 19% in 1980 and 22% in 1976 (C. Brecher & Horton, 1989).

The gathered mayors understandably set high on the postsummit agenda a coordinated campaign on urban budget issues aimed at the Congress and the presidency. But only a few months later, as the New York state and city budget processes came to a deadlock in spring 1991, the full complexity and acuteness of the city's fiscal distress came even more ominously into view. As states, major cities, and lesser localities have fallen into line with federal supply-side policy orientations regarding taxation, the capacity to respond to revenue shortfalls except through severe cutbacks in social programs and infrastructure spending has been undermined at every level. New York State, it turned out, ranks 49th in the nation in the percentage of combined state and local taxes raised by the state (States in Profile, 1990). Debate among tax experts, currently dominated by concern about the potentially dampening effects of any tax increases on investment, divided on the question of whether the regional economy would be damaged most by new state or city taxes (Kolbert, 1991).

According to the National League of Cities, urban fiscal crises in the 1990s, with places like New York in the lead, reflect an unprecedented complex of structural, demographic, and institutional problems that will keep cities in turmoil throughout the 1990s (Ledebar, 1991). New York

City is already a prime instance of this fiscal disarticulation. Urban-suburban disjunctures in tax policy and spending are as much complicating factors here as are the misfires and contradictions among city, state, and federal levels.

The "structural" forces behind this fiscal disarticulation are principally the interplay of competing economic development strategies aimed at enticing and rooting investments, and with them jobs and revenues, in particular localities. The favored mode for accomplishing and consolidating these connections, aside from tax concessions and other subsidies, are "public-private partnerships." Understandably, a prime strategy articulated at the mayors' summit conference (after the collective reassertion of claims at the federal level) was the building of ties with corporate peers. In fact, the meeting itself was at one time conceived of as one in which each mayor would be accompanied by a willing corporate associate or "buddy." The potential importance of these linkages has been reinforced in ensuing consultations, and a mayoral-corporate sector summit figures as a major next step in the process. These partnerships are seen as most promising in the field of education, building on the shared interest of localities and employers in developing the human resources most closely at hand. A key counterpart to the Competitive Cities Act of 1991 is therefore the Great Cities Education Act.

In January 1991 a Washington, D.C., conference of big-city school superintendents was in fact convened as a first follow-up to the New York City conclave. The mayors' commitment to get children into schools "safe, healthy and ready to learn" is part of a public sector compact with the corporate world intended to guarantee a work-ready labor force with the right combination of skills and without exaggerated expectations regarding "reservation" wages, that is, the wage rate that would draw them into the active labor force. Though the compact remains couched in the language of national security and economic competitiveness, it does freshly articulate commitments to preschool and early childhood education along with broader socially integrative and emancipatory goals not strictly tied to adequate performance in marginally rewarding employment. In the interim, the "mismatch" of the native work force and job demand now compromising competitiveness at various levels may be partly met by well-managed redeployments of production and services. Capital mobility, both within the United States and abroad, may be coupled with refinements in immigration policy to fine-tune the allocation of labor supplies to industries and regions that are in need of labor (Bach and Meissner, 1990).

New York is also among the top urban centers that are poles of attraction for immigrants, especially Latinos, but also for other Caribbean peoples as well as Asians. In this instance, fresh immigration and the attendant heightened diversification, cultural and political, occur against a background of total population loss and long-term regional decline. Political redistricting for the Municipal Council on the heels of the 1990 Census seems to foreshadow eventual African-American/Latino dominance of that body as it embarks on its functions with substantially enhanced powers (Community Service Society, 1991; Hanson & Falcon, 1992). Even earlier census results and projections had set off alarmed concern among politically dominant groups about possible gains of these constituencies at the state level (Bouvier & Briggs, 1988). The city thus constitutes one more distinctive setting in which, as the century ends, Latinos seem poised to take a role in changing the Americas by taking a hand in changing the United States from the inside (Rendon, 1989).

Whichever of the transformative scenarios sketched in our beginning paragraphs prevails, in New York the process seems destined to stretch beyond the 1990s and well into the next century, decidedly shaping life prospects for several generations. In fact, questions about the nature of the emergent economic order said to be in the offing have become more rather than less controversial. Clearly, the forces producing inequality and poverty are far from spent and figure centrally in all projections (Barnet, 1990; Mead, 1990). For Latinos, prototypical immigrants, an active presence in a broadly anchored movement to frame an urban agenda focused on inequality and poverty, as in the mayors' summit mentioned above, it is at least more likely that transnational as well as domestic issues of equity may figure more seriously in state and corporate agendas.

NOTES

1. Waldinger (1989a, p. 53) reports that New York City attracted over a million legal immigrants between 1966 and 1979. Glazer (1988, p. 56) notes a study that estimated a flow of 1.68 million immigrants between 1970 and 1986.

2. Recently, the New York City government sued an employment agency charging it with discrimination on the basis of race and age. The agency used codes on job application forms to distinguish black candidates (*New York Daily News,* 1990).

3. In her survey of Dominican immigrants Grasmuck (1984) found more than 40% were undocumented.

4. Annual earnings consist of total yearly income from employment and self-employment, regardless of hours worked. Note therefore that part-time workers are

included in the sample. Calculations of relative earnings in this study were based on Public Use Micro Data files of the U.S. Census for each year and based on residents of the New York City Standard Metropolitan Area. As SMSA-level data are not available in the PUMS file for the 1960 Census, state-level data were used. For descriptions of the data and variables used in this study see Carnoy, Daley, and Hinojosa Ojeda (1989) and F. Bonilla and Torres (1989).

5. For a description of the data, methods and results used in this analysis see the Appendix in an earlier draft of the present work, Torres and F. Bonilla (1991).

6. This section is based on an analysis of earnings distribution among wage/salary workers and the self-employed. The income distribution is formed for each race/ethnic group by arranging all earners in order of increasing incomes. It is then described by referring to the share of all incomes that goes to the poorest one fifth (quintile) of earners, the second quintile, the middle quintile, and so on.

Note that since the distributions are established separately for *each* group the dollar amount at each quintile cutoff point is different for each group. For example, the earnings level ending the poorest quintile for whites is higher than that for African Americans or Puerto Ricans. The method used here permits within-group analysis of changes in income distribution, but does not describe the absolute dollar amounts involved. Two recent discussions of changes in earnings distribution within the United States are presented by Levy (1988) and Harrison and Bluestone (1988).

7. Between 1970 and 1980, the rate of poverty among Puerto Rican families in the United States rose from 28.2% to 33.4%; in families headed by a single person it rose from 51.7% to 59.9% (Bean & Tienda, 1987; pp. 354, 356). By 1987, the rate of poverty among Puerto Rican families increased to 37.9% (Center on Budget and Policy Priorities, 1988, p. 11). Among New York Puerto Ricans, the rate of poverty had reached 47.5% in 1984; among Other Hispanics, it was 35.2% (Community Service Society, 1987, p. 30). For a recent journalistic account of the deteriorating conditions in the Puerto Rican community see Van Dyk (1990).

8. McCrate (1990) offers an analysis showing how poor educational quality and low probability of primary secondary employment feeds negatively on labor force participation rates for young women. In this context, teenagers who hold low expectations of employment tend to display higher rates of pregnancy.

9. Throughout the 20th century, there has been a Cuban presence in New York City, which historically has attracted people from the Caribbean. During the 1960s, the city became a major point of settlement for Cubans who left their homeland in the wake of the revolution. After a brief interlude of community formation in the Washington Heights section of Manhattan, this population increasingly resettled in other areas, such as northern New Jersey and Miami. Although a sizable number of Cubans continue to live in the city, they have not coalesced in dense residential concentrations as have the newer Latino immigrants.

10. Estimates of the probable loss of jobs in 1991 range from 40,000 to 70,000 (*New York Times,* April 7, 1991).

11. See earlier sections on relative earnings, shift share, and earnings distribution.

12. Gutierrez (1988) echoes earlier studies of the Puerto Rican and other migrations in his comment that Dominicans exhibit a "transient mentality" regarding their position within U.S. society. With thoughts of returning to the Dominican Republic still very strong among community residents, the necessary commitment to political and social involvement in the United States remains tentative.

5

Economic Restructuring and the Process of Incorporation of Latinos Into the Chicago Economy

John J. Betancur
Teresa Cordova
Maria de los Angeles Torres

INTRODUCTION

Soon after its incorporation in 1824, Chicago underwent one of the most impressive processes of economic growth in U.S. history. By 1910, Chicago was the second largest U.S. city and the manufacturing capital of the nation. Chicago industries recruited European workers by the thousands to satisfy the seemingly inexhaustible demand for labor.

The manner in which Latinos were incorporated into the labor force and the conditions under which they worked, however, have been markedly different from that of European immigrants. Unlike Europe, Latin America has been under greater U.S. influence. Whereas European immigrants came to partake in the development enterprise, Latinos were often imported as "colonial" labor. Hence, Latinos can be understood in the context of dependent development in certain instances.

U.S. foreign policies, political and military intervention, and capital investment in Latin America have and continue to displace large sectors of the population. Having limited, if any, options in their home countries, the displaced are then induced to emigrate to the United States. As Sassen (1988) shows, there is a close relationship between the form and intensity of U.S. intervention in specific countries in Latin America and the large immigration streams from those countries. Furthermore, immigration from the region has been highly selective and has played a key role in supplying the U.S. with low-wage labor (Sassen-Koob, 1990). The process and conditions under which that labor came and the limitations imposed upon it have shaped Latino workers into a distinct category within the U.S. labor market.

Another analytical model views the conditions of Latinos in the United States from the perspective of an internal colonial labor system (Barrera, 1979). In this system, workers are segmented along ethnic or racial lines with some segments, Latinos in this case, placed in a subordinate position. Subordinate segments suffer from labor repression (use of coercion and restrictions to limit their advancement), lower wages (within a dual system favoring dominant sectors), and occupational stratification (with minorities limited to certain jobs in the lowest rungs of the occupational ladder). Subordinate sectors are also used as a reserve labor force and as shock absorbers in times of economic dislocation. In fact, these sectors function as "ascriptive class segments." Although the system requires a reserve army of workers, the colonial version assigns that role to specific ethnic and racial groups, and establishes mechanisms to keep them in place.

In this chapter we argue that the history of the incorporation of Latino workers into the economy best explains the Latino experience in the Chicago area and provides a basis for understanding the impact of restructuring. Namely, the condition of ascriptive low-wage labor has prevented Latinos from developing the human capital and the political and economic power necessary for adapting to or benefiting from changes in labor demand. As a result, not only have Latinos been reproduced as low-wage labor within an ethnically and racially segmented labor market, but they are now losing ground to other groups.

The point of this chapter is to provide a backdrop to understand the role that Latino workers have played in the Chicago economy and the continuation of that role under economic restructuring. Thus, we first discuss the process of incorporation of Latinos into the Chicago economy, along with brief references to underlying conjunctures in U.S.-Latin American relations and conditions in the local economy. We then examine relevant characteristics of restructuring in the Chicago economy and the form in which they perpetuate the role of Latinos.

LATINO IMMIGRATION TO CHICAGO:
THE FIRST WAVE

Mexican immigration into the Chicago area reached large and steady proportions in 1916-1929 as a direct result of labor imports by Midwest and Chicago-area employers. A war-related economic boom coincided with a sharp decline of European migration, resulting in labor shortages, particularly in low-wage occupations and industries, as domestic workers moved into better paying opportunities. Satisfied with the performance of Mexicans in the Southwest, railroad and agricultural employers engaged very actively in the importation of Mexicans for Midwest jobs.

The first documented effort took place in 1916 when the railroads imported a group of Mexican workers for track labor (Año Nuevo Kerr 1976, p. 1; Reisler, 1976, p. 99). Recruitment continued steadily, and "by 1928, Mexicans constituted 43% of the track and maintenance workers on 16 major railroads in the Chicago-Gary region" (Mohl & Betten 1987, p. 162). Sugar beet companies also imported Mexicans during and after World War I for seasonal work in Michigan, Ohio, Indiana, Minnesota, Iowa, and the Dakotas (Reisler, 1976, p. 99). After the season, many of these workers were enticed by urban employers or entered the cities of the Midwest, attracted by higher wages and year-round employment.

The successful experience of the railroads was soon imitated by other industries in the Chicago area, particularly during the strikes of the steel (1919) and the meat-packing industries (1921). Recruiters from the Southwest and border towns provided Inland Steel, U.S. Steel, Youngstown Sheet and Tube Company, Wisconsin Steel, and other smaller firms with substantial numbers of Mexican recruits. By 1926, they constituted 14% of the work force employed in steel in the Chicago area (Rosales & Simon, 1978, p. 147). By 1928, Mexicans were also nearly 11% of all workers in 15 of the area's meat-packing industries (Mohl & Betten, 1987, p. 162). As a result, with the exception of the 1921-1922 recession, the Mexican population in Chicago increased steadily during this period from 1,224 in 1920 to 19,362 in 1930 (Reisler, 1976, p. 101). In East Chicago, Mexicans went from 20 or 30 in 1918 to 5,364 in 1930. This same year, there were 3,511 Mexicans in Gary (Taylor, 1987, p. 33-34). Slightly over 4% of the Mexican population in the United States or about 58,000 Mexicans, lived in the Midwest in the 1920s (Reisler, 1976, p. 101).

These imports provided the initial impetus for a steady immigration of Mexicans to the area. Once in place, workers brought their relatives, friends, or *paisanos*. The process took on a life of its own, and job networks linking Mexicans with jobs in the Chicago area were formed. Given the types of jobs available to Mexicans, these networks linked them to low-paying occupations or industries, hence reinforcing occupational segmentation and the reproduction of the same conditions for future Mexican immigrants.

OVERALL CHARACTERISTICS OF THE PROCESS

The importation and immigration of Mexicans for work in the Chicago area during this period bore three major characteristics that define the role assigned to the group in the local economy.

First, the process was closely conditioned and shaped by the form and content of international relations between the United States and Mexico, particularly the form and terms of U.S. investment in Mexico and the importation of Mexican labor as low-wage labor for the U.S. economy. Not only had Mexico been forced to "sell" about half of its territory to the United States in 1848, but it also became one of the main recipients of U.S. investment under the model of dependent development, especially since the government of Porfirio Díaz. Obtaining generous concessions, U.S. investors became heavily involved in railroad construction, oil extraction, mining, and agricultural exploitation in Mexico. By 1900, Mexico was among the largest recipients of U.S. foreign investment. Extensive programs of land expropriation and agricultural capitalization since the turn of the century, financed by foreign capital, produced massive displacement of Mexican peasants in search of jobs. Further displaced by the chaos of the revolution of 1910 and the ensuing counterrevolutions, many of them joined the stream of workers willing to work in the U.S. Southwest.

Continuing the policy of importation of low-wage workers from low-wage countries for development of the Southwest, the U.S. government and private employers turned to Mexico for the importation of workers to replace Chinese and Japanese workers banned from the country in 1883 and 1909, respectively. In an initial effort to screen immigrants, the Immigration Act of 1917 had required literacy and the payment of an entrance fee for all immigrants over 16 years of age. A few months after enactment of the act, under heavy pressure from the agribusiness and railroad industries claiming a war-related labor shortage, the secretary of labor temporarily waived the literacy and fee requirements for Mexican workers. The Immigration acts of 1921 and 1924 went even further in restricting the immigration of Europeans, but left the doors open for immigration from Latin America.

Repeated efforts by restrictionists to ban or limit the immigration of Mexicans throughout the 1920s were defeated by agribusiness and railroad interests (Reisler, 1976, pp. 198-226). U.S. expansionist policies and economic interests in Latin America were key in this outcome as presidents felt that restricting Latin American immigration would be deeply resented in Latin America and would set back U.S. gains in the region (Reisler, 1976, p. 212). As Secretary of State Frank Kellogg told the Senate Immigration Committee in 1927, "Two-thirds of the nation's total foreign investment and one-third of its trade went to Western Hemisphere nations" (Reisler, 1976, p. 212). In short, even as U.S.-assisted investment in Mexico produced a mass of unemployed peasants, the U.S. government and private businesses joined forces to import Mexicans as low-wage workers for agribusiness, railroad, and other interests and imposed the terms of their immigration, as discussed below.

The second characteristic was the extremely vulnerable immigrant status of Mexican workers. Mexicans had entered the United States freely before 1917. The requirements established that year turned those who could not prove legal entry before 1917 into undocumented workers (Año Nuevo Kerr, 1976, p. 146). Furthermore, those entering after 1917 under the waiver issued by the secretary of state, were admitted only temporarily. Many Mexican workers continued entering the United States illegally because they could not comply with the established requirements. In the absence of effective sanctions, employers profited from their vulnerability as undocumented workers.

The vulnerability of Mexican workers was aggravated by public prejudice and the bitter opposition of organized labor against their entry. During debate on the 1921 act, echoing the feelings among many of his colleagues and in other sectors in the United States, Congressman Martin Madden of Chicago argued that the bill left "open the doors for perhaps the worst element that comes into the United States—the Mexican peon." Adolph Sabath, also of Chicago, added: "I feel that there are very few of you who would be ready to go on record to prove that a Mexican makes a better citizen than the European immigrants." During this debate between restrictionists and employers, both sides coincided in their feelings about Mexicans as "inassimilable man-power," "masses of cheap laborers," "inferior racial stock," "serf, peon, and slave types," and "a serious racial menace" (Reisler, 1976, pp. 200-201, 205-218).

This condition was clearly reflected in repatriation during the short depression of 1921, and again in the Great Depression: Mexicans were asked or coerced to go back to Mexico as a means of alleviating the conditions of Americans. In 1930-1932, over 14,000 persons from Illinois returned to Mexico (Hoffman, 1978, p. 231). Rosales and Simon (1987, p. 146) illustrate the case of East Chicago, Indiana, where Latinos were reduced to half their pre-1930 numbers. A similarly bleak picture is painted for Gary, where "Mexicans bore the brunt of nativist hostilities and suffered massive deportations" (Mohl & Betten, 1987, p. 161). The Mexican population in the city of Chicago fell from 20,000 in 1930 to 14,000 in 1933 and to 12,500 in 1934. The proportion of Mexicans born in the United States increased substantially as a result— 9,000 out of the 16,000 Latinos in Chicago in 1940. Of particular importance during this period was the pressure on foreigners, Mexicans in particular, to prove legal immigrant status and to become naturalized in order to be eligible for public relief and employment (Año Nuevo Kerr, 1976, pp. 69-115).

The third characteristic relates to the status of Mexican workers as low-wage, disposable labor with minimal mobility and job tenure and extremely limited rights. Available evidence from the period indicates that they were used as strikebreakers and as an insurance against strikes; were set against other nationals (Taylor, 1987, p. 38); were hired for sporadic assignments, required to work long hours, laid off often; and suffered from unsteadier work and a higher unemployment rate than the other groups (Escobar & Lane, 1987, p. 11). Their occupational strati-fication was described by Taylor, who wrote that in 1932 the Mexican proportion of low-wage, unskilled workers was much larger than for other immigrant groups (Reisler, 1976, p. 103; Taylor, 1987, pp. 37-45). Their wages were also the lowest: Two thirds of Mexican families earned less than the poverty line, compared to half of black and one fifth of white families (Año Nuevo Kerr, 1976, pp. 25-26; Taylor, 1987). Finally, they recorded the highest unemployment levels during the 1921 recession and the Great Depression. In fact, 65% of Mexicans in the Chicago area lost their jobs during the economic downturn of 1921-1922 (Año Nuevo Kerr, 1976, p. 23). They also recorded higher levels of unemployment than whites and European immigrants in Chicago during the Great Depression. Latino workers retaining their jobs were subject to pressure, antagonism, and discrimination (Mohl & Betten, 1987, p. 169) and were accused of taking jobs from Americans. The position of Mexicans during the 1920s is illustrated by this quote from an employer: "What we need is 'hunkies' and lots of 'em. . . . The Mex does not come under the quota law and he's willing to work long and cheap, so we'll keep on importing them" (Mohl & Betten, 1987, p. 162).

These conditions extended outside the workplace. In fact, Mexicans were harassed by local police, abused by the courts, segregated into the worst and comparatively most expensive living quarters, limited in their rights, and abused in all manners as "temporary," second-class foreigners (Año Nuevo Kerr, 1976; Escobar & Lane, 1987; Reisler, 1976, pp. 109-110). The result was an exceptionally high mobility and instability for the Latino community, and a negative feeling about becoming U.S. citizens. As one Mexican immigrant put it: "If we become citizens, we are still Mexicans. . . . Even my boy who was born in the United States is a Mexican it seems. He has to go to the Mexican school. There is always a difference in the way he is treated" (Reisler, 1976, p. 113). Repatriation and discrimination during the Great Depression forced the most vulnerable and transient Latinos to leave, keeping those with more seniority, more stability, and roots in the area. Consequently, the Latino population became more balanced demographically, more stable, better represented in the semiskilled job category, more participant in non-Mexican organizations, and more "assimilated" (Reisler, 1976, p. 76; Rosales & Simon, 1987, pp. 154-155). According to Año Nuevo Kerr (1976), they became more Mexican American. In spite of this selection, by 1935 a mere 5% of Mexicans were skilled workers as compared to 35% of foreign-born whites. Fully 66% of Mexicans held unskilled jobs, compared to 58% of blacks, 35% of foreign-born whites, and 31% of native-born whites (Año Nuevo Kerr, 1976, pp. 69, 78).

WORLD WAR II AND THE BRACERO PROGRAM

War-related growth pushed the U.S. economy and manufacturing to new heights. In Chicago, manufacturing employment jumped from 402,840 workers in 1939 to 668,056 in 1947. Wholesale jobs increased from 95,494 in 1939 to 138,194 and retail employment from 184,449 to 248,763 during the period. Other industries also showed large increases (McDonald, 1984, pp. 10-18). Rural-to-urban migration and further migration of blacks from the South satisfied some of this demand. Labor shortages, however, left many vacancies, particularly in unskilled and low-wage occupations, as domestic workers were in a position to select the best paid jobs. A study by the railroads concluded that only 5% of track labor positions in that industry would be taken by domestic workers at the wage levels offered (Año Nuevo Kerr, 1976, p. 121).

The new conditions brought about by World War II reopened the door to Mexican immigration. The U.S. government formally contacted its Mexican counterpart in June 1941 to request a program of labor importation. Negotiations assumed an unusual speed and an agreement for an agricultural program was reached in less than a year. The agreement was extended in 1943 to include manufacturing and the railroads. Chicago became a major destination for Mexican immigrants, both documented and undocumented (Corwin, 1973, pp. 567-568). Approximately 15,000 Mexican railroad workers, or 11% of the total railroad imports into the United States, were brought to Chicago between 1943 and 1945. Another sizable number of railroad workers went to the suburbs of Blue Island and Norpaul (Año Nuevo Kerr, 1976, pp. 121-122).

The recruitment of bracero labor into the Chicago economy during and after World War II reinforced previous patterns of Mexican incorporation into the labor force.

INTERNATIONAL DIMENSIONS

The importation of Mexican labor, as documented by historians of the Bracero Program, was tied to U.S. interests and repeated earlier trends (Kirstein, 1977). If this time the United States agreed to demands from Mexico regarding minimum wages, lodging, and transportation, it was largely due to the urgent need for Mexican support. Yet, Congress never approved the agreement, and U.S. government agencies and private employers ignored and subverted many of its provisions, in practice opting for a virtual open border (Kirstein, 1977, p. 102). President Truman's Commission on Migratory Labor concluded that the U.S. government had "become a contributor to the growth of an illegal traffic which it has responsibility to prevent" (Kirstein, 1977, pp. 94-95). The same commission stated: "We have used the institutions of government to procure alien labor willing to work under obsolete and backward conditions and, thus, to perpetuate these conditions" (Corwin, 1978, p. 152). Meant only for wartime, the Bracero Program was renewed again and again until 1964. As U.S. labor representatives argued repeatedly and many analysts concluded, the program produced a cheap foreign labor supply for U.S. employers.

Immigrant Status. The Bracero Program reinforced the concept of temporary immigrant applied to Mexican workers in the war-related labor shortage of 1917 and in the restrictionist debates of the 1920s. To a large extent, it became a front for an ever-increasing influx of undocumented workers providing U.S. employers with their labor needs (Corwin, 1978, p. 152; Kirstein, 1977). Once Mexico agreed to the importation of Mexican workers, many employers circumvented the program and engaged in the illegal recruitment of Mexican workers, hence reproducing the undocumented problem (Corwin, 1978; Kiser & Kiser, 1979). Permanent immigration resumed, but it was minimal compared to the number of Mexican workers entering the country as braceros or undocumented workers. At the expiration of the agreement, the United States substituted it with arrangements that provided for the direct recruitment of Mexican workers by U.S. employers. "As a result, there was a gradual substitution during the 1950s of legally imported labor for Mexican wetbacks" (Kiser & Kiser, 1979, p. 99). Periodically, the United States enacted programs of legalization qualifying undocumented workers for permanent immigrant status. Employers also acted to "immigrate" their employees. Others became permanent immigrants through mechanisms contemplated in the law. These actions further encouraged "wetbacks" by sending the message that sooner or later they would become legal immigrants (Kiser & Kiser, 1979, pp. 151, 206).

Worker Status. The role assigned to Mexican workers in the Chicago economy in the 1920s was reproduced, and to a large extent, institutionalized by the bracero agreement, the undocumented-worker problem, and the related conditions.

Workers were imported only for places or industries with a certified labor shortage. Braceros were offered temporary contracts and were supposed to return to Mexico upon expiration of the contracts. But what was more limiting was the determination that they were not to compete in the open market for jobs. On the contrary, they were *to take only the jobs and occupations for which they were contracted.* This is to say that they were to perform the jobs that citizen workers did not want (Kirstein, 1977, pp. 15-24).

The program excluded mobility through the ranks and access to skilled industrial or clerical positions. A protest by Mexico addressing this issue resulted in jobs only "in all classifications of 'laborer,'

'helper,' 'assistant foreman,' and semi-skilled 'machine operators'."
According to many analysts, the justification of labor shortages was
inaccurate. An investigation of labor shortages in the railroads by the
War Manpower Commission concluded that "a shortage did not exist
but was attributable to low wages and rigid hiring specifications." The
claim has been repeatedly made that the underlying purpose of the
program was to produce a cheap foreign labor supply that met the
interests of employers against those of organized labor (Kirstein, 1977,
pp. 5, 23, 37-39).

These arrangements, and in general, the Bracero Program and the
related undocumented-workers problem, had a depressing impact on the
wages, conditions, and assignments of other Mexican workers. In fact,
not only were all Mexicanos suspected of an undocumented status but
the restrictions and role institutionalized in the Bracero Program were
extended de facto to them. Prejudices of the type mentioned earlier
contributed to this as did the bitter opposition of organized labor to the
immigration of Mexican workers. Coming from an underdeveloped
country with much less to offer to them, Mexican workers saw the
low-wage occupations they were being offered as an improvement.
Finally, documented workers could be easily passed up for undocumented workers that could be exploited and disposed of almost at will
(Kirstein, 1977, p. 103).

This process created a highly unprotected, transient, and vulnerable
segment of Mexican workers that supplied the U.S. economy with an
immense pool of cheap labor under ideal conditions for exploitation.
As much as Mexico tried to fight the abuse of its workers and improve
conditions, it was in a weak bargaining position after the war (Año
Nuevo Kerr, 1976, p. 157; Kirstein, 1977). In fact, after repeated
protests, unilateral cancellations of the Bracero Program, and multiple
interventions by Mexican consulates, Mexico realized that these efforts
did not make a difference, gave up, and allowed the United States to set
the terms.

Mexican workers in the Chicago area remained employed in low-
wage occupations in manufacturing. A 1944 survey of employers of
Mexicans in Chicago established that most Mexicans at that time were
still employed in the steel, railroad, and meat-packing industries (Año
Nuevo Kerr, 1976, p. 143), and their conditions did not markedly
improve. Anti-Mexican sentiment reemerged after the war and continued during the 1950s, culminating in "Operation Wetback" in 1954 and
in continuous "redadas" thereafter. Discrimination and segregation

continued. In 1947, Inland Steel imported nearly 250 Mexican workers from Texas 2 days prior to the calling of a strike. In 1963, speaking in support of the Bracero Program, a Chicago distributor argued about the lack of domestic workers for harvesting fruits and vegetables, as they "can only be picked on hands and knees and some items like melons are harvested . . . in hundred degrees temperatures. On some of these fast-maturing commodities over 90% of the pickers are Mexicans because they are adapted to this kind of work" (Año Nuevo Kerr, 1976, pp. 29, 143, 154, 169).

As a result of efforts to bring Mexican labor into the Chicago region, and despite undercounting of an estimated 20,000 persons, the U.S. Census Bureau reported 24,000 Mexicans in Chicago in 1950 and 35,000 in the metropolitan region (Año Nuevo Kerr, 1976, p. 132). In 1960 the census counted 55,597 Mexicans in the metropolitan area. By 1970, Chicago had the fourth largest urban Mexican population in the United States with 106,000 people. This figure increased to 255,770, or 60.6% of the Latino population in Chicago, in 1980 and to 352,560, or 64.6%, in 1990. Interestingly, the Latino population of Chicago was growing at a time when the population of the city as a whole was decreasing.

THE IMMIGRATION OF PUERTO RICANS

The immigration of Puerto Ricans to Chicago bears many similarities to the Mexican experience. Ceded to the United States by Spain in 1898 as a result of the Spanish-American War, Puerto Rico was transformed into a haven for U.S. investment. The system of principally small family farms was replaced by large industrialized sugar concerns owned by U.S. corporations (Matos Cintrón, 1980, pp. 54-72). Displaced from their farms, many unemployed peasants were recruited for work in low-wage occupations in the garment, hotel, cigar, and restaurant industries and domestic and personal service in the Northeast during and immediately after World War I.

In the Midwest, Puerto Ricans were first recruited for agricultural work, for seasonal or temporary manufacturing expansion, and generally, for jobs that employers had a hard time filling because of the wages and conditions they offered. According to Maldonado (1987), the first large wave of Puerto Rican immigrants to the Midwest and Chicago came as a result of contract labor. Increases in the seasonal farm labor system after the war produced a large demand for workers that braceros could not satisfy. Employers then turned to other sources of low-wage labor such as Puerto Ricans. Hence, many came as contract workers for agricultural jobs in Ohio, Pennsylvania, Indiana, Michigan, and Wisconsin, and then moved to cities such as Chicago, Milwaukee, and Detroit in hopes of getting manufacturing jobs, which they expected would pay higher wages and provide steadier employment (F. Padilla, 1947).

In 1946, Castle, Barton, and Associates, an employment agency in Chicago, worked in cooperation with the Department of Labor of the Puerto Rican government to recruit islanders for jobs in foundries and domestic work (F. Padilla, 1947). Similarly, the Puerto Rican Migration Division established an office in Chicago to promote the immigration of Puerto Ricans to the Midwest. Satisfied with these workers, many employers contacted this office for the importation of more Puerto Ricans. In the midst of postwar labor shortages, U.S. Steel Gary Works contacted the Samuel J. Friedman Farm Labor Agency to recruit Puerto Ricans for their plant in Gary, Indiana. U.S. Steel paid the agency for each worker recruited (Maldonado, 1987, p. 206).

The recruitment of Puerto Ricans in Chicago and the Midwest accelerated in the 1950s. Immigration into the United States became an escape valve for the island and was sanctioned by the Puerto Rican government as an official policy for dealing with social unrest and an ever-increasing unemployment problem. Unemployment reached such proportions that the government resorted to a new development approach including light manufacturing, social welfare, and further emigration. Puerto Ricans were urged by the United States and island governments to leave the island, and in some cases, were provided with the airfare (Sánchez Korrol, 1983, pp. 13-47).

Like Mexicans, Puerto Rican immigrants came from the lower social and economic strata. Such was the type of labor sought by employers, who preferred recruits from rural Puerto Rico "because they made better workers" (Maldonado, 1987, p. 209). They were, indeed, willing to work for lower wages and were less demanding with respect to work assignments and working conditions. Puerto Ricans entered "at the bottom of the occupational hierarchy of the secondary labor sector characterized by low-paying, short duration, dead end, often dirty and unsafe jobs" (F. Padilla, 1987, p. 104) and remained there as statistical evidence demonstrates. In 1960, nearly half of employed Puerto Ricans (45.7%) in Chicago worked as operatives and kindred, 13.7% as nonfarm laborers, 11.7% as service workers except household, and 9% as craftsmen, foremen, and kindred (F. Padilla, 1985, p. 44). In comparison, only 1.6%

were professional, technical, and kindred workers, and a mere 1.2% were managers and officials.

After the initial importation, immigration from the island took on a life of its own and increased quickly. Although the Puerto Rican population in the city in 1940 was only 240, it went to 32,371 in 1960, to 78,963 in 1970, to 109,736 in 1980 (26% of the Latino population), and in 1990, to 119,866, or 22% of all Latinos in Chicago. Puerto Ricans were limited in their housing choices to the most dilapidated areas and were charged comparatively higher rents (F. Padilla, 1987, pp. 117-123). They were harassed by police and the courts, and were subjected to many forms of racial prejudices (F. Padilla, 1987, pp. 123-125). Like Mexicans before them, they were the object of stereotypes portraying them as the opposite to the U.S. ideal. Puerto Ricans were depicted as lazy, dirty, black, violent, noisy, deviant, boastful, uncouth, and unable to form viable organizations and structures. Their cultural traits were viewed as backward and inferior (F. Padilla, 1987, pp. 59-75). In short, like Mexicans, Puerto Ricans were imported by employers as cheap and willing labor, were offered the worst jobs, and were discriminated against in their living and working places. Unlike Mexicans, Puerto Ricans were unilaterally made U.S. citizens in 1917, just in time for active military service, and did not have to face the same immigration difficulties. Nonetheless, their socioeconomic conditions very much resemble those of Mexicans.

THE IMMIGRATION OF CUBANS TO CHICAGO

Mass immigration of Cubans into the United States occurred under distinctive circumstances. After establishing a system of "tutelage" at the turn of the century, the United States had essentially appropriated control and ownership of the Cuban economy. This relationship ended with the Cuban revolution of 1959. The United States responded by offering political asylum to dissident Cubans and assisting them with "temporary" settlement. Assistance included financial packages such as relocation benefits of cash allotments, food, and scholarships sponsored by the U.S. Department of Health, Education and Welfare (HEW), among others.

Many Cubans used these opportunities to establish businesses. Moreover, many of them were able to move part of their assets to the United States and invest them. Cubans received special immigrant status, and in sharp contrast to Mexicans or Puerto Ricans, were helped with their settlement in the United States. Those Cubans who came during the 1960s were for the most part from the upper and middle classes. Among them was a large number of professionals, merchants, and business people with considerable experience, contacts, and material assets. Many had existing links with U.S. firms and the business community. Lower-income Cubans immigrating in the 1970s and 1980s were often able to work for established Cuban businesses, were also assisted with their settlement, and had generally higher educational levels than Mexican or Puerto Rican immigrants.

Cubans lived in Chicago before 1960, but their numbers were negligible and their presence in the city largely invisible. The first sizable wave arriving in the 1960s consisted largely of professionals and merchants. Some were recruited by HEW and churches to settle in the city. Some women who were teachers in Cuba were assisted in finding teaching jobs in the area. Other professionals and merchants benefited from the existence of a large Latino population in need of specialized services. Firms like Sears heavily recruited Cubans for their Chicago stores. They were even recruited to break a strike at Motorola by a former HEW employee who worked for Motorola. By 1970 there were 15,000 Cubans in the city and many others in the suburbs. In 1980 a group of "Marielitos" came to Chicago, but most did not settle permanently. The Cuban population decreased to nearly 11,400 in 1980, and again to 10,000 in 1990.

OTHER IMMIGRANT GROUPS

Other important Latino groups in the Chicago area are South and Central Americans. Each subgroup includes persons from various countries. For the most part, their immigration to the Chicago area is relatively recent.

With largely rural economies, Central American countries have depended on a few agricultural crops, particularly coffee and bananas, and have conducted most of their trade with the United States, particularly since World War II. Agriculture for export has been dominated by large U.S. firms. Not only have these firms displaced masses of peasants from their lands, but their centrality to those economies has given them key roles in the political and economic arena.

Generally lagging behind most of Latin America, these countries witnessed a large rural dislocation in recent decades. Extreme deprivation has exerted tremendous pressure on their political systems, which have responded with forced austerity, further exacerbating the situation. Heavily U.S.-supported, largely dictatorial regimes have been a common feature in the region and have fired the resistance of peasants and other alienated sectors of the population. Strong insurgency movements have flourished in countries such as Nicaragua, El Salvador, and Guatemala. Caught between contending forces, involved in a seemingly endless struggle and often its victims, many people looked for alternatives elsewhere. Moreover, increasing unemployment resulting from dependent development as well as the disruption of their communities produced large masses of jobless and underemployed. Many moved into neighboring nations, particularly Mexico, and finally joined the stream of political refugees, undocumented workers, or regular migrants to the United States.

Political turmoil also produced emigrants from middle and upper classes (e.g., in Nicaragua) who gravitated toward the United States. They were granted refugee status by the United States and gravitated toward urban areas with large Latino populations, including Chicago. As a result of these dual processes, Central American workers have a bipolar occupational structure with some educated and middle-class elements on the one hand and a majority of low-wage workers on the other. Tables 5.6 and 5.7 show the occupational and industrial distribution of Latino groups in the Chicago area in 1980.

Finally, a large number of persons have immigrated from South America into the Chicago area in the last 30 years. Legal immigrants benefited from immigration quotas allocated to their countries. Many professionals came due to the limited capacity of absorption of such occupations in their home countries. Health professionals were able to immigrate under special provisions of the law. Other would-be professionals came as students and remained. Still others used their networks to become permanent immigrants. The higher cost and distance of coming from South America resulted in a more selective process, but some came as undocumented workers using tourist visas or joining the routes of illegal immigration used by Mexicans and Central Americans. For example, the close relationship between Colombian immigration to the United States and U.S. intervention is discussed in detail by Sassen-Koob (1990).

Like Central Americans, South American immigrants have a highly polarized occupational structure with a higher-than-average representation in occupations such as professional and white-collar workers at one end, and a sizable concentration in blue-collar and other low-paid categories at the other. Tables 5.6 and 5.7 illustrate this. In spite of comparatively higher percentages in high-paying occupations, overall the conditions of Cubans and South and Central Americans are generally below those of whites and Asians in Chicago and resemble very much the average trends for Latinos.

ECONOMIC RESTRUCTURING IN CHICAGO

Soon after World War II, the Chicago area entered a period of economic restructuring. Its most dramatic impact has been felt since 1970 in city neighborhoods and old suburbs and among blacks and Latinos (Squires, Bennett, McCourt, & Nyden, 1987, pp. 25-44). Manufacturing jobs that had peaked in 1947 at 668,000 began a strong decline in the city (614,897 in 1954, 508,797 in 1963, 430,100 in 1972, 366,000 in 1977, and 295,992 in 1982). Restructuring initially took the form of suburbanization of both jobs and the white middle and upper classes. As a result, economic activity boomed in certain parts of the area while massive disinvestment depressed others. Factory jobs continued growing in the metropolitan area as a result of growth in the suburbs until 1967, when they registered an overall decline (Ranney, 1985).

Meanwhile, other economic sectors slowly displaced manufacturing as the leading economic sector. The so-called service economy emerged as the most dynamic activity (Commercial Club of Chicago, 1984). Led by corporate headquarters, banking, insurance, real estate, marketing, trade, research, and related industries, the "service economy" brought along a highly polarized labor market with a large group of highly skilled, highly paid positions in one pole and a vast number of low-paying, support occupations at the other. Even many occupations in the low end required higher educational and English-language levels and skills than prior manufacturing, warehousing, transportation, and other similar jobs (Mishel & Frankel, 1991, pp. 69-128).

Mass production manufacturing essentially moved out of the region. Many of the dynamic, cutting-edge service/manufacturing sectors remained, usually in the new suburbs and industrial parks. New forms of manufacturing started replacing the old "Fordist" assembly-line jobs. Firms engaged in vertical aggregation, subcontracting, out-sourcing, and specialization. Improvements in communications resulted in a higher mobility of firms, which were able to move their most labor-intensive, unskilled operations out of the area and even the country. A case in point are the *maquiladoras.* Many Chicago firms moved assembly operations to the U.S.-Mexico border, depriving the city of thousands of direct and indirect jobs (Merrion, 1990, pp. 15-21).

Out-migration of mass manufacturing and economic restructuring produced a large deskilling of workers as old processes were replaced or firms moved out. Masses of workers became unemployed overnight. Other economic changes called for a work force with higher levels of basic education and English-language skills. The emerging economic organization also demanded a flexible work force, with the ability to learn multiple skills and undertake a diverse array of jobs. Middle-class workers with strong educational, political, and economic backgrounds and access to resources and positions of control could better adjust to these changes by moving to the areas of growth or into the new occupations. In contrast, more vulnerable populations, strongly tied to the declining sectors, with lower educational levels, and traditionally relegated to the bottom occupations and industries, did not have the flexibility, resources, or opportunities to move into the new jobs.

THE IMPACT OF ECONOMIC RESTRUCTURING ON LATINOS IN CHICAGO AS REFLECTED IN CENSUS FIGURES AND OTHER EVIDENCE

Tied to unskilled or low-skilled occupations, particularly in the traditional manufacturing sector, deprived of the stability and wages needed to invest in education, lacking the resources to carry them through difficult times, and having no or weak political or institutional ties and jobs, Latino workers were the least prepared for economic restructuring, and indeed, have suffered the most from it. The bulk of the Latino work force remained tied to generally low occupations in the manufacturing sector, and in fact, their share of employment in this industry now increased. As shown in Table 5.1, even in 1980 Latinos were disproportionately represented in manufacturing compared to other major racial or ethnic groups in the Chicago area.

In 1960 in Illinois, Latinos also had the largest concentration in transportation. Meanwhile, they were disproportionately concentrated among operatives in manufacturing in 1970 and 1980 (Table 5.2).

The high-value manufacturing decline and restructuring had a devastating impact on Latino workers. While other groups increased their proportions

Table 5.1 Industrial Distribution of All Earners in the Chicago Metropolitan Area by Race and Latino Group, 1970 and 1980 (in percent)

Category	White 1970	White 1980	Black 1970	Black 1980	Latino 1970	Latino 1980	Asian 1970	Asian 1980
Agriculture	0.5	0.6	0.2	0.2	1.0	0.9	0.8	0.1
Mining	0.1	0.1	0.1	0.1	0.0	0.1	0.0	0.1
Construction	4.9	5.4	2.7	2.5	2.5	3.6	0.8	1.2
Manufacturing	31.1	24.8	31.3	24.1	61.6	48.3	22.3	25.4
Transportation	5.3	5.2	4.7	9.2	4.2	4.7	1.3	2.8
Communications	1.5	1.3	1.4	1.6	0.2	1.0	0.4	0.7
Wholesale Trade	5.1	5.6	2.9	2.9	3.2	4.3	2.9	4.6
Retail Trade	17.1	17.6	14.8	13.5	10.4	13.3	10.5	14.1
Fire	20.0	28.6	17.6	28.8	8.4	14.6	22.7	44.2
Services	9.3	6.0	13.8	8.6	6.8	6.5	31.5	4.9
Publ. Admin.	4.0	3.6	9.5	7.2	1.5	2.1	5.5	1.4
Defense	0.2	0.1	0.2	0.1	0.0	0.1	0.4	0.1
Utilities	1.1	1.1	0.9	1.3	0.2	0.6	0.8	0.3
Total	100.0	100.0	100.0	100.0	100.0	100.0	100.0	100.0

in high-paying industries and occupations, Latino earners stagnated in low-paying occupations and industries. Latinos often followed manufacturing jobs to the suburbs. They remained in manufacturing at higher rates than other groups, despite long and expensive commuting.

Table 5.2 Occupational Distribution for All Earners in the Chicago Metropolitan Area by Racial or Latino Group, 1970 and 1980 (in percent)

Category	White 1970	White 1980	Black 1970	Black 1980	Latino 1970	Latino 1980	Asian 1970	Asian 1980
Offic. & Mgrs.	10.7	12.9	3.3	5.1	2.4	4.2	8.8	8.2
Professionals	12.5	15.1	7.4	10.2	3.0	4.9	33.6	31.3
Technicians	1.5	2.3	0.9	2.4	0.8	1.1	4.2	6.7
Sales	8.9	10.5	3.4	5.8	2.8	4.2	4.6	4.9
Clerical/Admin.	24.2	23.5	23.7	25.4	11.7	17.2	17.6	19.1
Service	8.4	10.7	15.1	18.5	8.1	13.9	8.8	11.4
Craft	14.2	9.1	9.8	5.9	13.8	9.2	7.6	8.9
Operatives	15.7	11.2	29.5	19.2	48.4	33.2	12.6	6.9
Farm Laborers	0.1	0.4	0.1	0.2	0.6	0.9	0.4	1.2
Nonfarm Labor	3.8	4.4	6.8	7.3	8.5	11.2	1.7	1.6
Total	100.0	100.0	100.0	100.0	100.0	100.0	100.0	100.0

Though traditional manufacturing jobs moved to gain economic advantage, wages in the industry, and more particularly, in the occupations filled by Latinos have eroded. As manufacturing opportunities decreased, many Latinos have been absorbed into low-paying jobs as busboys and dishwashers in restaurants, as maids and cleaners in hotels, as security guards, messengers, maintenance workers, gardeners, and similar low-end jobs in the service industry.

Latinos have helped manufacturing stay in the area longer than it would have if it had to compete with other sectors for labor. They have helped the low-profit restaurant and hotel businesses and a downgraded manufacturing sector thrive on the basis of large pools of cheap labor. The highly competitive wholesale sector profited from the availability of Latinos. Displaced by conditions in their home countries, Latinos are giving new life to cities like New York, and in our case, Chicago with their willingness to work hard for low wages and lower living standards (Sassen, 1991).

Even though the concentration of Latinos in most industries and occupations increased, the largest increases for Latinos took place in highly polarized industries such as the retail and finance, insurance, and real estate industries (FIRE), and to a lesser extent, wholesale trade, and in occupations such as clerical, service worker, and laborer. However, their percentages in high-paying occupations such as officer and manager, professional, and technician were the lowest of all groups.

In 1980, Latino workers received the lowest average wages in all industries with the only exception being FIRE (ahead of blacks only), services (slightly ahead of blacks), public utilities (tied at the bottom with Asians), transportation (tied with Asians and blacks far behind whites), and retail (tied with blacks at the bottom). The lowest average wages in manufacturing, the largest employer of Latinos by far, confirm the traditional position of Latinos in this industry as low-wage workers. Latinos also received the lowest average wages in the occupations of operative, service (tied with Asians), craft, officials and managers (tied with blacks), and sales. In clerical they were ahead only of Asians. The only exception was the category laborer, in which they were only behind whites. The lowest wages received by the group in the category operatives, comprising the largest occupation of Latinos in the metropolitan area, testify to their role as low-wage labor (Tables 5.3a and 5.3b).

Table 5.4 suggests that there is a strong income differential for Latinos (and others as well) within the same educational level. In fact, given the same educational level, whites make more than any other

Table 5.3a Average Wages for Male and Female Earners by Industry and Racial or Latino Group in the Chicago Metropolitan Area, 1980

Industry	White Male	White Female	Latino Male	Latino Female	Black Male	Black Female	Asian Male	Asian Female
Construction	19,043	9,305	12,052	6,908	13,204	8,974	17,881	6,931
Trad. Mfg.	20,295	9,729	12,695	7,641	13,764	9,196	15,896	8,692
High Mfg.	21,824	10,927	12,963	8,682	13,836	9,902	18,527	9,629
Transportation	20,583	11,548	15,978	10,745	15,874	13,938	15,184	11,396
Communications	24,231	14,007	14,144	15,137	18,801	12,111	16,652	13,221
Wholesale	21,714	9,635	12,683	6,701	13,617	9,444	17,873	9,988
Retail	13,402	5,533	9,260	5,053	9,251	6,327	10,809	6,035
Fire	22,647	9,546	14,444	7,565	11,863	9,517	21,985	13,572
Services	13,295	6,104	9,740	6,021	9,094	6,513	11,301	6,879
Publ. Admin.	19,905	10,312	12,714	7,914	13,459	9,976	17,082	11,358
Defense	18,075	9,752	6,148	—	12,037	7,090	—	—
Utilities	22,152	12,806	15,620	8,429	16,749	12,073	15,424	—
Total Avg.	19,484	8,635	12,396	7,339	12,816	9,070	17,306	11,136

Table 5.3b Average Wages for Male and Female Earners by Occupation and Racial or Latino Group in the Chicago Metropolitan Area, 1980

Occupation	White Male	White Female	Latino Male	Latino Female	Black Male	Black Female	Asian Male	Asian Female
Office & Mgrs.	28,717	13,529	18,233	9,733	18,210	13,230	23,589	10,202
Professionals	24,628	11,678	20,556	10,771	16,063	12,744	24,853	17,354
Technicians	18,371	9,787	14,906	9,744	14,013	9,979	15,749	12,028
Sales	21,108	5,824	9,918	4,087	11,330	5,818	12,566	5,925
Clerical/Admin.	17,442	8,664	12,632	7,761	13,122	9,316	12,183	8,778
Service	10,758	5,003	8,745	5,887	9,043	6,543	8,130	7,105
Craft	17,744	8,285	14,394	7,686	14,664	9,001	15,483	7,729
Operatives	16,474	8,138	12,336	7,568	13,747	8,811	12,342	7,609
Farm Laborers	7,605	4,140	7,830	4,394	5,914	5,242	10,888	—
Nonfarm Laborers	9,731	7,088	10,317	6,449	10,112	7,830	7,266	6,159
Total Avg.	19,502	8,619	12,393	7,339	12,817	9,060	17,325	11,118

SOURCE: U.S. Bureau of the Census, PUMS (1980, Chicago).

group, followed by Asians and, far behind, by Latinos and blacks. This is particularly noticeable after high school.

Finally, all these conditions are reflected in income distribution, as Table 5.5 illustrates. Latino earners receive the lowest average wages of all groups and are concentrated in the lowest income quintiles. In

Table 5.4 Mean Income Compared to Level of Education for All Wage Earners, 1970 and 1980

Category	White 1970	White 1980	Black 1970	Black 1980	Latino 1970	Latino 1980	Asian 1970	Asian 1980
6 Years or Less	6,285	12,085	4,728	10,962	5,147	9,768	5,814	6,490
7 to 8 Years	5,858	9,376	4,716	8,581	5,061	9,173	48,94	6,562
Some High School	5,982	10,386	4,891	9,285	4,957	9,502	4,683	8,547
High School Grad	6,923	13,033	5,442	10,622	5,209	10,623	6,008	9,506
Some College	8,546	15,692	6,419	12,120	5,831	12,627	4,322	12,854
College Grad	13,101	22,359	9,650	16,500	11,377	18,616	7,645	19,161
Total Average	7,594	14,705	5,402	10,926	5,334	105,48	6,128	14,483

fact, in 1980 nearly three quarters of them were concentrated in the three lowest quintiles compared to nearly 70% of blacks, 58.8% of Asians, and 56.9% of whites.

There is, nonetheless, variation among Latino subgroups. Cubans and South Americans stand above the rest, with Central Americans in the middle and Mexicans and Puerto Ricans last. This is reflected in higher educational levels and average incomes, and in the occupational and industrial distribution. Mexicans, Puerto Ricans, and Central Americans were more concentrated in manufacturing and in the categories of operatives, service, and laborers, whereas Cubans and South Americans had higher percentages in FIRE and retail trade as well as in professional, manager, technician, and clerical occupations. In spite of their modest relative advantage, Cubans and South Americans had generally the same

Table 5.5 Income Quintiles by Ethnic Group, 1970 and 1980 (in percent)

Quintiles	White 1970	White 1980	Black 1970	Black 1980	Latino 1970	Latino 1980	Asian 1970	Asian 1980
1st Quintile	20.7	19.9	20.9	21.5	19.3	19.9	18.0	15.9
2nd Quintile	20.0	18.7	30.4	24.5	34.6	30.4	26.5	21.4
3rd Quintile	16.1	18.3	24.1	23.5	24.6	24.5	24.5	21.5
4th Quintile	20.3	20.5	18.1	21.0	15.8	17.1	17.6	22.6
5th Quintile	22.9	22.6	6.5	9.5	5.8	8.1	13.5	18.5
Total	100.0	100.0	100.0	100.0	100.0	100.0	100.0	100.0

SOURCE: U.S. Bureau of the Census, PUMS (1970 and 1980, Chicago).

average position as blacks. These results are consistent with the process of incorporation briefly discussed and reflect differences in the specific circumstances of immigration of the various groups. (See Tables 5.6 and 5.7.)

SUMMARY

The impact of economic restructuring on Latinos in Chicago is closely related to the process and form of incorporation of the group into the area's economy. The dominant presence of the United States in Latin America has not only influenced the conditions that have given rise to large-scale immigration but has also shaped the magnitude and composition of immigration flows. The U.S. government, in collaboration with employers, has facilitated the importation of Latino workers as sources of low-wage work. This role was largely reproduced over the years through a mixture of legislation (e.g., immigration laws), institutional practices (e.g., the INS, the Bracero Program), ideologies (ethnic stereotypes, racism), and labor and social practices (segmentation of the work force, job networks, discrimination, and segregation).

The same structures and practices continued reproducing the same type of Latino immigrant, the same types of jobs, and the same comparative conditions. Recent evidence, including 1980 and more recent statistics, show the continuation of occupational and industrial segmentation and lower wages. Latinos were handicapped politically by their limited immigrant status, and in the case of Chicago, by a political machine developed along ethnic lines that systematically excluded them from participation and opportunities.

Cuban elites and other refugees or educated groups from Latin America were given a somewhat different treatment, as evidenced by the U.S. government's political choices. Yet they were still treated as Latinos and were largely excluded from government jobs, high-paying and decision-making occupations, and other opportunities. The struggles in Chicago since the 1960s for better opportunities and against discrimination and exclusion of Latinos and the statistical evidence presented indicate that even these favored groups have also paid a "Latino" penalty in terms of lower wages, employment below their educational level and skills, segregation, and discrimination. The available data suggest that in the Chicago area Cubans and other Latino subgroups have been increasingly moving toward the average conditions of Mexicans and Puerto Ricans, rather than toward those of whites.

Table 5.6 Occupational Distribution by Latino Subgroup—1980

Occupation	Mexican	Puerto Rican	Cuban	South American	Central American
Offic. & Mgrs.	3.4	4.1	9.0	6.4	3.4
Professionals	3.4	5.0	11.8	13.2	6.5
Technicians	.9	1.1	2.2	2.3	.8
Sales	3.8	4.6	3.4	8.4	1.9
Clerical/Admin.	16.0	19.6	25.5	16.7	12.2
Service	14.4	2.8	13.3	11.0	18.7
Craft	9.3	8.4	10.6	9.1	14.1
Operatives	34.1	36.7	19.2	27.2	36.6
Farm Laborers	1.2	.2	—	.2	.4
Nonfarm Laborers	13.5	7.6	5.0	5.5	5.3

This situation made it particularly difficult for Latinos in Chicago to benefit from growth, to move up in or adapt to the process of economic restructuring. In fact, the conditions and limitations imposed on the group prevented the development of resources and political position, education, and networks and the accumulation of wealth necessary to

Table 5.7 Industry of Latinos by National Group—1980

Industry	Mexican	Puerto Rican	Cuban	South American	Central American
Agriculture	1.3	.1	—	.2	—
Mining	.1	—	—	—	—
Construction	4.0	2.6	2.8	2.5	4.2
Manufacturing	49.8	49.2	34.0	40.7	52.7
Traditional	45.9	45.4	28.1	35.2	45.1
Nontraditional	3.9	3.8	5.9	5.5	7.6
Transportation	4.6	5.5	3.7	3.0	2.3
Communications	1.0	.9	.9	.5	—
Wholesale Trade	4.7	3.5	4.0	4.1	3.4
Retail Trade	13.2	14.2	17.9	16.9	7.2
FIRE	12.5	15.6	2.9	23.1	17.8
Service	6.4	6.1	6.2	7.3	10.6
Public Admin.	1.8	6.0	1.5	1.6	1.5
Defense	.1	.1	.3	—	—
Utilities	.6	1.2	—	.2	.4

compete effectively, to live through the hardships and profit from the opportunities. Hence, economic restructuring extended, and indeed, reinforced the role of Latinos in the Chicago economy as low-wage, dominated workers.

Viewed from another perspective, in Chicago the availability of a large, subordinated, low-wage Latino work force has facilitated the development of the so-called service sector and has kept in business many manufacturing firms with low profit margins. As an employer in the westside of Chicago expressed to us: "I don't need to move to Mexico to get cheap labor. We have plenty of them here. By staying in Chicago I have the best of both worlds." In other words, Latinos have done for economic restructuring what they had previously done for the agribusiness, the railroad, and the manufacturing sectors. Latinos went from bad to worse as they moved from low-wage manufacturing jobs to lower wage, lower promising jobs in the restructuring economy.

This is not to say, however, that Latinos accepted this situation passively. A spirit of struggle is demonstrated in the formation of *mutualistas,* community organizations, active advocacy, projects and demonstrations, and political mobilization. Since the 1960s, with the formation of majority Latino neighborhoods and the enacting of affirmative action legislation, these struggles have been more focused and have led to greater job opportunities, educational progress for Latinos, improved services, and some community development. The growth of the Latino population since the 1960s, more comprehensive citywide efforts, coalitions with other minority groups, and voter registration drives have led to political representation at the local and state levels and are now producing federal representation. Community businesses in Latino neighborhoods have been the basis for some capital formation and the development of some businesses with a citywide market. Community organizations have provided the basis for more sustained struggles and for development of stronger Latino institutions. Indeed, were it not for the segmented and structured role that Latinos have played in the labor force, were it not for the parallel disruption and marginalization of communities that are an integral feature of this role, Latino communities would not be continuing to face the same problems that have plagued them since their arrival to Chicago. Our research indicates that the impact of recent economic restructuring on Latinos in Chicago is primarily a function of structured segmentation and discrimination and must, therefore, be mediated by policies that recognize this historical legacy of grinding inequality.

6

Cubans and the Changing Economy of Miami

Marifeli Pérez-Stable
Miren Uriarte

*In memory of Mauricio Gastón, who forged the way
in analyzing Cubans in a changing Miami.*

The experience of Cubans in Miami appears to stand apart from the Latino inequalities elsewhere in the U.S. economy. However mythical the "golden exile" (Portes, 1969) might have been, the perception of the successful Cuban is deeply ingrained among Cubans, other Latinos, and the general population. In important ways, the data back up these perceptions. Cubans earn higher incomes, have higher educational levels, and register lower poverty rates than other Latinos. Most Cubans in the United States, moreover, arrived as political exiles after the revolution of 1959. Thus, their migration differed markedly from that of Mexicans and Puerto Ricans.

Nonetheless, the "success story" has been "dysfunctional" for the characterization of Cuban communities, especially for those among them who do not quite live up to the prevailing image.[1] The other side

AUTHORS' NOTE: Research funded through the Inter-University Program for Latino Research and a 1989 Faculty Development Grant from the Research Foundation of the State University of New York to Pérez-Stable. Françoise Carre and Michael Stoll of the Gastón Institute at the University of Massachusetts provided invaluable help in analyzing the data. We thank Guillermo Grenier, Edwin Meléndez, Yolanda Prieto, and Andrés Torres for their comments. We are, of course, solely responsible for the analysis.

of the Cuban story, particularly in South Florida where most Cubans in the United States live, has clearly not received adequate attention. In this chapter we do not dismiss the predominant view of Cubans in U.S. society, but an analysis of their labor market participation in Miami over four decades delineates their profile in ways that allow for more meaningful comparisons with other groups.

The incorporation of Latino groups in the U.S. economy has elicited two sorts of explanations. The first focuses on human capital. Latinos—whether immigrants or long-time residents—are seen as having educational levels and work experience that do not easily fit the labor markets of the urban areas where they live and therefore being at a disadvantage in relation to other groups. Higher educational levels and labor market participation seem to place Cubans in a more advantageous position.

The second explanation emphasizes the centrality of economic structures from several different perspectives. One highlights the tendency of the labor market to segregate workers of different characteristics (i.e., race, ethnicity, and gender) into distinct economic sectors. Drawing upon structural theories of labor market segmentation, Portes and his colleagues have elaborated the primary paradigm for analyzing the Cuban economic experience in South Florida (Portes & Bach, 1985; Portes & Manning, 1986; K. L. Wilson & Portes, 1980). The Cuban enclave in Miami has provided a path of incorporation comparable to the primary sector and more beneficial to Cubans than the secondary labor market.

Other structural arguments underscore the overall transformation of the U.S. economy, marked by a sharp decline in production jobs and the rise of a service economy. Focusing on the role of U.S. cities in the international economy, Sassen (1991) notes the development of "global cities" (New York and Los Angeles) has expanded a segmented service sector where growing numbers of low-wage jobs are available for immigrants and minorities. Kasarda (1989) argues a "skills mismatch" greatly affects minorities, that is, their skills are best suited for the displaced industries and not appropriate for the ascending sectors. Waldinger (1986) contends an "ethnic queue" of minorities and immigrants has formed for the jobs vacated by whites; foreign-born workers are decidedly at the end (Waldinger, 1986). Regardless of their specific focus, these authors agree economic transformation has eliminated many manufacturing jobs, created low-wage employment, reinforced poverty, and resulted in growing income inequalities.

In this chapter we use the 1950, 1970, and 1980 U.S. Census Public Use Micro Data Sample and the 1988 Current Population Survey for the

Miami SMSA to describe the effect of economic transformation on the insertion of Cubans into the economy of Miami.[2] We start, however, by looking at Miami and Havana during the 1950s, with an eye for their emergent, though truncated, complementarity. Our purpose is to establish the structural context into which Cubans brought their human and other capital. The initial "skills match" was an important component of the relative ease with which the Miami economy incorporated the exiles. We next examine the extent of economic transformation in Miami in the light of industrial and occupational changes between 1950 and 1988. We then analyze the differential effect of these changes on the major racial/ethnic groups, paying particular attention to Cubans. Finally, we conclude with some suggestive notes on our findings and their implications for the paradigms used to understand the Cuban experience.

MIAMI AND HAVANA: DEVELOPMENT TRENDS BEFORE 1959

An often-ignored aspect of the Cuban experience in Miami is the complementarity in the patterns of development between the sending and receiving economies of the immigrants: those of Havana and Miami during the 1950s. These patterns and their aborted prospects constitute an important structural context for the entrance of Cubans into Miami after 1959. In Miami, Cubans, especially *habaneros,* stepped into familiar terrain. Their human capital and their know-how tapped the potential in the socioeconomic context of Miami, and consequently, their skills found their market match. These links and trends of the 1950s are an important, if so far overlooked, element in analyses of the formation of the Cuban enclave in Miami and the emergence of the region as the gateway to Latin America.

One of the consequences of the social revolution of 1959 was the migration of more than one-half million Cubans during the 1960s. The earliest exiles were especially unrepresentative of the Cuban population during the 1950s. They came from the wealthier, predominantly white, better educated, more urban, higher status occupational sectors of prerevolutionary society. Some arrived with little except a few personal belongings. Many managed to transfer some assets to the United States. A few had investments outside of Cuba well before the revolution. All came with substantial human capital, and just as important, with the insight that belonging to the Cuban middle class gave them into U.S. culture. During the 1950s, Cuba, particularly Havana, experienced substantial U.S. influence. At the time, no other group of Latin Americans could have entered the United States as prepared to succeed as middle-class Cubans were during the early 1960s. That Miami and Havana had been undergoing transformations that augured complementarity and competition, moreover, allowed the exiles to step into familiar territory.

Since the 1920s, tourism, real estate, construction, trade, and financial services had brought considerable expansion to Miami. The trade sectors were the most important employer, accounting for 31% of total employment in 1950. Services, especially the unskilled type supportive of tourism, were the second leading source of employment. Construction and transportation each accounted for about 7%-10% of Miami earners (Ballinger, 1936; Muir, 1953). Although manufacturing represented less than 10% of total employment, the city nonetheless had one of the fastest rates of industrial growth in the United States during the 1940s and 1950s.[3] Largely because of tourism, links to the Caribbean were growing. Miami was often the first stop before traveling farther south. But these expanding ties were also rooted in the developing importance of Miami as a financial center for foreign trade, particularly to Latin America. New Orleans, however, still retained preeminence as the U.S. gateway to the south. Some observers underscored the (then) 20 million potential customers in the Caribbean Basin as an incentive for South Florida manufacturing (Wolff, 1945, p. 66). The recession of the late 1950s hit Miami earlier, harder, and lasted longer than in the rest of the country (Center for Advanced International Studies, 1967). Thus, the profile of Miami when the Cuban exiles first arrived has been somewhat distorted. On the surface, Miami might have seemed not much more than a hard-pressed resort town. Underneath, however, longer term trends pointed to emerging transformations that the early influx of mostly upper- and middle-class Cubans undoubtedly encouraged.

During the 1950s, Havana was more decisively experiencing rapid changes. The capital was the motor behind the incipient transformation of dependent Cuban capitalism. With about 25% of the total population, Havana had nearly 31% of the economically active population. More disproportionate was its share of the more educated sectors of the labor force: 54% of all professionals, 40% of all managers, nearly 60% of all office workers, about 40% of all skilled workers, and 54% of all service workers (Oficina Nacional de los Censos Demográfico y Electoral,

1955, pp. 1, 183, 196). Havana was the principal site for the expanding industrialization then taking place in Cuba. Eight of the 14 industrial enterprises employing 500 or more workers were in its vicinity (U.S. Department of Commerce, 1955, pp. 73-74). Construction and tourism were also flourishing. During the 1950s, total wages in Havana province increased about 22%, even as those of all other provinces, especially Camagüey and Oriente, declined (R. C. Bonilla, 1983, pp. 416-417; Banco Nacional de Cuba, 1960, pp. 151-153).[4] Consumer culture was rapidly making inroads in the capital. Imports of consumer durables were growing significantly and most were destined for the *habanero* public (Banco Nacional de Cuba, 1960, p. 190). Moreover, *habaneros* were increasingly using credit to maintain their life-style.

In 1958, Havana certainly overshadowed Miami. Manufacturing, banking, construction, and tourism (as well as gambling and other underworld operations) were proliferating. All of these endeavors had actual or potential counterparts in Miami. During the 1960s, U.S. investments in Latin America increased rapidly and significantly contributed to the internationalization of the larger economies in the region (Cardoso & Faletto, 1979). We will never know how Cuba might have developed without the revolution. Given the special relationship with the United States, Cuba—and especially Havana—might have occupied a central space in the internationalization process of the 1960s and 1970s. The geographic proximity between Havana and Miami might also have meant that South Florida might have become the U.S. gateway to Latin America. Without the revolution, Havana and Miami would have likely shared that portal. Thus, even without the exiles, the days of Miami as just a tourist town might well have been numbered.

THE MIAMI ECONOMY, 1950-1988

Between 1950 and 1988, Miami underwent profound economic and demographic transformations. The restructuring process in the Miami SMSA entailed prodigious growth in the service sector, particularly in the high-end services, and the stagnation of the small manufacturing sector. In an industrial taxonomy of 94 metropolitan areas in the United States, Bluestone, Stevenson, and Tilly (1992) categorized them according to changes in aggregate employment levels and industrial structure. Between 1973 and 1987, Miami experienced trends similar to those of Boston and Los Angeles: significant expansion in nonagricultural sectors

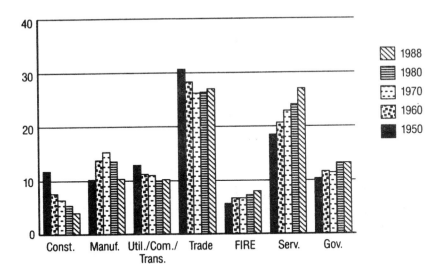

Figure 6.1. Industrial Distribution of Employment, Miami Metropolitan Area, 1950-1988 (in percent)

SOURCE: Florida Department of Labor and Employment Security.

and much smaller changes in total manufacturing employment. Until the 1970s, these trends, however, were not well established.

Between 1950 and 1988, total employment increased from just over 150,000 to more than 850,000. Miami experienced expansion and then decline in manufacturing, a steady decline in construction, and the rapid growth of the service sector (Figure 6.1). Manufacturing increased its share of workers through the 1950s and 1960s and started to decline during the 1970s. By 1988, the share of workers in manufacturing appears to have returned to 1950 levels. In contrast, construction has undergone sharp and steady declines over the four decades. By 1988 the share of earners in this sector was 40% of what it had been in 1950.

Trade and services have always been significant in the Miami economy, accounting for about half of all Miami workers through the four decades. During the 1960s, important changes in composition first became apparent. By 1970, the high-end services overtook the low-skilled jobs in personal services and the tourist industry. The restructuring process continued in favor of financial and other professional

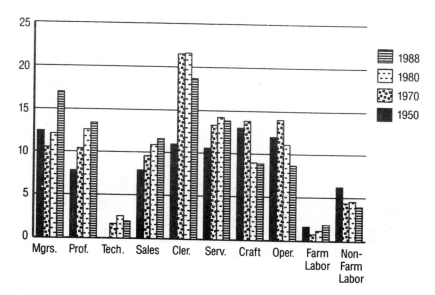

Figure 6.2. Occupational Distribution of Earners, Miami Metropolitan Area, 1950-1988 (in percent)
SOURCE: U.S. Census PUMS 1950-1980; CPS 1988.

services until 1988, when there appears to have been a slight reversal in the relationship between the two service sectors. Just as significant, high-end services displaced retail trade as the major employment sector. Although retail trade had recovered slightly from the decline occurring between 1970 and 1980, it remained well below the levels of 1950. During the 1980s, as Miami consolidated its place in the structure of international finance, the high-end service sector employed somewhat under a third of earners. The days of the tourist town were long gone.

Two major trends mark the changes in the occupational structure of Miami during these four decades (Figure 6.2). First, there has been a marked increase in the managerial and professional occupations at the expense of those occupations requiring lesser skills. Miami's share of workers in more highly skilled occupations has increased steadily from 20% in 1950 to 31% in 1988. By comparison, the share of earners in clerical and other low-end services appears to have stabilized after rising sharply during the 1960s. Craft, operative, and laborer occupations

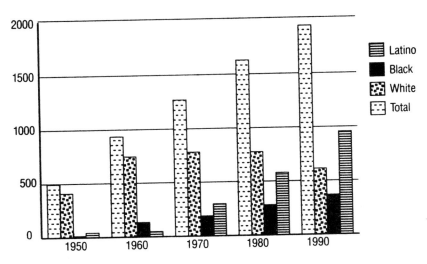

Figure 6.3. Population of Dade County, Florida, 1950-1990 (in thousands)
SOURCE: Research Division, Metropolitan Dade County Planning Department.

have undergone a significant relative decline. Second, the occupational opportunities for low-skilled workers have narrowed. By 1988, the Miami profile appears to have consolidated: Clerical occupations still accounted for the largest number of workers, with the sum of managers and professionals/technical personnel representing one third of earners in Dade County. Crafters, operatives, and laborers continued to decline.

Demographic changes, especially in racial/ethnic makeup, are even more significant (Figure 6.3). Between 1950 and 1990, the population of Miami nearly quadrupled from 495,084 to 1,937,094. In 1950, 83% of the population was non-Hispanic white, 13% black, and 4% Latino.[5] By 1970, blacks and Latinos had increased their share of total population, respectively, 15% and 23%. In contrast, the share of non-Hispanic whites had decreased by 21 percentage points.[6] After 1970, non-Hispanic whites continued to decline, representing only 32% of the Miami SMSA population in 1990, while blacks increased their share to 19%. By 1990, Latinos had become the largest group, accounting for 49% of the population.[7] During the late 1980s, Latinos were 40% of the working-age population; Cubans represented about 20% of Miami's workers. Diversification of the Latino population also characterizes the period

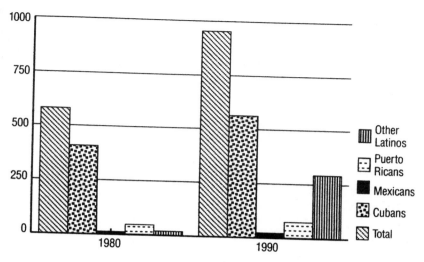

Figure 6.4. Latino Population of Dade County, Florida, 1980-1990 (in thousands)
SOURCE: U.S. Census.

(Figure 6.4). During the 1960s and 1970s, Cubans constituted about 70% of the Latino population. The remaining 30% were Central/South Americans and Dominicans (20%), Puerto Ricans (8%), and others (2%). By 1990, however, the Cuban share of the Latino population had decreased to 59% and that of Central/South Americans and Dominicans had increased to 31%. Puerto Ricans remained at 8%.

With the change in population came a transformation in the region's labor force. As the Latinization of Miami went forward, the proportion of non-Hispanic white earners across industrial sectors and occupations declined dramatically, while that of Latinos increased. Latino gains were particularly salient in manufacturing and high- and low-end services, all ascending sectors of the economy during the 1970s, and excepting manufacturing, during the 1980s as well. The black share of earners across sectors has largely remained constant. The composition of the labor force in different occupations adds another dimension to growing diversity. A clear racial/ethnic order emerged where non-Hispanic whites dominated the higher salaried and more prestigious occupations with Latinos beginning to make modest inroads. But both Latinos and blacks were more likely to be employed in occupations of lower socioeconomic status. During the 1970s and 1980s, these trends consolidated. By 1988, non-Hispanic whites were solidly ensconced in the expanding high-level management and professional/technical occupations. Blacks and Latinos, although increasing their share of earners in these sectors, continued to be underrepresented.

THE DIFFERENTIAL EFFECT OF ECONOMIC TRANSFORMATION: NON-HISPANIC WHITES, BLACKS, AND CUBANS IN MIAMI

How the three main racial/ethnic groups have fared in the restructuring of the regional economy is an important aspect of the recent history of Miami. According to industrial and occupational distributions by racial/ethnic groups as well as data on income and poverty, non-Hispanic white earners have fared the best. Between 1950 and 1980, they steadily increased their participation in the ascending economic sectors and in the highest status occupations in the new industries of South Florida (Tables 6.1 and 6.2). Non-Hispanic white workers have successfully made the occupational shifts concomitant to the new economic conditions. By 1988, 41% were employed as managers, technicians, and professionals; 43% labored as low-status white-collar workers in service, sales, and clerical occupations. Only 6% were still employed as operatives and laborers.

Rising incomes and declining poverty rates among non-Hispanic whites have resulted from the increase of their participation in the higher status occupations and the expanding sectors of the economy. Between 1950 and 1980, non-Hispanic whites experienced steady growth in their mean total income, although the rise was particularly dramatic among the men (Figure 6.5). During the 1980s, non-Hispanic white male income stagnated although that of females continued to rise. Non-Hispanic white poverty rates—low to begin with—declined slightly (Table 6.3). Poverty rates among non-Hispanic white earners, however, rose from 4.5% in 1970 to 5.3% in 1988, a local manifestation of national trends of growing numbers of working poor.

In contrast, blacks have fared much worse. Although increasing numbers of blacks have penetrated the ascending sectors of the economy, they have done so primarily in the lower status occupations. Black earners have particularly suffered because sectors where they were once strong and occupations they once dominated have declined. Construction,

Table 6.1 Selected Industries of White, Black, and Cuban Earners, Miami Metro Area, 1950-1988

	1950			1970			1980			1988		
	W	B	C	W	B	C	W	B	C	W	B	C
Agri	2.8	4.1	*	1.0	5.7	0.8	1.2	3.5	1.2	1.4	—	2.0
Constr	7.7	21.0	*	6.9	10.0	5.3	6.2	6.2	6.7	8.0	8.8	6.8
Trad Mfg	7.7	1.4	*	10.1	6.7	32.9	8.2	7.4	24.0	7.6	7.3	13.7
Trans	8.7	7.4	*	7.9	5.9	4.1	7.5	7.3	5.6	4.1	5.8	9.9
Commun	1.3	0.1	*	2.1	1.3	0.8	2.2	1.8	1.3	2.2	*	3.1
Wh Trade	6.9	6.3	*	5.5	4.1	4.7	5.2	3.7	6.9	4.9	*	5.8
Re Trade	21.2	14.4	*	19.5	13.3	17.8	19.8	15.8	16.9	20.0	14.6	16.4
Hi Serv	10.2	4.9	*	22.3	19.3	13.1	31.2	28.3	22.0	27.2	27.0	23.6
Lo Serv	11.9	20.7	*	16.4	27.6	16.8	10.0	15.3	10.2	9.8	18.2	13.0
Pub Adm	4.6	*	*	4.4	2.6	0.8	4.8	6.3	2.5	3.3	3.6	2.7
Hi Mfg	—	—	—	0.7	*	1.7	1.0	0.9	1.6	1.4	*	1.4
Utilities	1.5	3.3	*	1.0	0.5	*	1.3	2.4	0.6	1.0	*	1.4

SOURCE: U.S. Bureau of the Census, PUMS (1950, 1970, 1980), CPS (1988).
NOTE: (*) cell count too small; (—) data not available. Columns do not add up to 100% because of missing or not available data and because we did not include Mining and Defense. Moreover, the PUMS column totals are well below 100%.

143

Table 6.2 Selected Occupations of White, Black, and Cuban Earners, Miami Metro Area, 1950-1988

	1950			1970			1980			1988		
	W	B	C	W	B	C	W	B	C	W	B	C
Managers	13.3	3.0	*	13.0	1.5	6.1	15.4	5.3	9.9	22.4	6.9	17.5
Profession	8.9	1.4	*	12.4	5.8	5.2	15.3	9.2	8.3	16.4	12.2	11.6
Technician	—	—	—	1.6	*	2.6	3.1	2.3	2.1	2.5	2.3	2.1
Sales	9.7	1.4	*	11.6	2.7	6.5	12.8	5.9	9.6	12.3	6.1	11.6
Clerical	12.5	1.9	*	24.0	13.9	17.3	23.7	19.2	22.2	20.2	14.5	19.9
Service	8.3	16.3	*	10.5	32.4	10.3	11.9	26.6	11.4	11.2	23.7	9.6
Crafts	15.5	1.4	*	14.7	7.5	15.1	8.0	6.9	10.8	8.3	9.9	8.9
Operatives	11.5	12.5	*	9.0	18.7	32.7	5.8	13.0	19.3	3.8	11.5	14.4
Farm Labor	1.3	4.1	*	0.3	3.9	*	0.7	3.1	0.9	*	5.3	*
N-farm Labor	1.2	31.6	*	2.9	13.1	4.0	3.2	8.6	5.5	2.2	7.6	3.8

SOURCE: U.S. Bureau of the Census, PUMS (1950, 1970, 1980), CPS (1988).
NOTE: 1950 U.S. Census aggregated professionals and technicians; (*) cell count too small; (—) data not available. Columns do not add up to 100% because of missing or not available data and because we did not include Mining and Defense. Moreover, the 1950 PUMS column totals are well below 100%.

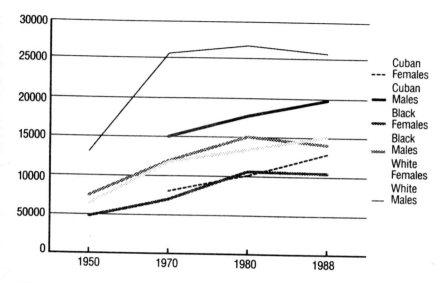

Figure 6.5. Mean Total Income of Earners, by Race and Ethnicity, Miami Metropolitan Area, 1950-1988 (in 1982-1984 dollars)
NOTE: *All figures refer to income in year prior to survey.
SOURCE: U.S. Census PUMS 1950-1980; CPS 1988.

for example, employed 21% of black workers in 1950 and only 6.2% in 1980. Similarly, 32% of black workers were laborers in 1950 and only 8.6% in 1980. The percentage of black workers in the low- and high-end services has increased rather sharply. In fact, the highest percentage increase among black earners has come among those in the high-end service sector. In 1950, 5% of black earners were employed in high-end services; by 1980 28% were so employed.

The changing economy of Miami has brought significant changes for black occupational opportunities. Black managers, technicians, and professionals increased sharply: More than one out of five black earners was employed in these occupations in 1988. Changes in occupational structures have, however, limited the jobs available to low-skilled workers, where blacks are disproportionately represented, and may thus have led significant numbers to abandon the labor force. Between 1950 and 1980, black operatives and laborers declined from 50% to 24%, and those in clerical, sales, and service jobs increased from 20% to 52%.

Table 6.3 Rates of Poverty in the Working-Age Population and Among Earners, Miami Metro Area, 1970-1988

	1970	1980	1988
White Population	10.7	8.9	8.7
Black Population	29.4	25.7	27.6
Cuban Population	13.4	15.2	17.2
White Earners	4.5	4.6	5.3
Black Earners	20.1	15.3	16.1
Cuban Earners	8.2	5.8	6.6

NOTE: 100% Federal Poverty Standard.
SOURCE: U.S. Bureau of the Census, PUMS (1970, 1980), CPS (1988).

This reversal may partially explain the decline of 15 percentage points in the labor force participation of black males and the rise by 21 percentage points in that of black women.

Black gains in the high-status occupations have not translated into a higher mean income relative to non-Hispanic white and Cuban males. Rising steadily between 1950 and 1980, mean income for black men has consistently remained below that of their counterparts in the other two main groups. In 1988, moreover, mean black male income was lower than that of non-Hispanic white females. Black female income also rose steadily throughout the period. Interestingly, the mean income of black women was lower than that of non-Hispanic white females and higher than that of Cuban females. During the 1980s, black women appear to have suffered significant losses in mean income, and by 1988, Cuban women surpassed them (Figure 6.5).

Not surprising, between 1970 and 1980, poverty rates for working-age blacks remained high. Although declining slightly during the 1970s, poverty rates were rising again during the 1980s. In 1988, black women had the highest poverty rates for working-age blacks: Nearly three quarters of all black poor were women and one third of all black women were poor. Poverty was also concentrated among the younger and oldest age cohorts: In 1988, 36% of blacks 16-24 and 46% over 60 were poor compared to 21% of those 25-59. The relative absence of jobs available to young blacks and the availability of low-paying jobs for black women seem to be contributing factors to the profile of black poverty in Miami. Black poverty rates have been about three times those of non-Hispanic whites. In contrast to non-Hispanic whites, however, poverty among black earners decreased from 20% in 1970 to 16% in 1988. This relative decrease notwithstanding, black earners suffer poverty rates three to four times greater than those of non-Hispanic whites. The Cuban experience lies somewhere between that of blacks and non-Hispanic whites. Cubans have generally been successful in entering the ascending sectors of the economy, particularly during the 1980s. During the 1960s, as manufacturing rose in importance in the Miami economy, it employed one third of all Cubans. During the 1970s, as the sector declined, so did the percentage of Cubans. By 1988, 14% of Cuban earners worked in manufacturing. During the 1970s, Cubans rapidly entered the high-end service sectors. By 1988, high-end services employed more Cubans than any other sector, 23.6%. In many ways, the sectoral experience of Cubans resembles that of non-Hispanic whites.

Occupationally, however, Cubans have had a different experience. Although Cubans have made substantial inroads in the high-status occupations, a large percentage of Cubans are still in the lower paying jobs. Between 1970 and 1988, Cuban earners in the high SES occupations registered the largest relative gains among the three groups: 14% to 31.2%. Nevertheless, a large percentage of Cubans still work in the lower paying occupations. In 1970, 71% of Cuban workers worked in sales or as clerks, service workers, operatives, and laborers. By 1988, 59% continued to do so, whereas 49% of non-Hispanic whites and 62% of blacks did.

In many ways, Cubans have also had to make occupational shifts similar to those of blacks: from operatives and laborers to white- and pink-collar employment. In 1970, Cuban earners were about equally employed in low-paying white-collar and service sectors (33.6%) as in operative and laborer occupations (36.7%). By 1988, only 18% remained in the declining operative and laborer occupations whereas 41% now had jobs in the low-paying service occupations. The shift is more rapid than that experienced by blacks and cushioned by a significant representation in the ascending occupational sectors. The labor force participation of Cuban men declined during the 1970s and subsequently stabilized; that of Cuban women remained stable and high throughout the period.

A closer look at the distribution of Cuban earners across the industries and occupations where they are most prevalent provides an illustration of their sectoral and occupational shifts (Table 6.4).[8] First, those industries and occupations historically representing the bulk of Cuban earners (80% in 1980) accounted for about 70% in 1988. Cubans appear to be moving into new sectors, primarily communications and transportation. Second, Cuban earners in 1988 manifest a sharp decline in the percent employed in manufacturing across all occupations. The trends in other sectors point to increases among the higher status occupations and declines among the lower paying ones. The only exception were the low-end services where Cuban earners increased their share among both high- and low-paying occupations. Third, distribution within each sector reveals a similar pattern of transition from the lower to the higher paying occupations. Manufacturing is the only exception where the remaining Cuban earners are concentrated in the lowest status occupations.

Finally, the distribution shows that only about 20% of Cubans conformed to the profile of success: managers and professionals in manufacturing, construction, the high-end services, and wholesale and retail trade. Most Cuban earners had a rather different experience: They worked as operatives and laborers in manufacturing and as office clerks, service workers, and salespeople in the service sectors and wholesale and retail trade. Although varying by sector, the difference in earnings between the high- and low-paying occupations is substantial. The 1988 Current Population Survey data appear to underscore widening income differentials between these two types of occupation.

Income and poverty trends support the indications of growing polarization. Between 1970 and 1988, earnings for Cuban workers as well as the rate of poverty among the working-age population and among earners increased. While incomes of non-Hispanic whites stagnated and those of blacks declined, those of Cuban males rose sharply. The mean income of Cuban females similarly rose, surpassing that of black women in 1988 but remaining well below that of non-Hispanic white females. Paralleling rising incomes were increases in poverty among the working-age population. In 1970, 13% lived in a poor household; by 1988, that rate was 17%. As among blacks, poverty among Cuban earners decreased during the 1970s and increased during the 1980s. Poverty among working-age Cubans appears to be concentrated among women and those over 60. Sixty-eight percent of all Cuban poor were women and 52% elderly. Women constituted 58% of low-wage earners: They made up 70% in the service and clerical occupations in the low- and high-end services and 54% of the operatives in manufacturing.

Table 6.4 Cuban Incomes by Industry and Occupation, Miami Metro Area, 1980 and 1988 (actual dollars)

Industry	Occupation	Distribution of Earners		% Sector's Earners		Mean Income	
		1980	1988	1980	1988	1980	1988
Manufacturing	Man/Prof/Tech	2.0	0.7	8.5	5	15,398	33,000
	Sal/Cler/Serv	4.4	2.1	18.2	15	9,395	15,900
	Oper/Lab	17.6	9.9	62.9	72.5	6,820	8,833
	Craft	2.5	1	10.2	7.5	8,861	18,333
Hi Services	Man/Prof/Tech	8.4	11	38.3	46.3	15,925	33,811
	Sal/Cler/Serv	13	11.6	57.2	49.2	8,377	12,163
Retail Trade	Man/Prof/Tech	2.8	4.1	16.7	25	14,057	28,226
	Sal/Cler/Serv	10.2	9.3	60.3	56.6	6,688	8,199
Lo Services	Man/Prof/Tech	1.6	3.1	15.4	23.7	13,007	16,504
	Sal/Cler/Serv	6.4	6.9	59.6	52.6	6,750	10,598
WH Trade	Man/Prof/Tech	1.5	2.1	21.2	35.3	18,469	23,416
	Sal/Cler/Serv	4.4	2.4	49.7	41.1	10,585	14,642
Construction	Man/Prof/Tech	1.2	2.1	17.9	30	17,340	40,308
	Oper/Lab	1.7	1	25.6	15	9,597	11,793
	Craft	3.2	3.1	46.9	45	11,207	14,957

SOURCE: U.S. Census PUMS 1980. CPS 1988.

EXPLAINING THE EXPERIENCE OF CUBANS IN MIAMI

The incorporation of Cubans into the Miami economy has been generally successful. Rising poverty levels and growing earnings polarization notwithstanding, the economic experience of Cubans differs radically from that of other Latinos in their cities of major concentration as well as from that of other minorities in Miami itself. Cubans have entered the ascending sectors of the regional economy at both higher and lower levels. Although there is a continued concentration of substantial numbers in the manufacturing sector and in low-level occupations, there is also evidence Cuban earners are making a steady transition to higher paying occupations throughout the economy.

Table 6.5 Educational Attainment of Earners by Race, Miami Metro Area, 1970 to 1988

	White			Black			Cuban		
	1970	1980	1988	1970	1980	1988	1970	1980	1988
6 yrs or less	4.5	2.4	*	17.6	8.4	*	20.2	16.2	11.1
7 yrs to H.S.	27.1	16.3	11.3	44.2	31.4	26.3	33.6	24.3	22.0
H.S. Graduate	35.1	33.4	38.4	25.0	32.4	36.5	23.7	27.6	28.9
Some College	19.2	24.3	24.1	7.2	18.6	17.5	12.5	17.8	20.6
College Graduate	14.1	23.6	25.8	2.7	8.6	13.9	9.7	13.4	17.4

SOURCE: U.S. Census PUMS 1970 and 1980, CPS 1988.
NOTE: (*) Cell Count too small.

Human capital explanations are the most prevalent. Educational attainment—higher for Cubans that for other Latinos—is often mentioned to explain their labor market success. However, in the context of Miami, the higher education levels do not appear to be as important as the earnings Cubans obtain at different levels of education in comparison with others in Miami. Between 1970 and 1988, the levels of educational attainment of Cuban earners have been closer to those of blacks than those of non-Hispanic whites (Table 6.5). In 1988, an equal percentage (67%) of black and Cuban earners had at least a high school degree; the rate for non-Hispanic whites was 88%. Cubans have a slightly higher percentage of college graduates (17%) than blacks (14%). The rate for non-Hispanic whites is 26%.

But, without doubt, Cuban earners are able to maximize the income potential of their educational attainment relative to other minorities. Across different educational levels, Cuban earnings are closer to those of non-Hispanic whites. For example, among earners with less than a high school education, Cuban earnings were more likely to approximate those of non-Hispanic whites whereas those of blacks tended to lag considerably (Figure 6.6). The gains are even more marked for those with a college education. In 1988, Cuban college graduates earned incomes slightly below non-Hispanic whites and substantially higher than black college graduates (Figure 6.7).

Human capital explanations also focus on the "business know-how" of Cubans as a factor in their higher rates of self-employment. Cubans

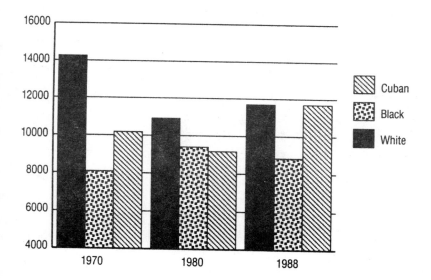

Figure 6.6. Earnings of Persons With Some High School Education in Wage and Self-Employment, Miami Metropolitan Area, 1970-1988 (in 1982-1984 dollars)

SOURCE: U.S. Census PUMS 1970, 1980; CPS 1988.

have, in fact, higher rates of self-employment than other groups in Miami (Figure 6.8). In 1988, rates of self-employment among Cubans (8.5%) surpassed those of non-Hispanic whites (7.4%) and were well above those of blacks (2.9%) in 1988.[9] Similarly, the mean self-employment earnings of Cubans relative to non-Hispanic whites has increased steadily. More important, among Cubans and non-Hispanic whites mean earnings from self-employment are higher than income from wage and salaries, whereas for blacks the reverse is the case.

The enclave economy appears to have enhanced the effect of education and work experience for Cubans in the Miami labor market. Although the data used in this paper do not allow the measurement of the effect of ethnic-owned enterprises on the incorporation of Cubans into the Miami economy, they do suggest the strength of the enclave. The occupational shifts that all Miamians have undergone appear to

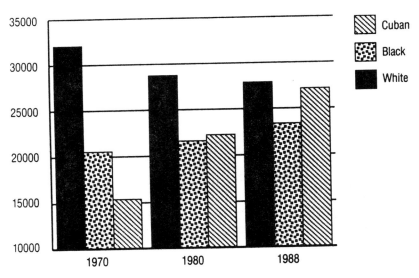

Figure 6.7. Earnings of College Graduates in Wages and Self-Employment, Miami Metropolitan Area, 1970-1988 (in 1982-1984 dollars)
SOURCE: U.S. Census PUMS 1970, 1980; CPS 1988.

have been buffered for Cubans as a result of the opportunities available to them, but not to others within the enclave. Although enclave earnings are lower than in the mainstream economy, the class diversity of the enclave has allowed Cubans across the occupational spectrum to exercise their human capital in a more protected environment. The enclave has thus facilitated the transition of Cubans into the mainstream sectors. During the 1980s, this transition appears to have accelerated and most likely explains the sustained increases in Cuban earnings.

Perhaps the most critical value of the enclave is the opportunity it affords for a mode of insertion that does not subject newcomers to the same degree of exploitation and discrimination as the primary and secondary labor markets. Enclave participation, even if exploitative, furnishes the immigrants with the opportunity to connect into a myriad of social networks, and consequently, gain more rapid social mobility. The high rates of self-employment for Cubans who left the island during

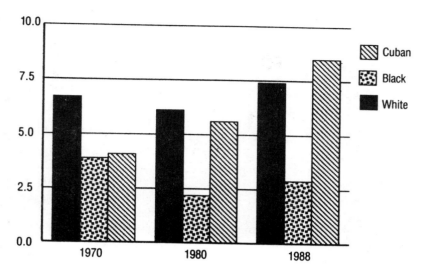

Figure 6.8. Self-Employment Rates, by Race and Ethnicity of Earners, Miami Metropolitan Area, 1970-1988
SOURCE: U.S. Census PUMS 1970, 1980; CPS 1988.

the 1970s and the Mariel boat lift in 1980 point to the preeminence of structural factors. Although largely lacking the endowed human capital of earlier immigrants, the more recent entrants have nonetheless had better economic outcomes than Latino immigrants with comparable qualifications in other areas of the country (Portes & Bach, 1985, pp. 205-216; Portes & Jensen, 1989).

Although the Portes paradigm is quite powerful, one of its relative weaknesses lies in the explanation for the origins of the enclave. This is no small matter. Understanding how Cuban exiles founded the businesses and established the networks that produced the enclave is a central question. Answering it allows the model to transcend the notion of "Cuban exceptionality." Where the original capital that formed the enclave came from is perhaps its most crucial starting point. Portes gives us several answers. First, and perhaps most evident, the Cuban migration included many persons who already had investments and savings in the United States or brought substantial capital that allowed them to become rentiers or start new endeavors. Moreover, many Cuban exiles, because of their pre-1959 dealings with U.S. companies, had useful business connections that served them well when applying for credit and establishing new enterprises. Next, Portes mentions a South American bank in Miami that, when the first exiles arrived, employed Cuban bankers. These bankers proceeded to issue loans to their conationals on the basis of prior knowledge about the applicants' record and experience in Cuba. In the same vein, Portes points to wealthy South Americans who invested their capital in Miami because of political upheavals in their native countries. Primarily in commerce and construction, this venture capital allowed small Cuban distributors and contractors the opportunity to grow beyond the enclave. Its extent and weight are understandably difficult to determine, but drug-related capital accumulation is mentioned. Finally, he underscores the role of individual savings in the smaller, more ethnic-oriented enterprises characteristic of the later entrants who lacked previous business experience and capital from Cuba (Portes, 1987).

These are all eminently convincing components of a structural explanation for the origins of the enclave. Nonetheless, a more complete framework needs to include at least two additional factors. In the first place, as outlined above, the patterns of Cuban development—particularly those of Havana—are crucial aspects of the context in which the initial migration occurred after 1959. Portes and Bach (1985) are quite right to insist on the "relational dynamics" within the international economy as the foundation for migrations. Following their lead, we are arguing for the importance of the specific regional context in establishing the structural framework for the development of the Cuban enclave in Miami after 1960.

The complementary development of Havana and Miami during the 1940s and 1950s allowed Cubans, especially the *habaneros,* to step into familiar territory. Manufacturing firms—not unlike the ones they had left behind in the industrial belt around Havana—came quickly to be controlled by Cubans at the top, and at the same time, offered a safe place for lower skilled Cubans to enter the labor market. The enclave also developed a service sector in which experienced entrepreneurs transplanted their business acumen from Havana to *la calle ocho* and provided entry level jobs for their compatriots.

The second set of considerations is the host of political and ideological factors that, although not exclusively determinant in the origins of the enclave, should be included in the analysis. Silvia Pedraza-Bailey (1985) rightfully focused on the role of the federal government. The United States invested nearly $1 billion in assisting the Cubans because they were fleeing communism. In many ways, it was a multifaceted community development strategy. In its 12 years of existence, federal assistance to Cuban refugees encompassed direct cash assistance, food subsidies, and guaranteed health care for needy individuals as well as college loans for Cuban students, training and retooling programs for professionals, and English-language instruction and financial assistance for those establishing small businesses. State intervention reinforced the advantages of the Cubans, and in turn, enhanced the ability of the exiles to contribute to the transformation of the South Florida economy. No other Latino group or community has had the benefit of similar levels of targeted investment and state intervention sustained over a significant period of time.

More recently, Carlos Forment (1989) has argued for the role of ideology within a political and structural context in the emergence of the enclave during the 1960s. The geopolitics of the Caribbean after the Cuban revolution and the interplay of the U.S. state and exile counter-revolutionary movements articulated a political discourse that significantly contributed to the development of a Cuban collective identity. Forment contends political convictions and activities are as important in community formation as the market forces and state intervention that Portes et al. and Pedraza-Bailey, respectively, emphasize. The role of the Central Intelligence Agency in providing some exiles with capital and business experience through the establishment of proprietary fronts should, for example, be mentioned, even if the full range of evidence is difficult to obtain (Argüelles, 1982; Forment, 1989). The downfall of Eastern European socialism, the disintegration of the Soviet Union, and current uncertainties about the future of Cuba itself, moreover, have reinforced the weight of ideological concerns in Cuban ethnic identity.

Two important questions in relationship to the future of the Cuban enclave are, first, the role of second-generation Cubans in the enclave economy, and second, the effect on the enclave on the growing diversity of the Latino population in Miami. There are indications from the data analyzed here that the retail enterprises in the enclave may serve as an entry point into the labor market for younger Cubans, particularly the retail trade sector. The question of whether they will fuel a second generation of the Cuban enclave, or as in other ethnic groups, the younger generation will immediately transcend it has not yet been answered. Similarly, there is evidence that "Other Hispanics" have very quickly attained even higher levels of self-employment than Cubans. Just a cursory observation of the main establishments of the enclave reveals that Central Americans are easily penetrating it both as owners and as workers. Nicaraguans are the main national group involved, which underscores the weight of the political and ideological factors framing the development and maintenance of the enclave.

CONCLUSIONS

In this chapter we bring out new facets of the images of Cubans in Miami. Although still impressive, the Cuban experience is considerably more complex than the success story would indicate. Miami developed very differently from the pattern anticipated during the 1930s and 1940s. As the U.S. gateway to Latin America was emerging, revolution convulsed Havana—Miami's Latin American counterpart. Consequently, many of the Cubans who were fueling the transformation of Havana during the 1950s made their way to Miami. Their presence in turn provided an added impetus to the development of Miami. During the 1960s, Miami and the exiles became an almost perfect match. Cubans thus look less like superachievers and more like a group intelligently transferring their skills to a propitious environment.

Our perspective allows underscoring some general lessons. First, the Cuban experience exemplifies successful state and private sector strategies on the adjustment and incorporation of immigrants. Encouraging the development of the enclave allowed Cubans the resources to control their own community. Far from the "social welfare" approach so characteristic of public and private sector policies toward other Latinos that so diminish and disempower individuals and communities, Cubans had the opportunity to exercise control over their community. Community development and community control, important pillars in the struggles of most Latino communities, have been critical factors in the attainments of Cubans in Miami. The fear of permanent separation from the mainstream that the independent development of Latino and immigrant communities often raises, as well as the concern that strong ethnic identity retards economic advancement, did not materialize in the Cuban case.

A second important lesson is the breadth of the Cuban Refugee Program and other federal initiatives to support the adaptation of Cubans. The range of programs offered are the top items in any Latino community's wish list: educational opportunities; retraining programs; English-language instruction; small business loans; college loans independent of need; and nonstigmatized direct cash benefits, health care, and food for those in need. Although these programs are not solely responsible for the Cuban success, they did provide a buffer against the initial, often traumatic experience of immigrants. No other Latino group has enjoyed similar favors. In this sense, the Cuban experience is indeed unique and needs to be underscored when comparing Cubans to other Latinos.

A growing concern is the state of race relations in Miami and our study likewise points to some insights. Three concurrent economic processes underlie relations among the three main groups. The first is the overwhelming success of non-Hispanic white workers who, after all, constitute the most important success story. Far from the sense of loss embodied in the slogan—"Will the last American to leave Miami, please bring the flag?"—non-Hispanic whites have been the principal beneficiaries of the economic transformations of the past four decades. Nevertheless, the Latinization of Miami has not been welcomed, the success of English-only legislation being but one example of non-Hispanic white dissatisfaction. Cuban attainments in Miami have undoubtedly most closely challenged the hegemony of non-Hispanic whites. Moreover, the ever-closer economic ties between Miami and Latin America underscore the importance of the Cuban success beyond the enclave. The prospects of continued Cuban advancement amid non-Hispanic white relative stagnation frame a most important backdrop to ethnic relations in Miami.

The second economic process underlying race relations is the marginalization of the black community. Blacks have not fared well in the processes of economic change in Miami. That change, set in motion well before the Cubans first arrived in the city, never took blacks' best interests into consideration. The advantages that some blacks have derived from their insertion in the ascending sectors of the economy are dwarfed by the severe disadvantages endured by the bulk of the black community. Although Cubans seem all-powerful from the perspective of blacks, Cubans are in fact less privileged than blacks think them to be. Up to the 1980s, the socioeconomic profiles of the two groups were more alike than different, especially when compared to non-Hispanic whites. However, as Cuban economic outcomes improved and those of blacks declined, and particularly as Cubans have attained more political power, the social separation and distrust between the two groups have become exacerbated.

The third process in understanding race relations in Miami is the changes within the Latino community itself. During the 1980s, the increase in the Latino population has been quite significant. Other Latinos, the principal contributors to that growth, appear to be taking advantage of the enclave. Not all, however, are doing so. Tensions between Cubans and Puerto Ricans may stem from the latter's lesser access to the protection of the enclave. For Cubans, now in titular control of the political structures, managing the demographic transition taking place in Miami is proving to be a more difficult task than achieving economic success. The future of group relations, indeed, depends on the economic and social development of the black and other Latino communities in Miami. Policies need to favor community-based economic development and employment and educational opportunities—policies similar to those that supported the successful incorporation of Cubans into the Miami economy.

NOTES

1. Prohías and Casal (1973) first pointed out the "dysfunctional" consequences of the "success story."

2. The 1950 PUMS is a 1/100 composite sample for Miami State Economic Area, Code 70 (sample size: 3,894). The 1970 PUMS is a 1% sample for the Miami SMSA, Code 3302 (Sample size: 9,347). The 1980 PUMS is a 5% 'A' sample of the Miami Metro Area (Dade County) Code 043-052 (sample size: 58,884). The PUMS data sets used in this study used the Miami Metropolitan Area defined in the 1980 PUMS for the extraction of the samples for 1950 and 1970. The 1988 March CPS is for the Miami SMSA (sample size: 1698). The 1960 PUMS is not used because data were reported statewide. The 1960 data reported were drawn from the sources noted.

3. *Psychosocial Dynamics in Miami* (Coral Gables, FL: University of Miami, January 1969, p. xxxvi). The report notes Miami led the United States in rates of increase in new manufacturing plants, new manufacturing payrolls, and new manufacturing value added.

4. The total wage bill excluded the salaries of sugar agricultural workers and only partially included other agricultural wages. See Pérez-Stable (1993) for a fuller analysis of Cuban development during the 1950s.

5. In 1950, there was no Latino identifier in the U.S. Census. The identification of Latino ethnicity in the 1950 PUMS was based on surname of the respondent or on Hispanic country of birth for respondent. Cubans are not identifiable as a distinct group in the 1950 PUMS.

6. The 1970 PUMS identifies Latinos by the birthplace of the parents.

7. Beginning in 1980, the U.S. Census contained a Latino identifier which asked respondents to identify their Latino background as well as the specific national group.

8. Because of the reduced cases in the cells, the figures for 1988 only provide an indication of trends and should be cautiously read.

9. Self-employment among Central Americans in Miami (8.7%) surpasses the high rates of Cubans.

7

The Changing Economic Position of Mexican Americans in San Antonio

Gilberto Cardenas
Jorge Chapa
Susan Burek

INTRODUCTION

San Antonio is the third largest city in Texas. It is known as a center of trade, tourism, biotechnology, and military bases—features that are rightly regarded as important to the economy of the city. The Mexican presence in the area spans several centuries, dating from the original settlement of the area by Spanish missionaries, farmers, and ranchers in the late 17th century. Anglo settlement occurred much later, in the early 19th century, as part of the general Anglo expansions and colonial wave that culminated in the declaration of Texan independence from Mexico in 1836 (Alvarez, 1985; Montejano, 1987). Population counts from the 1990 Census show that Mexican Americans constitute a majority of the population, and the city as a whole is of major importance to Mexican Americans in Texas. Unfortunately, San Antonio also has a higher than average poverty rate, 14.8% compared to 13.1% for Texas and 9.6% for the United States (Glickman & R. Wilson, 1985). The high poverty rate is often attributed to a poorly diversified economic base, weak manufacturing sector, and relatively low wage scale. In addition, San Antonio has a long history of ethnically exclusionary labor and development policies, and differential treatment of the Mexican-American population. Although Latinos constitute about 54% of the population, they represent more than 70% of persons living in poverty. According to one report, San Antonio's low-income population is nearly equal in size to the number of persons living in poverty in Houston, a city approximately twice its size. (Partnership for Hope, 1991).

San Antonio is located in Bexar County, which had more than 1 million residents in 1990, with Mexican Americans comprising approximately one half of the population. San Antonio plays a central cultural and economic role for the Mexican-American population in the Southwest. Along with Los Angeles and El Paso, San Antonio is a "capital" city for this population. Yet, the economic well-being of San Antonio's Mexican-American population is far below that of the Mexican-American population of Los Angeles. Regional economic variations between Texas and California are quite evident in the case of San Antonio. Contrasting with the diversified economy of Los Angeles and many other Latino cities, San Antonio continues to be dependent on tourism, commerce, military spending, and high-tech industries rather than industrial manufacturing. Although San Antonio does not attract large numbers of Latino immigrants from Central America and the Caribbean, a slow but steady stream of Mexican immigrants provides San Antonio with a continuing source of cheap human capital.

Our purpose here is to explore the economic condition of Mexican Americans and Mexican immigrants in San Antonio in comparison to their Anglo counterparts. We will examine their relative position in the labor force, access to educational opportunities, and prospects for the future within the regional economy of the Southwest. The overarching question is how to assess the lingering effects of racial discrimination and labor stratification. Empirical data from the U.S. Census Bureau Public Use Microdata Samples for the San Antonio SMSA civilian population age 16 and above for 1970 (15% 1/100 sample) and for 1980 (5% sample) are used to address these issues. These data have been weighted to approximate the population for each period.

HISTORICAL CONTEXT

San Antonio is the largest city in the United States in which the Spanish-origin population constitutes more than half of the population. Historically, it has been an important site for gauging the economic, social, and political well-being of the Mexican-American population in Texas. Although San Antonio is located in the south central region of Texas, it is understood as the social and commercial "capital" of South Texas, an area with 1.75 million Mexican Americans in 1980.

Since the mid-19th century, agriculture played a dominant role in shaping the economy of South Texas and in shaping the formation, composition, and relative social position of the Mexican-American labor force. The social impact of the South Texas agricultural economy on the Mexican-origin population is unique. Although the relative importance of agriculture in South Texas has diminished in the past 30 years, it continues to exert a strong influence in the southern part of the region along the Texas-Mexico border. Historically, a complex system of racial discrimination governed the insertion and devaluation of Mexican labor in San Antonio and throughout the Southwest. This system has had an extraordinarily harsh impact throughout the area (Montejano, 1987; Murgia, 1975; Tienda, 1988).

The shift from agricultural dominance to industrial manufacturing and other sectoral diversification since the 1940s has occurred more slowly in San Antonio and throughout South Texas than in other regions of the United States with high concentrations of Latinos. Although San Antonio is taking the lead in the region's economic development, it also must reckon with the realities and difficulties of the regional transition from agricultural to a more diversified economy. It is our contention that San Antonio's economic potential and rate of development is inevitably linked to the rate of development of the greater South Texas region. The city of San Antonio and South Texas as a whole have already passed a threshold and now are positioned to shed the legacy of agricultural dominance and move toward greater economic diversification. Nonetheless, agriculture is an important component of the regional economy, and it will continue to play a dynamic role in the development of the region.

Fred Schmidt's (1970) study of the employment of the Mexican-origin population in the Southwest documents the continuation into urban employment of the prejudice and discrimination that originated in agriculture. Schmidt describes this racial white-collar/blue-collar division of labor as a caste system that bars minorities from white-collar jobs and on-the-job training programs, especially in regions with large Mexican-origin populations, a condition similar to historical discrimination patterns against blacks in the South. Historically, the role of Mexican labor in the San Antonio urban economy paralleled its role in agriculture. Mexican labor was relegated to the lowest paying position in a racially based system of class stratification. The overwhelming majority of Mexican-American laborers did not own property in agriculture (Montejano, 1987). Medium- and small-sized Mexican-American entrepreneurial activity has been an important characteristic of the population's economic position, but it has not been as viable, as pervasive, or as well capitalized as the Anglo entrepreneurial sector. Until recently, the Mexican-American business sector has been largely supported by Mexican-origin clientele and was largely bypassed by the general economy during the post-1960s growth period (see Chapa & Cardenas, 1991).

Unlike the typical pattern of incorporation of European immigrants into growing industrial sectors and displacement during cyclical or (epochal) decline, the Mexican-origin population of San Antonio had a different history, as the agricultural origins of Mexican migration to San Antonio predate modern industry. Historically, San Antonio was founded on or near the site of five Spanish missions. It was the capital when Texas was a Mexican territory. Until 1930, San Antonio was the largest city in Texas. For these reasons, and for the social and familial networks between residents of Mexico and San Antonio, and its geographic proximity to the Mexican border, San Antonio has historically been a goal and a way station for Mexican migrants. Its size and geographic location would have made it a natural destination for migrants leaving Mexico during and following the revolution. Network and chain migration have accounted for much of migration since then.

DEMOGRAPHIC OVERVIEW

Initially, San Antonio's population was predominantly of Mexican origin. In the late 20th century, the Latino population again became a majority. Table 7.1 shows that the San Antonio SMSA civilian working-age population was approaching a Mexican-origin majority in 1970 and 1980. In 1970, 36.3% of the civilian San Antonio SMSA working-age population consisted of U.S.-born Mexican Americans, and 8.4% consisted of foreign-born Mexican immigrants. The proportion of both of these groups decreased slightly in 1980 to 33.9% U.S.-born and 6.2% foreign-born. This proportional decrease was due in part to the rapid growth of the Anglo population during the 1970s, and partly to procedural

Table 7.1 Ethnic Composition of San Antonio SMSA Working-Age Population
(age 16 and above)

	1970	Percent	1980	Percent
Anglo	279,900	48.7	357,220	52.9
Mexican American	208,500	36.3	228,720	33.9
Mexican Immigrant	48,300	8.4	42,000	6.2
Black	38,400	6.7	47,340	7.0
Total	575,100	100.0	675,280	100.0

SOURCE: U.S. Bureau of the Census, PUMS (1970 and 1980) for San Antonio SMSA civilian population age 16 and above, 5% Sample/1980; 15% Sample/1970. Data have been weighted to approximate the population.
NOTE: Other racial/ethnic groups not included.

changes in the census and perceptions and responses to census questions identifying Hispanics between 1970 and 1980.

Table 7.1 shows that both the number and proportion of Mexican immigrants over age 16 in the San Antonio SMSA decreased between 1970 and 1980. Two likely explanations for these changes include increased mortality and increased out-migration among these cohorts, both of which are normal processes. However, given the increased migration to the United States from Mexico during the 1970s, it is surprising that the Mexican immigrant count did not increase significantly in number. This might be related to recent changes in immigrant migration patterns from traditional rural receiving areas along the Mexican border to urban areas farther away from the border that offer growing employment opportunities in manufacturing industries.

LABOR FORCE

Table 7.2 shows that the number of Anglos, blacks, and both U.S.-and Mexican-born Latinos in the San Antonio SMSA full-time civilian labor force increased between 1970 and 1980. A comparison of Table 7.1 with Table 7.2 indicates that in 1980 Anglos comprised a higher proportion of the civilian full-time labor force, 57.6%, as compared to their proportion within the civilian working-age population, 52.9%. For blacks, the 1980 proportions were just about the same; 6.6% of the civilian full-time labor force and 6.2% of the civilian working-age population. The proportion of U.S.-born Mexican Americans in the

Table 7.2 Ethnic Composition of the Full-Time Labor Force in San Antonio SMSA

	1970	1980
Total Labor Force		
Anglo	107,700	141,020
Mexican American	69,800	76,420
Mexican Immigrant	10,800	11,120
Black	12,900	16,240
Total	201,200	244,800
Percent Distribution		
Anglo	53.5	57.6
Mexican American	34.7	31.3
Mexican Immigrant	5.4	4.5
Black	6.4	6.6
Total	100.0	100.0

SOURCE: U.S. Bureau of the Census, PUMS (1970 and 1980) for San Antonio SMSA civilian population age 16 and above, 5% Sample/1980; 15% Sample/1970. Data have been weighted to approximate the population.
NOTE: Other racial/ethnic groups not included; full-time employment defined as working 35 or more hours per week and 50 or more weeks in the previous year.

civilian full-time labor force was 31.3%, slightly less than their 33.9% composition of the civilian working-age population. The difference between foreign-born immigrants, *Mexicanos,* in the labor force and the general population was greater; *Mexicanos* comprised 7.0% of the civilian population, but only 4.5% of the civilian labor force.

Many factors could explain the higher proportions of Anglos in the full-time civilian labor force. One may be the privileged or preferential access to the labor market as compared to the situation of discriminatory labor market practices for Hispanics (Barrera, 1979; Montejano, 1987; Tienda, 1988). Another explanation might include gender differences in the full-time civilian labor force participation of Anglo and Latina women. Table 7.3 indicates that the number of Anglo women in the civilian labor force grew by 42.5% between 1970 and 1980, whereas the number of U.S.-born Chicanas in the civilian labor force increased by only 17.8%. It should be noted, however, that the gender composition of the work force is almost the same for Anglos and Mexican Americans. In 1980, 42.4% of the Anglo work force was female as compared to 42.2% of the Mexican-American work force. As these proportions are virtually identical, they cannot be used to explain the differences in full-time employment noted above.

Table 7.3 Gender Composition of the San Antonio SMSA Full-Time and Part-Time Labor Force

	1970	*1980*	*Percent Growth*
Anglos	196,000	245,840	25.4
Males	122,900	141,680	15.3
Females	73,100	104,160	42.5
% Females	37.3	42.4	
Mexican American	133,900	148,080	10.6
Males	80,900	85,640	5.9
Females	53,000	62,440	17.8
% Females	39.6	42.2	
Mexican Immigrant	23,800	22,440	−5.7
Males	14,500	14,600	0.7
Females	9,300	7,840	−15.7
% Females	39.1	35.0	

SOURCE: U.S. Bureau of the Census, PUMS (1970 and 1980) for San Antonio SMSA civilian population age 16 and above, 5% Sample/1980; 15% Sample/1970. Data have been weighted to approximate the population.
NOTE: Other racial/ethnic groups not included; full-time employment defined as working 35 or more hours per week and 50 or more weeks in the previous year; part-time is defined as working less than 35 hours per week or less than 50 weeks per year.

In addition to the lower proportions of full-time workers, the Mexican-origin San Antonio SMSA population also has higher unemployment rates in comparison to Anglos. Table 7.4 shows that the 1980 Mexican-American male unemployment rate, 5.4%, was almost twice as high as the Anglo male unemployment rate, 3.0%. The unemployment rate for male Mexican immigrants was 4.2%, about halfway between the Anglo rate and the Chicano rate. Unemployment rates among women were slightly different. The unemployment rate among Mexican immigrant women was the highest at 5.9%. The rate for Anglo women was the lowest at 3.4%, and Chicanas had a rate of 4.1%. The above unemployment distinctions between Anglos and the two Mexican-origin groups also hold for the figures on duration of unemployment. To illustrate, 85.3% of Anglo males in the civilian work force in 1980 were unaffected by unemployment (unemployed for zero weeks), as compared to only 82.4% of Mexican-American males and 81.4% of Mexican immigrant males. Conversely, both Mexican-American males and Mexican immigrant males experienced more short-term (1-4 weeks) and long-term (5 or more weeks) spells of unemployment than Anglos.

Table 7.4 San Antonio SMSA Unemployment Statistics, 1980

	Anglo	Mexican American	Mexican Immigrant
1980 Unemployment Rats			
Males	3.0%	5.4%	4.2%
Females	3.4%	4.1%	5.9%
Population Estimates			
Males	141,720	85,660	14,600
Females	104,300	62,540	7,860
Weeks Unemployed, 1979			
Males			
0 weeks	85.3%	82.4%	81.4%
1-4 weeks	8.9%	10.9%	12.0%
5 or more weeks	5.8%	6.7%	6.6%
Females			
0 weeks	83.1%	80.9%	81.2%
1-4 weeks	11.3%	12.1%	11.9%
5 or more weeks	5.6%	7.0%	6.9%

SOURCE: U.S. Bureau of the Census, PUMS (1970 and 1980) for San Antonio SMSA civilian population age 16 and above, 5% Sample/1980; 15% Sample/1970. Data have been weighted to approximate the population.
NOTE: Other racial/ethnic groups not included.

EDUCATIONAL CHARACTERISTICS

There are marked differences in the educational attainments of Anglos, Mexican Americans, and Mexican immigrants in the San Antonio SMSA. Table 7.5 shows that the average years of school completed by Anglo males, 13.7, is much higher than the average, 11.0 years, completed by Mexican-American males, but both of these groups far exceed the 7.8 years completed by Mexican immigrant males. A similar pattern is found among females. An interesting observation, however, is that although Anglo females on the average complete slightly fewer years of school than Anglo males, 13.3 years as compared to 13.7, respectively, the trend for Mexican-American and Mexican immigrant females is the opposite, with both completing more schooling than their male counterparts. Chicano females on the average completed 0.2 years more schooling than Chicano males (11.2 and 11.0 years, respectively), whereas Mexican immigrant females attain a full year of additional schooling as compared to Mexican immigrant males (8.8 and 7.8 years, respectively).

Table 7.5 Educational Characteristics of the San Antonio SMSA Working-Age
Population (age 16 and above), 1980

	Anglo	Mexican American	Mexican Immigrant
Mean Years of Schooling			
Males	13.7	11.0	7.8
Females	13.3	11.2	8.8
Percent With High School Degree			
Males	81.5	51.8	24.2
Females	78.0	47.0	22.9
Percent With College Education			
Males	14.7	2.7	1.3
Females	7.4	1.5	1.5
Population Estimate			
Males	173,040	108,000	19,700
Females	184,180	120,720	22,600

SOURCE: U.S. Bureau of the Census, PUMS (1970 and 1980) for San Antonio civilian population age 16
and above, 5% sample/1980; 15% sample/1970. Data have been weighted to approximate the population.
NOTE: Other racial/ethnic groups not included.

In many analyses, educational credentials are a more meaningful
measure of educational attainment than the number of years of schooling completed. A high school degree or diploma is a basic educational
credential that often serves as a minimum qualification for entry level
jobs. Table 7.5 dramatically illustrates the educational disparity between Anglo and Mexican-origin groups in the San Antonio SMSA.
Although approximately 80% of Anglo males and females in the San
Antonio SMSA had completed high school in 1980, only about 50% of
Mexican-American males and females had this credential. And the high
school completion rate for Mexican immigrants, less than 25%, was
significantly lower than either of these two groups. In addition, the
proportion of college attendance in 1980 was far greater among Anglo
males, 14.7%, than for any other group. It exceeded the 7.4% of Anglo
females who had attended college and was substantially greater than the
minuscule college attendance proportions among the Mexican-origin
groups; less than 3% for Mexican-American males and females and less
than 2% for Mexican immigrant males and females.

Very low levels of educational attainment continue to characterize
both the U.S.-born Chicanos and Mexican immigrants in San Antonio.
The 1991 report published by Partnership for Hope documents the

clearly discriminatory educational structure of San Antonio. In fact, inequality in school funding has been the focus of two major lawsuits initiated in San Antonio, *San Antonio Independent School District v. Rodriguez* (1971) and *Edgewood Independent School District v. Kirby* (1988). Excluding the three public school districts located on military bases, Bexar County has 12 publicly funded independent school districts. During the 1989-1990 school year, its student population exceeded 229,000, with a racial composition of 31% Anglo, 60% Hispanic, 8% black, and 1% Asian and other students. The Partnership for Hope report shows the 12 district boundaries to be divided along clear socioeconomic and racial lines, with sharp differences among the districts in expenditures per pupil, teacher salaries, graduation rates, college aspirations, test scores, dropout rates, literacy problems, and teen pregnancy rates. Wealthier, predominantly Anglo districts reported the highest test scores, graduation rates, and college attendance rates, and the fewest attrition and educational problems; the poorest, predominantly Hispanic southside and westside districts reported, not surprisingly, the lowest test scores, graduation rates, and college attendance rates, along with the highest attrition and educational problems. The report concludes that the severe economic inequality that pervades the San Antonio area also invades its educational institutions, reproducing the same patterns of inequality within each new generation.

EMPLOYMENT BY INDUSTRY AND OCCUPATION

In contrast to many other major cities with high concentrations of Latinos, San Antonio never developed strong manufacturing industries in either durable or nondurable goods. Table 7.6 displays employment statistics for the San Antonio SMSA by industry and gender. It indicates that in both 1970 and 1980, less than 14% of the San Antonio male or female civilian work force held jobs in manufacturing. An examination of U.S. Census Bureau publications shows that the number of jobs related to manufacturing was even lower as far back as 1940. Instead, most of the San Antonio SMSA civilian jobs are concentrated in the "Other Services" category, which is comprised of business, personal, entertainment, and professional services. Our unpublished tabulations of the 1980 Census data files show that 31.8% of civilian employment in the San Antonio SMSA was found in this aggregate category. The second largest single source of employment was the retail trade industry, which employed 19.9% of civilian workers in 1980; and the third largest employer was government, which employed 9.7% of the civilian labor force.

Table 7.6 shows that female workers are particularly concentrated in the services sector, including almost 43% in the Other Services category. This female concentration was almost twice the male concentration of 22%. A similarly high relative concentration of females existed in the finance and real estate industry, which employed 8.5% of the SMSA's female civilian work force but only 4.6% of the male civilian work force in 1980. In the same vein, women were also relatively more concentrated than men in retail industries (23.0% versus 17.6%, respectively) and in nondurable goods manufacturing (6.6% versus 5.0%, respectively).

The occupational distributions shown in Table 7.7 indicate that the manual-based Craft and Operative occupational categories do not occupy a major part of the San Antonio SMSA civilian work force, and that between 1970 and 1980, employment in these occupations decreased in number and proportion. Employment in craft occupations decreased from 13.7% in 1970 to 9.8% in 1980, and employment in operative occupations decreased from 14.1% to 10.0%, respectively. These changes represent substantial reductions in the importance of these occupations during a period in which the size of the San Antonio SMSA civilian work force grew rapidly. The drop in the percentage of males found in craft and operative occupations paralleled that discussed above for all workers. At the same time, male employment increased moderately in clerical, sales, professional, and managerial occupations.

Table 7.7 further indicates that the proportion of all San Antonio SMSA civilian workers employed in managerial, professional, technical, and service occupations increased moderately between 1970 and 1980. However, it should be noted that although the number of clerical workers increased significantly (by 17%) between 1970 and 1980, the proportion of clerical workers in the total SMSA labor force decreased slightly, from 23.3% to 21.1%, respectively.

In part, the decrease in the proportion of clerical workers was associated with improved opportunities for women in other occupations. In 1970, almost two out of every five female workers, 38.9%, were employed in clerical occupations. By 1980, this proportion had decreased to 31.5%. The proportion of female operatives also diminished sharply, from 11.4% in 1970 to 6.9% in 1980. Conversely, female employment in managerial, professional, technical, and sales occupations increased during the 1970s. By 1980, the number and proportion of females in

Table 7.6 San Antonio SMSA Employment by Industry and Gender

	1970	Percent	1980	Percent	Percent Change
Female Workers					
Agricultural	1,300	.9	1,380	.6	6
Mining	200	.1	900	.4	350
Construction	900	.6	3,500	1.5	389
Durable Manufacturing	1,700	1.2	6,180	2.7	264
Nondurable Manufacturing	11,000	7.8	14,860	6.6	35
Trans./Com./Util.	6,200	4.4	8,040	3.5	30
Wholesale	3,700	2.6	6,880	3.0	86
Retail	32,000	22.7	52,160	23.0	63
Finance/Real Estate	12,200	8.6	19,160	8.5	57
Other Services	57,800	41.0	97,160	42.9	68
Business	4,400	7.6	9,100	9.4	107
Personal	14,300	24.7	14,680	15.3	3
Entertainment	1,800	3.1	2,220	2.3	23
Professional	37,300	64.6	71,160	73.2	91
Government	14,200	10.1	16,380	7.2	15
Total	141,200	100.0	226,600	100.0	60
Male Workers					
Agricultural	4,400	2.4	4,300	1.7	−2
Mining	1,100	.6	2,400	0.9	118
Construction	21,400	11.5	33,060	12.9	54
Durable Manufacturing	12,100	6.5	19,980	7.8	65
Nondurable Manufacturing	13,200	7.1	12,860	5.0	−3
Trans./Com./Util.	16,300	8.7	22,360	8.7	37
Wholesale	11,800	6.3	17,540	6.8	49
Retail	34,300	18.4	45,040	17.6	31
Finance/Real Estate	7,500	4.0	11,820	4.6	58
Other Services	32,900	17.6	56,720	22.0	72
Business	9,400	28.6	15,720	27.8	67
Personal	4,500	13.7	5,160	9.1	15
Entertainment	1,000	3.0	2,960	5.2	196
Professional	18,000	54.7	32,620	57.8	81
Government	31,600	16.9	30,320	11.8	−4
Total	186,600	100.0	256,140	100.0	37

SOURCE: U.S. Bureau of the Census, PUMS (1970 and 1980) for San Antonio SMSA civilian population age 16 and above, 5% Sample/1980; 15% Sample/1970. Data have been weighted to approximate the population.

professional occupations exceeded that of males, with 32,100 female professionals (14.2% of the female work force) as compared to 28,480

Table 7.7   San Antonio SMSA Employment by Occupation

	1970		1980		Percent
	N	*Percent*	*N*	*Percent*	*Change*
All Workers					
Managers	33,000	8.8	51,480	10.7	+56
Professionals	39,600	10.6	60,580	12.5	+53
Technical	4,700	1.3	13,340	2.8	+184
Sales	34,200	9.1	52,100	10.6	+52
Clerical	87,100	23.3	102,000	21.1	+17
Service	48,000	13.0	76,000	15.8	+58
Craft	51,200	13.7	47,380	9.8	−8
Operative	52,800	14.1	49,280	10.0	−7
Laborer	23,000	6.1	31,280	6.5	+36
Total	374,400	100.0	482,740	100.0	+29
Male Workers					
Managers	25,900	13.2	35,680	13.9	+38
Professionals	18,400	9.4	28,480	11.1	+55
Technical	3,000	1.5	6,660	2.6	+122
Sales	17,300	8.8	22,540	8.8	+30
Clerical	17,800	9.1	30,730	12.0	+73
Craft	48,600	24.7	44,240	17.3	−9
Operative	32,500	16.5	32,800	12.8	+1
Laborer	19,600	10.0	25,940	10.1	+32
Total	196,400	100.0	256,140	100.0	+30
Female Workers					
Managers	7,100	4.0	15,800	7.0	+123
Professionals	21,200	11.9	32,100	14.2	+41
Technical	1,700	1.0	6,680	2.9	+292
Sales	16,900	9.5	29,580	13.1	+75
Clerical	69,00	38.9	71,280	31.5	+3
Service	35,500	19.9	47,100	20.8	+33
Craft	2,600	1.5	3,140	1.4	+21
Operative	20,300	11.4	15,580	6.9	−23
Labor	3,400	1.9	6,280	2.3	+85
Total	178,000	100.0	226,600	100.0	+27

SOURCE: U.S. Bureau of the Census, PUMS (1970 and 1980) for San Antonio SMSA civilian population age 16 and above, 5% Sample/1980; 15% Sample/1970. Data have been weighted to approximate the population.

male professionals (11.1% of the male work force). However, the data also indicate that males still far exceeded females in managerial occupations, with 35,680 males as compared to 15,800 females in 1980, whereas females continued to significantly outnumber males in clerical

Table 7.8 San Antonio SMSA Employment Distribution by Industry and Occupation, 1980

	Anglo	Mexican American	Mexican Immigrant
Males			
% Durable Manufacturing	7.5	8.3	11.1
% Nondurable Manufacturing	4.0	6.0	6.6
% Craft Occupations	14.0	20.0	31.1
% Operatives/Laborer	14.6	31.1	35.3
Population Estimate	582,600	412,700	72,300
Females			
% Durable Manufacturing	2.3	2.9	3.6
% Nondurable Manufacturing	3.0	10.6	21.2
% Craft Occupations	0.9	1.8	4.1
% Operatives/Laborer	3.6	14.4	27.1
Population Estimate	1,966,000	1,243,600	156,000

SOURCE: U.S. Bureau of the Census, PUMS (1970 and 1980) for San Antonio SMSA civilian population age 16 and above, 5% Sample/1980; 15% Sample/1970. Data have been weighted to approximate the population.
NOTE: Other racial/ethnic groups not included.

occupations, with 71,280 females as compared to 30,730 males in 1980. These last two facts show that women have made strides toward occupational parity, but that they still have a long way to go.

MEXICAN AMERICANS AND MEXICAN IMMIGRANTS IN THE LABOR FORCE

The most striking characteristic of Mexican-American and Mexican immigrant civilian workers in the San Antonio SMSA has been their high concentration in manual occupations relative to Anglos. Table 7.8 shows that in 1980, more than half of all Mexican-American males, 51.1%, and nearly two thirds of Mexican immigrants, 66.4%, worked as craftsmen, operatives, or laborers. This is significantly higher than the 28.6% Anglo employment in these occupations. The relatively high proportion of Mexican-American and Mexican immigrant males in craft occupations has fewer positive implications for earnings and employment stability in a right-to-work state like Texas than it would in a region with strong unions.

The high concentration of Mexican-American and Mexican immigrant males in manual occupations has not been replicated in the durable and nondurable goods manufacturing industries. Given the high concentration of Mexican-American and Mexican immigrant males in manual occupations, it should be expected that they would also dominate the manufacturing industry. But Table 7.8 shows that only 6% of Mexican-American males and 6.6% of Mexican immigrant males worked in nondurable goods manufacturing, compared to 4.0% of Anglo males. Durable goods manufacturing shows a slightly different pattern, with 8.3% of Mexican-American males and 11.1% of Mexican immigrant males, as compared to 7.5% of Anglo males. The expected domination of Mexican-American and Mexican immigrant males over Anglo males did not occur.

This same general pattern appears to apply to women working in durable goods manufacturing and craft occupations, although the pattern and degree of concentration is very different for females working in nondurable goods manufacturing and in operative or laborer occupations. The percentage of Mexican-American females employed in nondurable goods manufacturing, 10.6%, is three and a half times greater than the corresponding percentage of Anglo females, 3.0%; the percentage of Mexican immigrant females, 21.2%, is seven times greater than the Anglo percentage. The high and increasing concentration of Mexican-American and Mexican immigrant females relative to Anglo females in operative and labor occupations is even more pronounced. The proportion of Mexican-American females found in this occupational grouping, 14.4%, was four times that of Anglo females, and the Mexican immigrant female concentration, 27.1%, was seven and a half times higher.

Overall, the concentration of Mexican Americans and Mexican immigrants in manual occupations, but not in manufacturing industries, indicates that a set of Mexican-American and Mexican immigrant jobs may exist, but not a Mexican-American and Mexican immigrant manufacturing industry. Although craft workers, operatives, and laborers are highly represented in a few industries, that is, construction, manufacturing, and so on, these occupations are also found within a broad range of industries. The data in Table 7.8 show that Mexican-American and Mexican immigrant males are predominantly employed as manual laborers in nonmanufacturing industries. Mexican-American and Mexican immigrant females are also comparatively highly concentrated in operative and laborer occupations, but these jobs are more evenly spread within the nondurable goods manufacturing industry. The relative absence of Mexican-origin males and females from San Antonio SMSA manufacturing industry employment was probably the result of discrimination, stereotyping, network failures, and low educational attainment levels. However, the concentration of the Latinas in nondurable goods manufacturing suggests that the history of this industry might follow the classic pattern of utilization and recruitment of immigrant labor into the secondary labor market and economically marginal enterprises.

Mexican-American and Mexican immigrant earnings also follow the classic pattern of being substantially less than those of Anglos. Table 7.9 shows the average hourly pay for Mexican-American males, $5.77, was 70% of the average Anglo hourly pay of $8.23; the average pay rate for Mexican immigrant males, $5.15, was only 63% of the Anglo rate. The ratio of Latino annual earnings compared to Anglos is even lower, reflecting the lower wages and the higher unemployment rates discussed earlier. Table 7.9 shows that Anglo males in the San Antonio SMSA earned an average of $17,384, whereas Mexican-American males earned only $11,440, and Mexican immigrant males earned even less, $9,803. Latinas earn considerably less than Anglo females, but all women, including Anglo women, earn much less than Anglo men. The hourly wages of Anglo females, $5.34, were less than two thirds of the Anglo male pay of $8.23. Mexican-American females earned an average of $4.27, a little more than half as much as Anglo males, and Mexican immigrant females earned $3.84, a little less than half. The annual earnings of all women compared to Anglo men resulted in even smaller fractions. Table 7.10 shows the results of a regression analysis that indicates that education, experience, and number of hours worked are important determinants of annual earnings.

MEXICAN IMMIGRATION

The absence of a strong manufacturing sector probably explains the relatively small proportion of Mexican immigrants in the city. The proportion of San Antonio's population that is foreign-born has remained about 12% throughout the 1980s. In comparison to the city of Los Angeles, where the Mexican foreign-born population constitutes 78% of the total adult Mexican origin population, we may conclude that at best, Mexican immigration has only moderately affected San Antonio since 1970 (cf. Chapter 3).

Table 7.9 San Antonio SMSA Wages and Earnings, 1979

	Anglo	Mexican American	Mexican Immigrant
Males			
Means			
Hourly pay	$8.23	$5.77	$5.15
Annual earnings	$17,384	$11,440	$9,803
Distribution			
$4 or less per hour	26.5%	37.7%	45.0%
Over $11 per hour	18.3%	4.2%	2.8%
Less than $10K per year	40.1%	56.1%	64.0%
Over $25K per year	15.8%	3.1%	1.8%
Population Estimates	131,940	81,720	13,420
Females			
Means			
Hourly pay	$5,34	$4.27	$3.84
Annual earnings	$9,182	$7,113	$6,249
Distribution			
$4 or less per hour	46.2%	62.6%	72.7%
Over $11 per hour	2.8%	1.5%	1.3%
Less than $10K per year	70.2%	84.5%	88.5%
Over $25K per year	1.2%	0.4%	0.1%
Population Estimates	100,560	60,920	7,440

SOURCE: U.S. Bureau of the Census, PUMS (1970 and 1980) for San Antonio SMSA civilian population age 16 and above, 5% Sample/1980; 15% Sample/1970. Data have been weighted to approximate the population.
NOTE: Other racial/ethnic groups not included.

The comparison of San Antonio to Los Angeles is striking with respect to the new immigration patterns, particularly the movement and settlement patterns of Mexican immigrants. Mexican immigration to Los Angeles has been phenomenal, and since the 1970s has had a tremendous effect on the size and composition of the total Mexican-origin population there. The insertion of legally admitted Mexican immigrants into the Los Angeles labor market has been matched by the presence and insertion of large numbers of undocumented workers. In part, the massive flows of immigrants from Mexico and Asia have converged to sustain growth in the Southern California economy. In the case of San Antonio, however, Mexican immigration has not been massive, nor has it resulted in a recomposition of San Antonio's Mexican-origin population. Rather the insertion of Mexican immigrant workers into San Antonio's labor markets has, at best, been moderate.

Table 7.10 Regression Analysis of 1979 San Antonio SMSA Earnings
Dependent Variable, Log of Annual Earnings

| Independent Variables | Estimated Coefficients | | | |
| | Total | | Anglo | Mexican-Origin |
	1	*2*	*3*	*4*
Constant	2.729*	6.689*	2.311*	3.340*
Years of Education	.109*	.126*	.114*	.116*
Years of Experience	.029*	.032*	.026*	.034*
Years of Experience Squared	−1.059*	−1.146*	−1.381*	−5.869*
Log of Hours Worked	1.173*	—	1.287*	.949*
Limited English Dummy	−.083	—	−.062	−.160*
Chicano Dummy	−.003	−.009	—	—
Adjusted *R*-square	.321	.154	.350	.257
F-ratio	1476.27*	852.99*	1255.40*	493.99*

SOURCE: U.S. Bureau of the Census, PUMS (1970 and 1980) for San Antonio SMSA civilian population age 16 and above, 5% Sample/1980; 15% Sample/1970. Data have been weighted to approximate the population.
NOTE: Other racial/ethnic groups not included.
*Coefficient is significant at .01 level.

DISCUSSION

As the "capital" city of South Texas, San Antonio plays an important role in regional integration. Currently, San Antonio is entrenched in *maquiladora,* or twin-plant border industrialization. Although *maquiladoras* are exerting a tremendous impact on the border, this impact has been more closely related to industrial development and economic exploitation in Mexico than in the United States. Specifically, *maquiladoras* have profited from the extremely low labor costs of the relatively unskilled, unorganized, and predominantly female Mexican assembly workers, who earn only about $1 per hour; their high turnover rates; the ample supply of new, unskilled replacement workers who guarantee low-wage rates; the continual peso devaluation; the related favorable peso- dollar exchange rates; low overhead, land, and plant costs; and attractive customs regulations (Glickman & R. Wilson, 1985). Nevertheless, Mexican border industrialization initiatives have generated some growth within the skilled high-tech and electronic research and development industries on the U.S. side, which has had a moderate effect on the economic growth of South Texas, where industrialization activities had previously been nonexistent or low.

In addition, San Antonio itself has experienced steady growth in high-tech and biotechnology industries, due in part to the strength of its existing biomedical-health sciences complex. Examples of this growth are the recent creation of the Institute of Biotechnology and the development of the Texas Research Park. The strong research and development focus of these groups is expected to benefit the San Antonio area by increasing employment among skilled professional and technical workers. Mixed with this benefit, however, is the tendency of these industries to contribute to the "vanishing middle" syndrome by creating bifurcated occupational structures made up of a highly paid professional and technical work force in which minorities and women are underrepresented; a larger, lower paid service, assembly, and clerical work force characterized by limited wage and occupational mobility; and a small segment of the skilled or semiskilled workers who traditionally formed the core of the U.S. work force (Glickman & R. Wilson, 1985; Markusen, 1983). Although the creation of new jobs represents an obvious advantage to the community, the unequal spread of rewards does little to improve traditional patterns of discrimination and labor stratification in San Antonio. In addition, from a national perspective, job creation in high-tech industries fails to compensate for critical losses of prime jobs in other regions of the country and sections of the economy. Ultimately, high-tech employment and production innovations are expected to create 3 million new jobs nationally by 1990, but they are also expected to directly or indirectly displace about eight times as many workers. It is questionable whether the high-tech industry can adequately retrain redundant workers or provide employment opportunities for new, relatively unskilled entrants to the labor market (Markusen, 1983).

The service sector of San Antonio's economy has traditionally been strong and has experienced rapid growth since 1970. In both 1970 and 1980, the service industry was the largest sector of the economy, representing 33.7% in 1970 and 38.3% in 1980. Similarly, the clerical and service sectors employed over one third of the work force in both periods, with 36.3% in 1970 and 36.9% in 1980. The service sector includes financial, real estate, business, personal, legal, entertainment, tourism, social, and professional services, and it also supports many of the other industries in the area. Studies show that for every job created in tourism, entertainment, and recreation industries, about two other jobs are added indirectly to the economy through the multiplier process. In addition, these industries have provided dependable job markets for minorities, women, and youth, who often have difficulty finding jobs. The rapid growth of the service industry stimulates opportunity for entrepreneurial development, particularly among small- and medium-sized firms. Even in San Antonio, however, much of this opportunity has bypassed the minority community due to the limited availability of the necessary startup or expansion capital. Finally, service sector jobs often provide relatively low pay scales and limited benefits, which tend to widen existing income maldistributions, limit occupational advancement and mobility, and ignore the skills and needs of the middle class (Glickman & R. Wilson, 1985).

In addition to the moderate profit potential offered in connection with the *maquiladora* and industrialization projects, there is a strong expectation that this new industrialization will stimulate economic growth through job creation on both sides of the U.S.-Mexico border and in places such as San Antonio if it is able to achieve and sustain a favorable position vis-à-vis border industrialization.

The state of Texas has supported free trade initiatives with Mexico. Former Governor Bill Clements was particularly active in this area. In addition to the many border conference symposia and seminars that the state sponsored, efforts have been made to establish closer economic linkages with Mexico. But it is difficult to predict the results of these initiatives. Most trade with Mexico involves intermediate products (Weintraub, 1990), and San Antonio and South Texas may merely become the points of the final assembly of parts manufactured elsewhere.

To succeed, San Antonio must become more competitive. The city did not become a major player in the Sunbelt as some expected. Former mayor Henry Cisneros played a highly visible role in San Antonio's high-tech development strategy, attempting to attract high-tech industry to San Antonio. In addition to various state and city incentives, Texas and San Antonio have a large labor pool of unemployed, underemployed, and skilled Mexican-origin labor. Translated into industrial terms, the job creation initiatives supported by San Antonio's leadership were based on the availability and exploitation of low-cost labor. The effort to attract high-tech industry to San Antonio resulted in limited success. San Antonio has not been able to attract enough firms away from existing high-tech centers in the Sunbelt such as Phoenix, Austin, Denver, and Albuquerque. Obviously, San Antonio's low wages and low levels of unionization due to Texas right-to-work laws would be attractive to potential employers. But the state's overall disregard for workers, particularly evident in low levels of public education, may mitigate the attractiveness of the labor pool.

The limited success of the high-tech Sunbelt strategy continues to rest on a shaky foundation. San Antonio has been much more successful in developing and promoting tourism. River Walk, the Convention Center, the Sports Arena, and Sea World all have worked to position the city as a major tourist attraction for the United States and Mexico. The hotel, retail, restaurant, and service industries have grown. The entertainment, professional service, and transportation industries have also been affected by the success of tourism. Although the Mexican-origin population has benefited through the increased availability of jobs, the types of jobs available generally involve low pay and limited opportunity for advancement.

In contrast to the Sunbelt industrialization initiatives, the growth of tourism, retail trade, and investment have significantly contributed to the San Antonio economy. These developments have also positively affected the regional economy of South Texas, particularly at the border.

Tourism in other South Texas locations has also increased, particularly along the lower Gulf Coast and Padre Island. Moreover, the Lower Rio Grande economy of South Texas has benefited from the seasonal snowbird phenomenon of retired winter vacationers. The depressed economies of South Texas and Mexico allow the tourists and snowbirds to stretch their vacation or retirement dollars.

The devaluation of the Mexican peso and oil crisis of the 1980s greatly reduced the relative importance of Mexican expenditures and investments in the San Antonio and South Texas regions. Should the Mexican economy improve, it is reasonable to expect a renewal of Mexican expenditures and investments. Heretofore, Mexican expenditures and investments have played a moderate but important role in the San Antonio economy. They have exerted a lesser impact on the Los Angeles economy due to its much greater size and economic complexity. Further research in this area may help to clarify the degree to which Mexican Americans are connected to the expenditures and investment of Mexican money in the San Antonio economy.

The Mexican-origin population of San Antonio has grown significantly since the turn of the century. In contrast, Los Angeles's immigrant population shot up after World War II. San Antonio has continued to rely heavily on military and defense installations and expenditures to sustain its economic vitality.

Military growth has been a vital feature of San Antonio's economy since World War II. Construction of the military bases at one time provided lucrative employment opportunities for Mexican-American workers. The five local military bases also provided new employment opportunities, better jobs, and greater economic stability for Mexican Americans than had been available previously. San Antonio's economic viability has been dependent on military expenditures, particularly on defense-related employment and income. Military bases continue to play a large role in the economic life despite economic growth.

San Antonio's economy did not diversify, nor did it become an industrial center as did Los Angeles. The construction boom in the 1970s generated considerable growth, but by the mid-1980s this boom ended in Texas and was replaced by stagnation in construction and housing and commercial real estate markets. Although the boom in construction provided jobs for Mexican-origin laborers in the 1970s, it also created the conditions for subsequent high rates of unemployment.

Despite apparent growth, the Sea World amusement park, a key to San Antonio's attraction as a center of tourism, announced in 1990 that it would shut down seasonally for more than a third of the year, November through March. This change will dramatically affect the economic status of workers in entertainment service occupations, who comprise the highest proportion of part-time workers, greater even than agricultural workers. In addition, the five military bases are also facing budget cuts and layoffs in the near term and may shut down altogether in the now uncertain future. The three occupations with the largest number of openings are janitors, retail salespersons, and office clerks. Growth in biotechnology may be a positive force in San Antonio's future, but how many jobs will it create for Latino dropouts and how far will the 5% Latino college graduates go?

SUMMARY AND CONCLUSION

The history and pattern of economic change in San Antonio is different from the experiences of Chicago, New York, Miami, and Los Angeles, but it provides an important perspective on a large and predominantly Latino urban area. San Antonio is the ninth largest city in the United States, and over 50% of the SMSA's 1.1 million inhabitants are Latino. Its economic and social patterns apply in general to many of the cities of South Texas, including Corpus Christi, McAllen, Brownsville, and Laredo. Together, these cities and the surrounding towns comprise possibly the largest concentration of Mexican-origin Latinos outside of Southern California.

The principal difference between San Antonio and the other major cities in this study is that as compared to Chicago, New York, or Los Angeles, San Antonio never became highly industrialized. In San Antonio, the highest concentration of manufacturing employment within the last 50 years was 12.2%. Instead, service industry employment has played a larger role in the economy and comprised more than one third of the jobs in 1980. The retail trade and service industries are the sources of more than one half of all jobs in the city. In 1980, government was the third largest employer of civilians.

The largest single occupational group in the San Antonio SMSA in 1980 was clerical workers, with a gender ratio of 70% female to 30% male workers. The second largest occupational category was service occupations, with a gender ratio of 62% female to 38% male workers. Overall, 47% of the San Antonio SMSA labor force is female. The single, striking difference in the distribution of Latinos and Anglos by industry is in manufacturing, where Latinos appear to be seriously underrepresented in relation to their strong presence in craft, operative, and labor occupations. The biggest difference between Latinos and non-Latinos in industrial employment was the proportion found in construction—66% Anglos, 13% Latinos. It should be no surprise that the Anglos are concentrated near the top and Latinos at the bottom. For example, in 1988, among managers and professionals, the Anglo/Latino ratio is 4:1. In technical occupations the Anglo/Latino ratio was 6:1, in sales 2:1. In service occupations the ratio was 1 Anglo to 3 Latinos and among operators and laborers, it was 2 Anglos to 5 Latinos. Even though 90% of San Antonio's Latino population is U.S.-born, Mexican male immigrants are highly concentrated in operative and laborer positions.

An examination of the largest plant closing in San Antonio's history might prove instructive. In early 1990, the Levi Strauss plant in San Antonio closed, displacing 1,115 workers in light manufacturing, 93% of whom were Latinos. The plant was moved to Costa Rica, where the company pays its Costa Rican workers $6 per day as compared to the $6 per hour paid to workers in San Antonio. Seven hundred of the laid-off workers enrolled in community job training and Job Training Partnership Act (JTPA) placement programs. According to newspaper reports 10 months later, only 14 of these persons had found jobs through JTPA, 45 others found jobs on their own, and the rest, more than 1,000, were still unemployed (*San Antonio Light*, 1990). The most striking fact is that illiteracy is higher in San Antonio than it is in Costa Rica, and Costa

Rican workers have life-styles similar to those of San Antonio's Latinos (*San Antonio Light,* 1990).

San Antonio has slowly been coming out of the throes of the repressive Southern regional economic structure in which Hispanic and black minorities are relegated to the lower positions of an Anglo-dominated caste-like social, political, and economic system. Segregated communities and segregated labor markets are beginning to become more diversified, yet relative to Anglos, Latinos are still not sharing equally in the new economic order.

There is evidence of change and hope for the future, however. The previously restricted and still limited participation of Mexican Americans in San Antonio's economy will change as Mexican Americans receive more education and eventually find or create positions in a wider array of options in all of San Antonio's various markets: labor, consumer, residential, and credit. Mexican-American entrepreneurship and self-employment will continue to offer greater potential in comparison to the restricted and limited employment opportunities available in the mainstream economy. Another option for Mexican Americans is migration away from San Antonio to other, more prosperous areas of the country.

Given the class structure of San Antonio described above, it is likely that we will see three distinct mobility paths. A proportionally small, but slowly growing segment of the Mexican-American population will be able to take advantage of the existing opportunities and become moderately successful in creating new channels for those who follow. At the same time, a large segment of the Mexican-American population of San Antonio will experience downward mobility and become part of an urban underclass. The bulk of the Mexican-American population of San Antonio are neither upwardly mobile professionals nor persistently poor members of the underclass. Instead, they will continue to form a disadvantaged working class that is able to hang onto but not move up the ladder.

The new Latino leadership and organizational structures developed in the 1980s continue to erode the old Southern system. Latino political muscle has the potential to translate political strength into economic strength in ever-increasing political and cultural pluralism initiatives that require Anglos to share economic and political power with Latinos. Whether this new sharing achieves the goals promised by the new Latino leadership for rank-and-file workers remains to be seen.

8

Urban Transformation and Employment

Saskia Sassen

Over the last two decades, the United States has moved to a service-dominated economy, not only in terms of job numbers but also in the broader sense of a new economic regime. This transformation assumes specific forms in different types of locations. Here we will focus particularly on major cities. These cities have come to be characterized by finance and specialized services, sectors considered to be among the most advanced and dynamic. Correspondingly, the cities experienced a sharp increase in the demand for highly qualified and highly paid white-collar workers. Many cities, especially New York, Los Angeles, and Chicago, contain large numbers of workers who lack such high educational attainment levels and who have typically held low-wage jobs in services or middle-level supervisory jobs, often in manufacturing industries now in severe shrinkage. Many of these cities also contain large numbers of Latino and African-American workers who lack the traits historically associated with workers in the leading sectors, or at least have typically not functioned as a labor supply for high-income white-collar jobs requiring advanced qualifications.

This situation raises a number of questions. One concerns the impact of this form of growth on the broader social and economic structure of major cities. We know that when manufacturing was the leading sector of the economy it created the conditions for the expansion of a vast middle class because: (a) it facilitated unionization; (b) it was based in good part on household consumption, hence wage levels mattered in that they created an effective demand; and (c) the wage levels and social benefits typical of the leading sectors became a model for broader sectors of the economy. A second question concerns the place of workers lacking the high levels of education required in the advanced sectors of the economy in these major cities. Have these workers become superfluous? Yet another question concerns the place in an advanced urban economy of firms and sectors that appear to be backward or lack the advanced technological and human capital base of the new leading sectors. Have they also become superfluous? Or are such workers, firms, and sectors actually articulated to the economic core, but under conditions of severe segmentation in the social, economic, racial, and organizational traits of firms and workers? This raises yet another question. To what extent is this segmentation produced or strengthened by the existence of ethnic/racial segmentation in combination with racism and discrimination?

In this chapter I focus on these general questions about the organization of work and its impact on cities and jobs. The purpose of examining these trends is to understand whether there are forms of economic growth today that promote polarization in cities, and if so, how this affects employment opportunities. A central proposition is that cities and jobs cannot be examined in isolation of the larger economic and political system. That is to say, at least some of the conditions for inequality are systemwide, even though specific social and economic characteristics of cities may strengthen some of these inequalities and diffuse or resist others.

First, I offer a discussion and interpretation of trends and conditions promoting polarization in an advanced economy, with a special focus on cities. Some of these trends and conditions exist at the level of the national political economy, others at the level of major cities. Whether this interpretation holds for other advanced economies and their major cities is a question for research, though there is evidence that it does (Sassen, 1991). Second, I discuss changes in the organization of work in major cities, focusing on labor market dynamics and how economic changes affect the sphere of consumption, which in turn has a feedback effect on the organization of work. Finally, I examine the overall impact of these conditions and trends on the minority population in major cities.

CONDITIONS FOR POLARIZATION IN SERVICE-DOMINATED ECONOMIES

The consolidation of a new economic core of professional and servicing activities needs to be viewed alongside the general move to a service economy and the decline of manufacturing. New economic sectors are reshaping the job supply. But so are new ways of organizing work in both new and old sectors of the economy. Components of the work process that even 20 years ago took place on the shop floor and were classified as production jobs today have been replaced by a combination of machine/service or worker/engineer. Activities that were once all consolidated in a single-service retail establishment have now been divided between a service delivery outlet and central headquarters. Finally, a large array of activities that were being carried out under standardized forms of organizing work a decade ago are today increasingly characterized by customization, flexible specialization, networks of subcontractors, and informalization, including sweatshops and industrial homework. In brief, the changes in the job supply evident in major cities are a function both of new sectors and of the reorganization of work in both the new and the old sectors.

The historical forms assumed by economic growth after World War II, which contributed to the vast expansion of a middle class—notably capital intensity, standardized production, and suburbanization-led growth—deterred and reduced systemic tendencies toward inequality by constituting an economic regime centered on mass production and mass consumption. (So also did the cultural forms accompanying these processes, particularly as they shaped the structures of everyday life insofar as a large middle class contributes to mass consumption and thus to standardization in production.) These various trends led to greater levels of unionization or other forms of workers' empowerment that can be derived from large scales in production and the centrality of mass production and mass consumption in national economic growth and profits. It is in the postwar period, extending into the late 1960s and early 1970s, that the incorporation of workers into formal labor market relations reached its highest level. The formalization of the employment relation carries with it the implementation (albeit frequently precarious) of a set of regulations that have had the overall effect of protecting workers and securing the fruits of frequently violent labor struggles. But this formalization also entailed the exclusion of distinct segments of the work force, particularly in certain heavily unionized industries.

It is now clear that in the 1970s the share of services as final output (e.g., consumer services) actually declined relative to the production of services as intermediate outputs, that is, producer and distributive services (Browning & Singelmann, 1978; Denison, 1979; Ginzberg & Vojta, 1981; Noyelle & Stanback, 1985). This shift from final to intermediate services is another indicator of restructuring. National trends in the United States show that total employment increased by 15% from 1977 to 1981 and by 8.3% from 1981 to 1985, but that total employment in producer services for those same periods increased by 24% and 22%, respectively.[1]

Second, producer services have emerged as a key sector in major cities. The evidence shows that FIRE, business and legal services, and the communications group accounted for 26.4% of all workers in New York City in 1985, 20.3% in Chicago, and 17.8% in Los Angeles, compared with 15% for the United States as a whole (Sassen, 1991).

A third trend is that the national employment share of producer services in major cities is at least a third higher and often twice as large as the share of these cities in total national employment. But the degree of concentration as measured by locational quotients is declining, signaling growth of such services in nonmajor cities as well.

There is clearly overrepresentation of these industries in major cities, notwithstanding relative declines in their shares over the last decade. The levels of overrepresentation and growth tend to vary considerably among industries. Thus New York City, with 3.7% of all U.S. employment in 1985, accounted for 11% of U.S. employment in banking and 9% in legal services but only 5.2% in insurance. Boston and Chicago have a greater share of insurance than of the other major producer services or of their share of national employment in producer services.

Organizing this information by location quotients underlines the extent to which major cities have overrepresentation of most of these producer services, but with considerable variation in the degrees and type of industry. New York City is the premier banking center in the country, with a location quotient of 2.5 over the last decade, reaching 2.9 in 1985. Boston is a major insurance center, with location quotients of 3.2 in 1977 and 2.7 in 1985. It is also the city with the second highest location quotient in banking, going from 1.9 in 1977 up to 2 in 1985. These quotients have magnitudes that clearly are describing a market that extends significantly beyond average overrepresentation and reveals a highly specialized spatial organization of a sector.[2]

The pattern of concentration of producer services in large urban areas and manufacturing in small urban areas raises the possibility of a transformation in the urban system or hierarchy.[3] Thus it is not enough to know that New York City has the highest location quotient for producer services. We also need to ask whether there are significant differences among these cities in the composition and market orientation of their industries. We need to know whether Boston is as specialized in international banking and finance as New York and Los Angeles, and if so, whether it is the same type of international finance. Second, the absolute weight of transactions is going to diverge dramatically given the much smaller employment base of Boston, under one-half million, compared with 3 million each in New York and Los Angeles, and 2.1 million in Chicago. Houston has overrepresentation in certain business services but underrepresentation in two such key industries as banking and insurance, which is quite surprising given that it is a major hub in the Southwest, an area that has seen much growth over the last decade. It is evident that the sectors in which Houston has overrepresentation are linked to the oil industry and the real estate boom that came about with the large domestic migration of people and firms to the South and Southwest of the United States in the 1970s (Feagin, 1985). At the same time, the underrepresentation in banking and insurance is an indication of the extent to which firms in Houston and the Southwest generally use the large banks and insurance companies of the Northeast (Sassen, 1991). Detroit, once the premier manufacturing city of the country, has unexpectedly low representation of real estate, an indication of its acute manufacturing losses (Hill, 1989). Given that it is still the home of major car manufacturers, it is worth noting its underrepresentation in business services, legal services, real estate, and insurance. The very low relative representation of banking in Detroit, only slightly above the national norm, indicates that to a large extent this may be consumer banking. This situation is reminiscent of that in Great Britain, where the former major manufacturing centers now have underrepresentation of producer services (Daniels, 1985). The high incidence of business services in Los Angeles is related to its vast and dynamic industrial sector (Cohen & Zysman, 1987; Soja, Morales, & Wolff, 1983). The incidence of producer services in Chicago probably follows a more expected pattern, somewhere between the acute overrepresentation of some producer services in New York, Los Angeles, and Boston and marked underrepresentation in Houston and Detroit. Chicago is the financial, marketing, and insurance center for the once powerful agro-industrial complex in the Midwest (Markusen, 1987). Two questions raised by the Chicago case are to what extent the composition of the producer services is quite different from that in New York or Los Angeles because it is directly related to servicing the agroindustrial base of the region, and second, to what extent the decline of the agroindustrial complex and the growth of the futures market have reoriented Chicago to the world market and finance (Sassen, 1991)?[4]

An important aspect we should not lose sight of is that although quantitatively significant in major cities, producer services do not account for the majority of all jobs. Thus one could posit that the power they have had in reshaping broad areas of economic life may point to the existence of a new service-based economic regime, one with effects going beyond the actual number of jobs in the producer services (Sassen, 1991).

THE EARNINGS DISTRIBUTION IN A SERVICE-DOMINATED ECONOMY

A major question arising from this sectoral shift concerns the earnings distribution in a service-dominated economy and more generally the income structure. There is a growing body of studies on the occupational and earnings distribution in services. These studies find that services produce a larger share of low-wage jobs than manufacturing, though the latter may increasingly be falling to the level of services; and second, that several major service industries also produce a larger share of jobs in the highest paid occupations (Harrison & Bluestone, 1988; Nelson & Lorence, 1985; Sheets, Nord, & Phelps, 1987; Silver, 1984; Stanback & Noyelle, 1982). Much attention has gone to the importance of manufacturing in reducing income inequality in the 1950s and 1960s (Blumberg, 1981; Garofalo & Fogarty, 1979; Stanback et al., 1981). Central reasons typically identified for this effect are the greater productivity and higher levels of unionization found in manufacturing. But clearly, these studies tend to cover a period largely characterized by such conditions. The organization of jobs has also undergone pronounced transformation in manufacturing. In what is at this point the most detailed analysis of occupational and industry data, Harrison and Bluestone (1988) found that earnings in manufacturing have declined in many industries and occupations. Glickman and Glasmeier (1989) found that a majority of manufacturing jobs in the Sunbelt are low wage and Fernandez-Kelly and Sassen (1991) found growth of sweatshops and homework in several industry branches in New York and Los Angeles (see also Carnoy et al., 1990; Fernandez-Kelly & Garcia, 1989; Morales, Ong, & Payne, 1988; National Council of La Raza, 1990; Portes & Sassen-Koob, 1987; Torres-Saillant, 1989).[5]

There is now a considerable body of studies with a strong theoretical bend (Hill, 1989; Lipietz, 1986; Massey, 1984; Sassen, 1988; Scott & Storper, 1986) that argue that the declining centrality of mass production in national growth and the shift to services as the leading economic sector contributed to the demise of a broader set of arrangements. In the postwar period, the economy functioned according to a dynamic that transmitted the benefits accruing to the core manufacturing industries on to more peripheral sectors of the economy. The benefits of price and market stability and increases in productivity could be transferred to a secondary set of firms, including suppliers and subcontractors, but also to less directly related industries. Although there was still a vast array of firms and workers that did not benefit from the shadow effect, their number was probably at a minimum in the postwar period. By the early 1980s the wage-setting power of leading manufacturing industries and this shadow effect had eroded significantly.

The importance of this combination of processes for the expansion of a middle class and generally rising wages should conceivably be evident in a comparison of earnings and income data for the postwar period with the last two decades. Yet different analysts have produced different results, often due to methodological or definitional differences. One can identify broadly three strands in the literature: those that show there has been no increase in earnings and/or income inequality; those that show there has been such an increase and explain it mostly in terms of demographic shifts; and those that find an often significant increase in earnings and/or income and explain it mostly in terms of economic restructuring, including prominently the intrasectoral reorganization of work.

The evidence showing inequality is substantive. Blumberg (1981) found increases in the degree of equality in the earnings distribution up to 1963. Inflation-adjusted average weekly wages peaked in 1973, stagnated over the next few years, and fell in the decade of the 1980s. Harrison and Bluestone (1988) used CPS data to show that the index of inequality grew 18% from 1975 to 1986. Other studies found the same trend (Bell & Freeman, 1987; Organization for Economic Cooperation and Development, 1985, pp. 90-91). The data show a clear increase in low-wage full-time year-round jobs since the late 1970s and a less pronounced increase in high-income jobs compared with the decade from 1963 to 1973 when 9 out of 10 new jobs were in the middle earnings group and high-paying jobs actually lost share. After 1973 only one in two new jobs was in the middle earnings category.[6]

Central to the literature on the earning distribution has been the demography versus structure debate. Several analysts maintain that increases in earnings inequality are a function of demographic shifts, notably the growing participation of women in the labor force and the large number of young workers due to the baby boom generation, two types of workers traditionally earning less than white adult males (Lawrence, 1984; Levy, 1987). But recently reviewing the latest data, Levy, a leading exponent of the demography side (Levy & Murnane, 1992), has found that earnings dispersion is indeed also structural. Harrison and Bluestone (1988, Chapter 5) analyzed the data controlling for various demographic factors as well as the shift to services and found that within each group, that is, white women, young workers, white adult men, and so on, there has been an increase in earnings inequality. They found that the sectoral shift accounted for one fifth of the increase in inequality, but most of the rest of the growth in inequality occurred *within* industries so that, as with demographic groups, there is a growth in inequality in the earnings distribution within industries (see their appendix Table A.2 for 18 demographic, sectoral, and regional factors). The authors explain the increased inequality in the earnings distribution in terms of the restructuring of wages and work hours (Chapters 2 and 3).

There are several detailed analyses of the social impact of service growth in major metropolitan areas (Bergman & Goldstein, 1983, Fainstein, Fainstein, Hill, Judd, & M. P. Smith, 1986; Hawley, Long, & Rasmussen, 1978; Hirsch, 1982; Maume, 1983; Nelson & Lorence, 1985; Ross & Trachte, 1983; Sheets et al., 1987; Silver, 1984; Noyelle & Stanback, 1985). Using the 1980 Census PUMS file, Sheets et al. (1987) found that from 1970 to 1980 several service industries had a significant effect on the growth of what they label underemployment and define as employment paying below poverty level wages in the 100 largest metropolitan areas. The strongest effect was associated with the growth of producer services and retail trade. The highest relative contribution resulted from what the authors call "corporate services" (FIRE, business services, legal services, membership organizations, and professional services) such that a 1% increase in employment in these services was found to result in a 0.37% increase in full-time, year-round low-wage jobs; a 1% increase in distributive services, in a 0.32% increase in such jobs. In contrast, a 1% increase in personal services was found to result in a 0.13% increase in such jobs and a higher share of *part*-time low-wage jobs. The retail industry had the highest effect on the creation of part-time, year-round low-wage jobs, such that a 1% increase in retail was found to result in a 0.88% increase in such jobs.

But what about the impact of services on the expansion of high-income jobs? Nelson and Lorence (1985) examined this question using census data on the 125 largest urban areas. In order to establish why male earnings are more unequal in metropolises with high levels of service sector employment they measured the ratio of median earnings over the 5th percentile to identify the difference in earnings between the least affluent and the median metropolitan male earners, and the ratio at the 95th percentile to establish the gap between median and affluent earners.[7] Overall, they found that inequality in the 125 areas appeared to be due to greater earnings disparity between the highest and the median earners than between the median and lowest earners (Nelson & Lorence, 1985, p. 115). Furthermore they found that the strongest effect came from the producer services and that the next strongest was far weaker (social services in 1970 and personal services in 1980).[8]

All these trends are operating in major cities, in many cases with greater intensity than national average data describe. This greater intensity can be rooted in at least three conditions. First, there is the locational concentration of major growth sectors with either sharp earnings dispersion or disproportionate concentration of either low- or high-paying jobs. Second, there is a proliferation of small, low-cost, service operations made possible by the massive concentration of people in such cities, in addition to a large daily inflow of nonresident workers and tourists. The ratio between the number of these service operations and the resident population is most probably significantly higher in a very large city than in an average city. Furthermore, the large concentration of people in major cities tends to create intense inducements to open up such operations as well as intense competition and very marginal returns. Under such conditions, the cost of labor is crucial and hence the likelihood of a high concentration of low-wage jobs. Third, for these same reasons, together with other components of demand, the relative size of the downgraded manufacturing sector would tend to be larger in big cities like New York or Los Angeles than in average-sized cities.

The overall result is a tendency toward increased economic polarization. The argument put forth here is that although the middle strata still constitute the majority, the conditions that contributed to their expansion and politicoeconomic power—the centrality of mass production and mass consumption in economic growth and profit realization—have been displaced by new sources of growth. This is not simply a quantitative transformation; we see here the elements for a new economic regime (Sassen, 1991). This tendency toward polarization assumes distinct forms in (a) its spatial organization, (b) the structures for social reproduction, and (c) the organization of the labor process. How do these trends play themselves out in a major city like New York? We will start with the last.

TRANSFORMATIONS IN THE ORGANIZATION OF THE LABOR PROCESS

The economic and social transformations in the economy since the mid-1970s assumes specific forms in urban labor markets. Changes in the functioning of urban labor markets since the mid-1970s have a number of possible origins. The most evident stems from the long-term shifts in the occupational and industrial balance of employment, which directly affects the mix of job characteristics, including earnings levels and employment stability, and the types of careers available to local workers. On the demand side these developments include the new flexibility that employers have tended to seek under the pressure of international competition, unstable product markets, and a weakening of political support for public sector programs. On the supply side a key factor has been the persistence of high unemployment over a decade in many large cities, which notably altered the bargaining position of employers, and the insecurity or marginalization of the most disadvantaged groups in the labor market. In many leading cities a factor of importance has been the rapid growth of a new immigrant population since the late 1960s, occupying quite distinct positions in the labor market. In combination these major developments on the two sides of the labor market, all of which have operated most strongly in the urban core, seem likely to have induced, on one hand, a growing destabilization of employment, with increasing casualization and/or informalization of jobs, and on the other hand, an increasing polarization of employment opportunities with new forms of social divisions. The extent to which either of these outcomes has in fact materialized needs to be examined in relation to possible countervailing forces.

Metropolitan labor markets will tend to reflect a variety of background factors beyond particular restructuring effects. The most important include their sheer size and density, the particular industrial and occupational mix of their employment base, the overall state of tightness or slack in labor demand, and in many cities the representation and characteristics of immigrant groups. Two key characteristics of the labor markets in major cities, today as well as a century ago, are the fluidity and openness that influence the types of activity prospering there, as well as the labor market experiences of their residents. But equally important is that the labor markets in and around the cities are *structured,* with particular sets of jobs having attached to them distinctive combinations of rewards, security, and conditions of access.

The market characteristics of many important industries in major cities evidence tendencies toward shorter term employment relationships. Whether in fashion-oriented industries such as the garment trade, in private consumer services, historically in trades associated with mass production, or currently in the more speculative finance houses, there is a significant share of establishments operating in competitive and often highly unstable markets. Again the evidence is that turnover rates in these activities are much higher than in large establishments and monopolistic, bureaucratized organizations. And one of the attractions of cities to these more unstable activities must be the ease with which, in the fluid labor markets, employment levels can be adjusted up and down. High rates of turnover also have implications on the supply side, adding to the attractions of the city for speculative migrants, particularly minorities with difficulty gaining access to more closed sectors of employment, and young single workers for whom job security may be a lower priority. The availability of these particular labor supplies must then have further implications for employers' strategies. The actual structure of urban labor markets has been more complex and changeable than agglomeration economies and the "natural selection" of activities and groups of workers can account for.

There have been objective transformations in the forms of organizing production, with a growing presence of small batch production, small scales, high product differentiation, and rapid changes in output. These have promoted subcontracting and the use of flexible ways of organizing production. Flexible forms of production can range from highly sophisticated to very primitive and can be found in advanced or in backward industries. Such ways of organizing production assume distinct forms in the labor market, in the components of labor demand, and in the conditions under which labor is employed. Indications of these changes are the decline of unions in manufacturing, the loss of various contractual protections, the increase of involuntary part-time and temporary work or other forms of contingent labor. An extreme indication of this downgrading is the growth of sweatshops and industrial homework. The expansion of a downgraded manufacturing sector partly involves the same industries that used to have largely organized plants and reasonably well-paid jobs, but replaces these with different forms of production and organization of the work process, such as piecework and industrial homework. But it also involves new kinds of activity associated with the new major growth trends. The possibility for manufacturers to develop alternatives to the organized factory becomes particularly significant in growth sectors. The consolidation of a downgraded manufacturing sector, whether through social or technical transformation, can be seen as a politicoeconomic response to a need for expanded production in a situation of growing average wages and militancy, as was the case in the 1960s and early 1970s.

A good part of what I am here calling the downgraded manufacturing sector is an instance of informalization, or a component of the informal sector. We need to distinguish two spheres for the circulation of goods and services produced in the informal sector. One sphere circulates internally and meets mostly the demands of its members—that is, small immigrant-owned shops in the immigrant community that service the latter; the other circulates throughout the "formal" sector of the economy. In this second case, informalization represents a direct profit-maximizing strategy, one that can operate through subcontracting, the use of sweatshops and homework, or direct acquisition of goods or services. This second aspect is somewhat lost when we use the concept of the informal sector, whereas it comes to the fore with the notion of a downgraded manufacturing sector—and increasingly, downgraded mass consumer services, whether public or private, alongside increasingly upgraded non-mass consumer services.

These conditions suggest that there are inducements to informalization in the combination of several trends, particularly evident in major cities: (a) the increased demand for highly priced customized services and products by the expanding high-income population; (b) the increased demand for extremely low-cost services and products by the expanding low-income population; (c) the demand for customized services and goods or limited runs from firms that are either final or intermediate buyers with a corresponding growth of subcontracting; (d) the increasing inequality in the bidding power of firms in a context of acute pressures on land due to the rapid growth and strong agglomerative pattern of the leading industries; and (e) the continuing demand by various firms and sectors of the population, including demand from leading industries and high-income workers, for a range of goods and services typically produced in firms with low profit rates that find it increasingly difficult to survive given rising rents and costs of production.

The argument is that the transformation of final and intermediate consumption and the growing inequality in the bidding power of firms and households for space creates inducements for informalization in a broad range of activities and spheres of the economy; the existence of an informal economy in turn emerges as a mechanism for reducing costs, even in the case of firms and households that do not need it for survival, and for providing flexibility in instances where this is essential or advantageous.[9]

The potential importance of the presence or absence of a large immigrant labor force extends to a range of issues including the level of wages in the lower part of the labor market, and its implications for the cost of living and competitiveness of local activities, as well as for patterns of segmentation and opportunities of advancement for indigenous workers. Furthermore, given typical concentration of new migrants in central cities, immigration has also contributed to changes in spatial patterns in labor supply. There has been a marked decentralization of the white population into the outer rings of the metropolitan regions. In major cities mostly white flight to the suburbs was counterbalanced by mostly Third World immigration from the mid-1960s on.

The rapid growth of industries with strong concentration of either high- and low-income jobs or both has assumed distinct forms in the consumption structure that in turn has a feedback effect on the organization of work and the types of jobs being created. The expansion of the high-income work force in conjunction with the emergence of new cultural forms has led to a process of high-income gentrification that rests, in the last analysis, on the availability of a vast supply of low-wage workers. As I have argued at greater length elsewhere high-income gentrification is labor intensive, in contrast to the typical middle-class suburb that represents a capital-intensive process—tract housing, road and highway construction, dependence on private automobile or commuter trains, marked reliance on appliances and household equipment of all sorts, large shopping malls with self-service operations (Sassen, 1988). High-income gentrification replaces much of this capital intensity with workers, directly and indirectly. Similarly, high-income residents in the city depend to a much larger extent on hired maintenance staff than the middle-class suburban home with its concentrated input of family labor and machinery.

The delicatessens and specialty boutiques that have replaced the self-service supermarket and department store have a very different organization of work from that prevalent in large, standardized establishments. This difference in the organization of work is evident both in the retail and in the production phase (Morales & Mines, 1984; Sassen, 1988). High-income gentrification generates a demand for goods and services that are frequently not mass produced or sold through mass outlets. Customized production, small runs, specialty items, fine food dishes are generally produced through labor-intensive methods and sold through small, full-service outlets. Subcontracting part of this production to low-cost operations, and also sweatshops or households, is common. Proximity to stores is of far greater importance with customized producers. The overall outcome for the job supply and the range of firms involved in this production and delivery is rather different from that characterizing the large department stores and supermarkets, which rely on mass production and hence on large, standardized factories located outside the city or the region. Mass production and mass distribution outlets facilitate unionizing.

The magnitude of the expansion of high-income workers and the high levels of spending contributed to this outcome. All major cities have long had a core of wealthy residents or commuters. But by itself, this core of wealthy people could not have created the large-scale residential and commercial gentrification in the city. As a stratum, the new high-income workers are to be distinguished from this core of wealth, or upper class. Their disposable income is, still, not enough to make them into major investors. It is, however, sufficient for a significant expansion in the demand for highly priced goods and services; that is to say, to create a sufficiently large demand so as to ensure economic viability for the producers and providers of such goods and services. Furthermore, the level of disposable income is also a function of life-style and demographic patterns, such as postponing having children and the larger number of two-earner households.

The expansion in the low-income population has also contributed to the proliferation of small operations and the move away from large-scale standardized factories and large chain stores for low-priced goods. In good part the consumption needs of the low-income population are met by manufacturing and retail establishments that are small, rely on family labor, and often fall below minimum safety and health standards. Cheap, locally produced sweatshop garments, for example, can compete with low-cost Asian imports. A growing range of products and services, from low-cost furniture made in basements to "gypsy" cabs and family day care is available to meet the demand from the growing low-income population.

In any large city, there also tends to be a proliferation of small, low-cost service operations made possible by the massive concentration of people in such cities and the daily inflow of commuters and of tourists. This will tend to create intense inducements to open up such operations as well as intense competition and very marginal returns. Under such conditions the cost of labor is crucial and contributes to the likelihood of a high concentration of low-wage jobs. This tendency was confirmed by Sheets et al. (1987) when they found that each 1% increase in retail jobs resulted in a 0.88% average increase in below poverty level jobs in the 100 largest metropolitan areas in 1980.

There are numerous instances of how the increased inequality in earnings reshapes the consumption structure and how this in turn has feedback effects on the organization of work. Examples are: the creation of a special taxi line for Wall Street that only services the financial district and the increase of "gypsy" cabs in low-income neighborhoods not serviced by regular cabs; the increase in highly customized wood work in gentrified areas and low-cost rehabilitation in poor neighborhoods; the increase of homeworkers and sweatshops making either very expensive designer items for boutiques or very cheap products.

MINORITIES AND THE URBAN TRANSFORMATION

The consequences of these various processes have become particularly evident in the largest cities, partly because they had large manufacturing sectors, and partly because they had disproportionate concentrations of low-income blacks, and eventually Latinos, likely to be employed in manufacturing. In this context of large cities, several studies have posited the expansion and consolidation of distinct social forms, such as an underclass (Ricketts & Sawhill, 1988; W. J. Wilson, 1987), an informal economy (Portes, Castells, & Benton, 1989; Sassen, 1989), and the renewed growth of immigrant communities with strong entrepreneurial elements (Light & Bonacich, 1988; K. L. Wilson & Portes, 1980).

As has been widely recognized, in the 1970s and 1980s our large cities became poorer, blacker, and more Latino (Cortina & Marcada, 1988; Hayes-Bautista, Schink, & Chapa, 1988; National Council of La Raza, 1990b; Peterson, 1985). From 1969 to 1979, the share of black families in cities with populations over one-half million increased sharply while that of white families dropped, and from 1979 to 1986 the most pronounced change was the increase in the share of Latino and Asian families. In 1969, 75.8% of families in cities with over one-half million population were white; by 1979 the share was down to 68.6%. The percentage of black families went from 22.7% in 1969 to 27.5% in 1979 and 26.1% in 1986. Latinos, for whom there is no figure for 1969, increased from 11.7% in 1979 to 16.3% in 1986. Both black and white families in large metropolitan areas have higher median incomes than those of nonmetropolitan families. Yet within these areas there is a strong difference for both whites and blacks between cities and suburbs. There has been a relative decline in city median family income from 1969 to 1976. After 1979, white city families maintained their relative standing, but black families' median income declined further and their poverty rate increased significantly (Drennan, 1988).[10] In 1986, the poverty rate was 10.8% for white families in cities and 5.6% in suburbs, and for blacks respectively 29% and 19.4%. In nonmetropolitan areas whites had a poverty rate of 12.6% and blacks 36.8%.

The most detailed information on urban poverty comes from the 1980 Census. Using census data for the 100 largest cities in the United States and a measure for concentrated poverty tracts developed by Ricketts and Sawhill (1988), Mincey (1988) found that 73% of all underclass tracts with a majority of blacks were in the 50 largest metropolitan areas of the United States. This share rises to 83% for the 100 largest areas. The highest level of concentration was among Latinos, with 95% of such tracts in the 50 largest cities, for whites the share is under 50%. Clearly, black and Latino poverty is disproportionately concentrated in the largest cities. Furthermore, Mincey (1988) found that nonminority poor were more likely to gain access to housing in nonpoverty and nonextreme poverty tracts than minorities. Finally, poor Latino whites are less concentrated in extreme poverty tracts than blacks or nonwhite Latinos, which leads Mincey to posit that racial differentials in access to housing among the poor may be more important to explain the high concentration of minority poor than ethnic differentials (Enchautegui, 1990; Massey & Denton, 1987; Mincey, 1988, p. 5; Santiago, 1989; Torres, 1989).

In sum, the concentration of poor in large cities has increased and median family income is lower in large cities than in their suburbs. Controlling for race we can see increasing differentials between whites and blacks as of 1969, with the urban poverty rate of blacks reaching a level triple that of whites in 1986; median income of black families in the cities has lost ground relative to that of blacks in the suburbs and to whites generally, and the concentration of blacks in large cities has increased while that of whites has decreased.

The growing urbanization of poor blacks and Hispanics has occurred at a time of pronounced transformations in the occupational distribution in major cities (F. Bonilla & Campos, 1986; Carnoy et al., 1990a; Kasarda, 1988; Orfield, 1985). Using the 1980 Census PUMS file, Kasarda (1988) found that large northern and northeastern cities all had severe losses in clerical and sales occupations and in blue-collar occupations, and they all had gains in managerial, professional, technical, and administrative support occupations.[11] The suburban rings had gains in these occupational groups, but they also gained blue-collar jobs. This left cities with net job losses ranging from 46,480 in Boston to 104,860 in Detroit and net gains in suburban rings ranging from 97,060 in Cleveland to 489,080 in New York.[12] The evidence clearly indicates sharp declines among job holders with a high school degree or less, and sharp increases among job holders with some college and college graduates. At the same time it is important to note that about half of all job holders in major cities in 1980 had only a high school degree or less. This was the case for half or more of all job holders in New York City, Baltimore, Chicago, Cleveland, Detroit, St. Louis, Philadelphia (Kasarda, 1988). Thus the rates of change do not necessarily mean that a vast majority of all jobs in cities are now held by individuals with advanced educations. In fact, 10% of black male job holders in these cities had only a high school degree or less, but of black males not working, 80% had a high school degree or less. For all regions of the United States the share of black males of working age without a high school degree has increased sharply over the last 20 years in both central cities and suburban rings of metropolitan regions. From about a fifth in cities in 1969 it increased to almost half by 1987, ranging from a "low" of 44% in the Northeast to a high of 60.8% in the West. The figures for suburbs are considerably lower, but still reveal a sharp increase and are far higher than those for whites, going from about a sixth in 1969 to well over a third by 1987, from a "low" of 30.8% in the Northeast to a high of 41.3% in the Midwest.

W. J. Wilson (1985, 1987) finds that various types of social dislocation have acquired catastrophic dimensions in the inner areas of large cities and further widened the gap between these and the growing successful black middle class. Since the mid-1960s there has been a doubling in the share of black births outside marriage—from one quarter to over half by 1980—in the share of black families headed by women, in black crime rates, and in joblessness, all disproportionately concentrated in what Wilson describes as the underclass, "a heterogenous grouping of inner city families and individuals who are outside the mainstream of the American occupational system" (1985, p. 133). Although only one in nine persons was black in the United States, one in every two persons arrested for murder and nonnegligent manslaughter was black and 44% of the murder victims were black.

This severe deterioration in the significant share of the black population concentrated in cities occurred at a time when major antidiscrimination legislation was in place and growth of a strong black middle class emerged, partly through increased access to well-paying public sector jobs. Wilson argues that although discrimination will explain part of this deterioration, one must bring into account the structural transformation of the economic base in the large cities where disadvantaged blacks are concentrated.[13]

A key debate centers on the weight of spatial factors in the rise of joblessness among urban blacks (Ellwood, 1986; Freeman & Holzer, 1986; Hughes, 1987; Kasarda, 1985; Leonard, 1986; Orfield, 1985). Some emphasize that the suburbanization of blue-collar and other low-skill jobs has worked to the economic disadvantage of blacks who remain residentially constrained to inner-city housing (Farley, 1987a).[14] Ellwood (1986) presents strong evidence that race, not spatial factors (differential proximity to jobs), is the key variable explaining employment differentials (see also Fainstein, 1987).

In these same large cities, many of the new immigrants have made disproportionate "gains" into declining manufacturing industries (Fernandez-Kelly & Sassen, 1991), and typically show much lower joblessness than blacks. One key difference is the centrality of the immigrant community with its resources of people, small capital, markets, the possibility of pooling resources, and extended households (Light & Bonacich, 1988; NACLA, 1992; K. L. Wilson & Portes, 1980, to name but a few titles of a vast literature). This has meant many things, from job generation in the immigrant community to the possibility of surviving—through household income pooling—on extremely low-wage jobs in declining manufacturing industries. A recent development in immigrant communities in large cities that contrasts sharply with Wilson's (1987) description of the underclass in black neighborhoods in these same cities, is the expansion of an informal economy (Portes et al., 1989; Sassen, 1989). The informal economy is defined as the production and distribution of (mostly) licit goods and services outside the regulatory apparatus, covering zoning, tax, health and safety, minimum wage laws, and other types of standards in a context where such activities are usually regulated.

An important question for theory and policy is whether the formation and expansion of informal work in advanced economies is the result of conditions created by these economies. Rather than assume that Third World immigration is causing informalization, we need a critical examination of the role it may or may not play in this process. Immigrants, insofar as they tend to form communities, may be in a favorable position to seize the opportunities represented by informalization. But the opportunities are not necessarily created by immigrants. They may well be a structured outcome of current trends in advanced industrial economies. Several studies attempt an analytic differentiation of immigration, informalization, and characteristics of the current phase of advanced industrialized economies in order to establish the differential impact of (a) immigration and (b) conditions in the economy at large on the formation and expansion of informal sectors (Castells & Portes, 1989; Fernandez-Kelly & Garcia, 1989; Sassen, 1989; Stepick, 1989).

The sectoral and occupational transformation in large cities and the associated expansion of low- and high-income strata have brought about (a) a proliferation of small firms engaged in the production and retail of both highly priced and very cheap products for firms and for final consumers and (b) a partial concentration of such small firms in major cities due to the critical mass of both high- and low-income residents and commuters in cities, and further, the need for small firms to be close to suppliers and buyers. These growth trends contain inducements toward the informalization of a whole range of activities. In contrast to standardized mass production, informal work arrangements are not conducive to unionization and high wages.

CONCLUSION

Developments in cities cannot be understood in isolation of fundamental changes in the larger organization of advanced economies. The combination of economic, political, and technical forces that has contributed to the decline of mass production as the central driving element in the economy brought about a decline in a broader institutional framework that shaped the employment relation. The group of service industries that were the driving economic force in the 1980s and continue to be into the 1990s are characterized by greater earnings and occupational dispersion, weak unions, and mostly a growing share of unsheltered jobs in the lower paying echelons along with a growing share of high-income jobs. The associated institutional framework shaping the employment relation is very different from the earlier one. This contributes to a reshaping of the sphere of social reproduction and consumption that in turn has a feedback effect on economic organization and earnings. Whereas in the earlier period this feedback effect contributed to reproduction of the middle class, currently it reproduces growing earnings disparity and labor market casualization.

The growth of service employment in cities and the evidence on the associated growth of inequality raises questions about how fundamental a change this shift entails. Several of these questions concern the nature of service-based urban economies. The observed changes in the occupational and earnings distribution are outcomes not only of industrial shifts but also of changes in the organization of firms and of labor markets. A detailed analysis of service-based urban economies shows that there is considerable articulation of firms, sectors, and workers who may appear as though they have little connection to an urban economy dominated by finance and specialized services, but in fact fulfill a series of functions that are an integral part of that economy. They do so under conditions of sharp social, earnings, and often racial/ethnic segmentation.

NOTES

1. Considerable disparity between the level of overall national employment growth and growth in producer services is evident in several major industrialized countries. For example, total national employment in Japan grew by 5% from 1977 to 1985 but the FIRE sector grew by 27% in 1975-1985; in Great Britain total employment grew by 5% from 1978 to 1985, while FIRE increased by 44% (Sassen, 1991).

2. The figures for Los Angeles are underestimates of the extent of concentration because they cover the whole county, which in this case corresponds far less closely to the city than is the case of other counties, e.g., Cook County and Chicago. The massive industrial complex and active harbor are central to the growth of producer services in the area, but will tend to create a demand for different types of services from that engendered by Los Angeles's expanding financial activities.

3. Intersecting this question is another one concerning the type of urban system formed by the leading finance and business centers in the world economy today. New forms of interdependence among the cities with a strong world market orientation in some ways disconnects these cities from their national context and strengthen their interdependence, a sort of Hanseatic league at the global level (Sassen, 1991, p. 310). In his major new

book, *The Informational City,* Castells (1989) posits the emergence of a "space of flows" whose logic supersedes that of the nation, region, and city.

4. New York's is a producer services sector catering to a world market and heavily internationalized, servicing or making transactions at the axis between a firm and the international market. Chicago's would seem to be much less so. Chicago's large export-oriented firms were typically highly integrated with extensive internal production of the necessary services. Now we may be seeing the beginnings of a free-standing producer services industry fed by the growth of foreign investment in the region and of the futures market.

5. The numbers of workers who are not employed full-time and year-round has increased. Part-time work rose from 15% in 1955, to 22% in 1977, and 24% in 1986. Over the last few years the government has implemented a number of decisions that promote the growing use of part-time and temporary workers (U.S. Congressional Budget Office, 1987). Circular A-76 by the Office of Management and Budget ordered all agencies to raise their use of private firms for service work unless the agency could demonstrate that it could do it more economically in-house. The result has been a growing subcontracting out of such services as food preparation, building maintenance, warehousing, data processing. They involve types of jobs that can be organized in part-time or temporary work hours, and being labor intensive, can cut costs significantly by reducing wages. In 1984 the government implemented a two-tiered wage system in the U.S. Postal Service, one of the largest employers among government agencies. The purpose was to create more flexible work schedules. The second tier paid wages 25% below the previous standard. In 1985 the government implemented a regulation authorizing the employment of temporary workers at all levels for up to 4 years and in fact urging agencies to do so "whenever possible." This represented a severe erosion of the contractual arrangement regulating the civil service guarantee of permanent employment after a probationary period. Finally, in 1986 the government implemented regulations that make it easier for companies to use homeworkers. This is reminiscent of the privatization of these types of services in London, where many of these jobs went from being full-time, year-round regulated government jobs with fringe benefits to part-time or temporary jobs in subcontracting firms with no fringe benefits and lacking the regulatory protection of the state (Sassen, 1991).

6. It should be noted that notwithstanding an increase in multiple-earner families and an increase in transfer payments, several studies found the family income distribution has also become more unequal. Using CPS data on family income, Blumberg (1981) found that family income adjusted for inflation increased by 33% from 1948 to 1958, by 42% in 1958-1968, by 9% in 1968-1978. Median family income kept growing throughout the postwar period but stagnated after 1973. By 1984, the Gini coefficient, the inequality measure used by the U.S. Bureau of the Census, stood at its highest since the end of World War II. The increase in inequality began sharply in 1980, after slight increases in the 1970s. A report prepared by the staff of the House Ways and Means Committee released in July 1989 found that from 1979 to 1987 the bottom fifth of the population had a decline of 8% in private income and the top fifth, an increase of 16% in private income. Adjusting income for inflation and family size, the bottom fifth of the income distribution suffered a 1% decline from 1973 to 1979 and a 10% decline from 1979 to 1987; for the top fifth, there was an increase of 7% from 1973 to 1979 and a 16% increase from 1979 to 1987. Both 1979 and 1987 were years of prosperity and low unemployment. Most recently, the staff of the House Ways and Means Committee compiled data showing increasing inequality in the distribution of income. From 1977 to 1988 the incomes of the bottom

fifth of families sank by 13%; by contrast, the top fifth of families earned 27% more, while the top 1% saw their incomes nearly double. Tax changes further raised the 96% pretax income gain of the top into a 123% after-tax gain.

7. A larger ratio between the upper end and the median indicates that the more affluent have a greater economic advantage over median earners than high earners in another metropolitan area. They disaggregated service employment into four major groups following Browning and Singelmann (1978) and included a number of control variables (race, age, education, unemployment).

8. The authors regressed the various income and percentile measures on the other four service sectors and select control variables and found that the producer services sector had the most substantial relationship to overall inequality of the four service sectors and were more highly related to inequality than most of the control variables associated with the traditional explanations of inequality.

9. A small but growing body of evidence points to the expansion of informal sectors in major cities of the United States over the last decade (Columbia University, 1987; Fernandez-Kelly & Garcia, 1989; Sassen-Koob, 1989; Sassen & Grover, 1986; Stepick, 1989). These studies are mostly based on ethnographic research. They are to be distinguished from studies that aim at overall estimates of the underground economy based on aggregate figures for the supply and circulation of money (Gutmann, 1979; Spitznas, 1981; Tanzi, 1982). As categories for analysis, the underground economy and the informal sector overlap only partly. Studies on the underground have sought to measure all income not registered in official figures, including income derived from illicit activities such as drug dealing. Studies in the informal sector focus on the production and sale of goods and services that are licit, produced and/or sold outside the regulatory apparatus covering zoning, tax, health and safety, minimum wage laws, and other types of standards.

10. The 1969 median income of white families in cities was 84.5% of those in suburbs of large metropolitan areas; by 1979 this had fallen to 78.5% and 77.9% by 1986. That of blacks stood at 85.5% in 1969, 71.9% in 1979, and 65.6%.

11. In the 1970s black migration into large cities subsided and there was in fact a net out-migration to the suburbs; but in the 1980s this out-migration also declined and there was little movement in either direction. Births accounted for most of the increase in the urban black population (Hauser, 1981). Census data (Hauser, 1981) indicate that blacks migrating from nonmetropolitan areas in the South are now going predominantly to the large cities in the South such as Atlanta and Houston, where we are seeing the formation of large inner-city ghettoes that resemble the northern ghettoes. This will further add to the disproportionate concentration of poor blacks in large cities who are particularly vulnerable to the changes brought about by restructuring. Wilson points out that this would mean that for the first time in the 20th century "the ranks of central city blacks are no longer being replenished by poor migrants" (Wilson 1985, p. 14).

12. Blue-collar jobs did grow in particular industries in cities: notably in producer services in New York and Chicago and in the public sector.

13. This is clearly a highly complex and difficult issue with a wide range of theoretical and empirical lines of inquiry. W. J. Wilson (1987) argues that present-day discrimination cannot be seen as the main culprit for this severe deterioration, but that it is rather the legacy of historic discrimination in combination with contemporary social and economic forces. Lieberson (1980) found that the large and prolonged influx of southern black migrants was a central factor in producing economic disadvantages in the large ghettoes of the northeastern cities.

14. Farley (1987a) found that black unemployment is higher relative to whites where jobs are most suburbanized and black population least so. Goldsmith and Blakely (1991) compiled data showing that African-Americans hold disproportionate concentrations of low-wage jobs even controlling for job characteristics, education, age, and other demographic characteristics. Vrooman and Greenfield (1980) found that 40% of the black-white racial earning gap could be closed by the suburbanization of central city black labor. And Strazheim (1980) found a positive wage gradient from city to suburb employment among lesser educated blacks in contrast to whites.

9

An Unnatural Trade-Off: Latinos and Environmental Justice

Paul M. Ong
Evelyn Blumenberg

INTRODUCTION

Economic restructuring, discussed elsewhere in this book, plays a key role in reproducing racial inequality. The restructuring of the U.S. economy has had an impact on workers by both maintaining and strengthening labor market segmentation. With increased global competition and the squeeze on profits, capital has sought to offset the tide of market forces by seeking cheaper labor. New cost-cutting measures not only promote offshore production but also involve the incorporation of low-wage immigrant labor within the United States through the expansion of secondary labor markets and the weakening of organized labor and labor laws. In addition to the direct economic threats of job loss or reduced wages, workers are also increasingly threatened by environmental hazards—in the workplace and in their communities.

AUTHORS' NOTE: This research was partially supported by a grant from the California Council for the Humanities through the project "The California Dilemma: Economic Development, Environmental Quality, and Economic Justice." We are indebted to the Data Archives at the UCLA Institute for Social Science Research for access to computer data files and to the UCLA Graduate School of Architecture and Urban Planning for computer support. We alone are responsible for all interpretations and conclusions, and for any errors.

Restructuring is not limited to the labor market, however. The adjustment process also has an environmental dimension: Many firms avoid the cost of conforming to U.S. environmental and occupational safety laws and regulations. One industrial strategy utilized is offshore production; firms relocate to countries where regulations are less stringent or nonexistent. Other enterprises adopt a second strategy, shifting their domestic production to marginal firms that are more likely to use hazardous production processes and to evade government regulations. Not surprisingly, these firms are often those that employ a disproportionate number of minority or Latino workers.

The environmental risks and damage to Latinos are not confined to the workplace. Latino and minority communities are adversely affected by the siting of hazardous production and hazardous waste facilities in their neighborhoods. In their search for cheaper locations within the United States, hazardous industries often locate in neighborhoods with low land values, neighborhoods that often house the city's minority residents. But "economic restructuring"—the search for lower operating costs, the widening gap between the rich and the poor—is not the entire explanation for the disparate impact of environmental hazards on Latinos. Economic inequality and racism have a long history in the United States. They have shaped residential location patterns and determined the holders of political power. Latinos are largely segregated in distinct areas of metropolitan regions and lack the political clout to prevent hazardous sitings. Their communities often suffer from their inability to influence and capture the benefits of environmental and growth control policies. Economic restructuring, then, has reinforced and compounded racial and economic inequalities.

Our interest in environmental inequality is based not only in the desire to show conceptually how economic restructuring has implications beyond those covered in previous chapters. We believe that to understand the position of Latinos in the changing economy of the United States, it is necessary to recognize that the very definition of what constitutes our concerns must extend beyond the labor and product markets. In addition to income inequality and unequal access to material goods, Latinos suffer from the harmful externalities generated through agricultural and industrial activities—costs that are not reflected in market prices, but nonetheless are real costs to individuals and communities. Job hazards and environmental degradation, two major by-products of our advanced economy, are not new, but their cumulative impact on people's health and quality of life are so high today that a full accounting of the economic status of Latinos must also take into account these external costs.

Although one could argue that environmental inequality is rooted in economic inequality, the inequality in the environmental arena also has a logic and form of its own, shaped by the inequality embedded in our political and policy-making processes. Indeed, it is in the latter two areas that much of the struggle for racial justice is now taking place. In recent years, the environmental crisis has reached such an alarming level that it has set off a powerful political movement in the form of environmentalism. The debate over our economy and state intervention has expanded to the environmental arena. Although the ideological response to economic re-structuring has been to reembrace capitalism, to let markets rather than regulations shape the new U.S. economy, the environmental arena has been one of the few policy areas where the notions of market failure, collective responses, and state intervention are still seriously discussed. One indica-tion of its importance is President Bush's claim to being the environmental president, although a reading of the position put forth in the chapter on "The Economy and the Environment" in the 1990 *Economic Report of the President* does not support this claim. Instead, the Bush administration has reframed the environmental issue into one of balancing economic growth with costly regulation, frequently arguing on behalf of business that many environmental policies have been more detrimental than helpful to the national interest. Nonetheless, the political discourse in the environmental arena remains unique.

In this chapter we examine the impact of environmental inequality on California Latinos. California is in the midst of a dramatic demo-graphic transformation, with the state's minority population growing from 22% of the total in 1970 to 44% in 1990. The California Depart-ment of Finance projects that by the end of the century, minorities will constitute over half of California's population (California Department of Finance, 1988). Latinos have comprised and will continue to consti-tute the largest minority population in the state, constituting 12% of the total population in 1970 and 26% in 1990. At this rate of increase, Latinos will make up one third of the state's population by the year 2000. Like most Californians, Latinos wish to live in a state abundant in clean air, fresh water, and pristine land. However, they face another issue: *Who* bears the costs of hazardous conditions and expensive cleanup? Latinos work in California's most hazardous jobs, live in California's most polluted neighborhoods, and shoulder a dispropor-tionate share of the costs associated with environmental regulations.

The remainder of this chapter is organized into four parts. The first part documents the economic roots of environmental inequality confronting California Latinos, the process through which the concentration of Latinos in low-wage jobs and the residential segregation of Latinos translate into higher environmental risks. The second part discusses the de facto disparate impact of "racially neutral" environmental policies on Latinos. This situation is not likely to change soon given the political disenfranchisement of Latinos. Third, we examine environmental politics through the controversy over growth control. Unless checked, the environmental racism embedded in some growth control movements has the potential to reinforce the existing racial hierarchy. The chapter concludes with a general discussion of the production of racial inequality.

ECONOMIC ROOTS
OF ENVIRONMENTAL INEQUALITY

The environmental problems of Latino communities are rooted in California's persistent economic segmentation, a segmentation defined along racial lines and heightened by economic restructuring. This segmentation determines the life chances of minorities. Contemporary racial inequality results from historical racism and the institution of new discriminatory practices that maintain and perpetuate a long legacy of injustice. Latinos are more likely than nonminorities to find themselves at the bottom of the economic ladder employed in low-status occupations and living in low-income neighborhoods, two visible manifestations of our system of racial stratification. Racial segregation in the labor and housing markets form the basis for inequalities in the degree of exposure to environmental hazards.

Racial inequality is part and parcel of the recent widening gap between the haves and have-nots, a gap which has been documented both nationally (Harrison & Bluestone, 1988) and in Los Angeles (Research Group on the Los Angeles Economy, 1989). Economic restructuring produces disproportionately more jobs at the high and low ends of the wage distribution, with far fewer jobs in the middle-income range, particularly in manufacturing. As most Latinos are excluded from employment in the high-wage sector because of the lack of education, limited English-language skills, and discrimination, many remain trapped in low-wage jobs or become completely alienated from the

Table 9.1 California Economic Status by Ethnicity

	1969	*1979*	*1987*
Poverty Rates			
NH White	8.6%	7.6%	7.6%
Latino	19.5%	18.8%	25.4%
African Americans	25.4%	22.7%	22.2%
Asians/Others	12.8%	11.2%	19.8%
Median Family Income			
NH White	34,400	36,800	38,300
Latino	22,000	22,900	23,600
African Americans	24,800	25,000	23,000
Asians/Others	31,000	35,100	37,100

SOURCE: U.S. Bureau of the Census, CPS (1988), PUMS (1970, 1980).
NOTE: Income data adjusted to 1987 dollars.

formal labor market. As a result, the poverty rates of Latinos remain high and income inequality persists, as reflected in the historical data on California's poverty rates and median family income (Table 9.1). By both measures, Latinos have fared substantially worse than non-Hispanic whites (NH whites) declining in economic status during the eighties. Although immigration has contributed to this deterioration, studies indicate that even U.S.-born Latinos have lost ground during this period (Forsyth, 1989; Ong & Morales, 1992; Van Houten, 1989).

Racial inequality manifests itself in the labor market. Latino workers are more likely to be employed in menial jobs and less likely to be employed in management and professional jobs than NH whites, African Americans, and Asians (Table 9.2). Latinos earn approximately one

Table 9.2 Occupational Distribution (in percent)

	Management/Professional	*Menial*	*Others*
NH White	33	8	59
Latino	10	35	55
African Americans	19	13	68
Asians/Others	27	15	58

SOURCE: U.S. Bureau of the Census, CPS (March 1988).
NOTE: Menial category includes private household workers, farm laborers, operators and assemblers, and laborers.

third less than NH whites and experience an unemployment rate twice as high as that for NH whites. Differences in educational attainment and training account for part of the racial gap, reflecting inequalities in our public education system. At the same time, Latinos earn wages below those of NH whites with comparable levels of education and labor market experience, suggesting the impact of discriminatory practices on income (Ong, 1990; Van Houten, 1989).

Racial differences are also the cause of California's segregated neighborhoods. Although Latino segregation is less severe than the segregation of African Americans, more than a majority of Latinos would have to relocate to achieve full housing integration (Farley, 1987b). In Los Angeles, home to the largest Latino population in the United States, Latinos have grown more segregated over time, becoming by one measure the most racially isolated group in the area (Ong, Lawrence, & Davidson, 1991). Housing segregation, however, is not merely a product of the lower economic status of Latinos. Housing segregation is reinforced by cultural differences and by the social networks that incorporate Latinos into the economy. Immigrants, who are a majority of Latinos, depend on the services and employment system available in ethnic enclaves (Dagodag, 1984; Garcia, 1985).

Poor Latinos are further isolated into poor neighborhoods and thus suffer from both racial and class segregation. In Los Angeles, low-income areas are predominantly a minority phenomenon (Ong, 1989). Among poor NH whites in 1980, only 1% lived in poverty areas (where 40% or more of the residents lived below the poverty line), and another 18% lived in poor areas (where 20%-39% of the residents lived below the poverty line). The respective figures are 5% and 54% for Latinos. The net result is that many of the poor and poverty neighborhoods of Los Angeles are Latino neighborhoods.

Racial inequality in employment and housing forms the basis for other forms of inequality. For example, residential segregation produces the uneven quality of education. In Los Angeles County, students from low-income, Latino communities receive a poor education and experience higher dropout rates than their counterparts in affluent, NH white communities (Castellanos, Echavarria, & Galindo, 1989). This educational inequality severely handicaps children, thus perpetuating economic inequality across generations.

Racial inequality in employment and housing also engenders disparities among individuals and communities who assume the consequences of environmental degradation. Limited employment opportunities and

Table 9.3 Job Hazard by Ethnicity in California, 1988

	Industrial	*Occupational*
NH White	7.5	0.66
Latinos	9.3	1.28
African Americans	7.6	0.92
Asians/Others	7.6	0.68

NOTE: The estimates of industrial and occupational risks were developed by merging individual data from the 1988 Current Population Survey with hazard rates from the Bureau of Labor Statistics. The industrial rates are the number of injuries and illnesses per 100 full-time workers; the occupation risks are the weighted averages of the occupational hazard index, which is the percent injured divided by the percent employment.

restricted residential mobility result in the disproportionate exposure of Latino workers and communities to pollution and other environmental hazards. Specifically, Latinos more than NH whites work in hazardous conditions, breathe contaminated air, and live in close proximity to toxic waste dumps. Latino workers experience more work-related hazards, including occupational diseases due to exposure to dangerous chemicals (see review by Robinson, 1989; see also Friedman-Jimenez, 1989). According to the National Safe Workplace Institute (1988), the deadliest jobs in the United States are in agriculture, construction, mining, transportation, and manufacturing. Our analysis of the 1988 Current Population Survey shows that 28% of California's NH whites and 47% of Latinos are employed in these five industries.[1] The greatest concentration of Latinos occurs in durable and nondurable goods manufacturing, where 27% of Latino workers are employed.

Table 9.3 reports industrial and occupational risk rates by ethnicity in California.[2] The figures indicate that Latinos, more than the other three groups, are concentrated in industries and occupations with higher job hazards. Studies of individual industries or specific types of poisoning confirm that Latinos work at a significantly higher risk than other groups of workers. In agriculture, where Latinos comprise a majority of the migrant and seasonal farm workers, workers are exposed to high levels of pesticides known to produce chronic illness, such as cancer, adverse reproductive outcomes, and delayed neuropathy and neurobehavioral effects (Moses, 1989). In addition, Latinos are disproportionately exposed to industrial lead poisoning. An analysis of California's lead poisoning registry shows that persons with Spanish surnames are overrepresented, accounting for 44% of the registrants (Alexander,

1989). These findings are confirmed in a study conducted by the California Department of Health Services that indicates excessive lead exposure in workers in a few high-risk occupations; 44% of the exposed employees were Latino (Roan, 1990).

In addition to job hazards, Latinos are more likely to be exposed to environmental hazards in their communities. Minority neighborhoods have served as dumping grounds for solid waste. A report by the Commission for Racial Justice concludes, "Communities with the greatest number of commercial hazardous waste facilities had the highest composition of racial and ethnic residents" (United Church of Christ, 1987). Within California, the report demonstrates that Latinos in cities throughout the state are significantly more likely to live in communities with hazardous waste sites. In Los Angeles, 35% of whites and 60% of Latinos live in communities with waste sites. In Oakland, the respective percentages are 24% and 69%.

As with the employment patterns, the siting of toxic waste facilities arises from both economic and institutional forces. Latinos live in areas where land values are low, thus these communities are financially attractive to firms and public agencies seeking sites for the disposal of hazardous materials. In addition, Latinos have fewer opportunities to move away from environmentally hazardous neighborhoods, because of limited economic resources and housing discrimination. But the location of hazardous waste sites cannot be explained by economic differences alone. In fact, the racial composition of the neighborhood is the most important predictor of whether a community contains a hazardous waste site—the greater the percentage of minorities, the higher the probability of a toxic site (United Church of Christ, 1987).

Residential segregation not only results in greater exposure to hazardous wastes, but also to higher levels of air contaminants. Latinos live in communities where air pollution is worse than in NH white neighborhoods. According to one estimate for the South Coast air basin (the greater Los Angeles area), 50% of Latinos reside in areas with the most polluted air, whereas only 34% of NH whites do (South Coast Air Quality Management District [SCAQMD], personal communication, January 19, 1990). It appears that the environmental situation for Latinos has deteriorated in recent years. Forty-six percent of minority respondents to the Southern California Social Survey (1988) state that pollution was worse at the time of the interview than 5 years earlier.

Latinos are more exposed to lead in paint and water because of poor housing, more exposed to the externalities generated by increased traffic because they live in close proximity to heavily congested free-ways, and more exposed to the stresses of high-density living. These employment and residential problems only begin to scratch the surface of the health and environmental crisis facing California's Latinos. California's Latinos, therefore, have a vital interest in promoting a safer and healthier environment.

These environmental problems have not escaped the attention of Latinos, and are slowly emerging as major concerns. For most Latinos, environmental problems are still less pressing concerns than the myriad of economic and social ills they face. In a 1987 *Los Angeles Times* survey that asked respondents to name the most important issue in Los Angeles, 11% of NH whites mentioned the environment, whereas only 6% of Latinos did. Proportionately more minorities identify economic problems, crime, and drugs as major issues, an understandable pattern given their more precarious economic position and the state of their neighborhoods. This is not to say that Latinos are against environmental programs. When Southern California residents were asked about gov-ernmental expenditure on environmental problems, 76% of NH whites and 78% of nonwhites, a fair proportion of whom were Latinos, stated that more should be spent (SCSS, 1988). And for the segment of the Latino population that faces extremely high risks, environmental con-cerns now outweigh economic concerns. In a study conducted by agri-cultural economists and social science researchers at California State University, Fresno, 33% of agricultural workers, predominantly Lati-nos, identified "pesticides" as the most serious problem faced by farm workers, 23% identified "low wages," 8% other "work hazards," and 4% "abusive labor contractors" (Alvarado, Riley, & Mason, 1990).

DISPARATE POLICY IMPACTS

Like other states, California faces a number of critical environmental hazards that seriously threaten the quality of life for residents—poor air quality, traffic congestion, adverse effects of rampant growth, offshore oil drilling, toxic waste dumps. To solve these environmental problems, indi-viduals and communities have increasingly intervened in the operation of the free market; state intervention in the form of government regulation and "populist" movements in the form of grass roots environmental and slow growth initiatives attempt to redirect our environment.

Many of the proposed policies and programs to lessen or eliminate environmental problems can benefit society as a whole by improving the "commons," but they will be costly. A well-designed policy prevents firms and individuals from freely passing on the environmentally damaging consequences of their actions. Whether we alter these undesirable actions through regulation or by pricing mechanisms that force agents to internalize the cost of their actions, the transition to a cleaner world will be disruptive and expensive. The efforts to improve environmental quality are justified because California will be a better place in which to live. But we must consider the distribution of the costs and benefits of environmental policies and growth control measures. Latinos can potentially gain from policies to improve the environment, but the same forces that situate them in marginal economic positions also position Latinos at a greater risk from the adverse impacts of environmental and growth control measures. Although the policies and programs may officially be "race blind," they nonetheless have disparate impacts across social groups.

We can begin to understand the equity problems of current policies by examining the effort to improve air quality. The drive to achieve clean air is one facet of the environmental crisis that has been highly institutionalized, both in legislation (the Clean Air Acts of 1970, 1977, and 1990) and in the establishment of local regulatory agencies, the single-purpose air districts.

Studies of the South Coast Air Quality Management District's (SCAQMD) Tier I requirements for stationary pollution and additional studies on the employment of Latinos and Latino firms suggest that air quality regulations disproportionately affect the jobs and businesses of Latinos more than those of NH whites. Latinos have a more difficult time adjusting to economic disruptions; they are less likely to capitalize improvements in the environment; they are more susceptible to economic downturns; and finally, they lack the political clout to influence the formation of public policy.

Implementation of the SCAQMD Tier I requirements for stationary pollution sources is likely to displace workers in industries in which Latino workers are overrepresented, such as furniture manufacturers, auto body and paint shops, metal finishing, and other industries that use chemical solvents.[3] The level of displacement that will occur as a result of these requirements is a matter of debate; the estimates are sensitive to underlying assumptions regarding the capability and willingness of firms to adopt the required technology, and the propensity of firms to relocate their businesses to escape stricter local standards. One study estimates that there will be less than a 1% drop in employment in the industries and occupations where minorities are overrepresented (Planning Institute, 1988). A competing study estimates the loss of approximately 62,000 jobs in metal products and 45,000 jobs in furniture manufacturing (S. Padilla, 1990), which represent about 9% and 11% respectively of the total employment in those two industries (calculated from base employment data from the California Employment Development Department, 1989). Although there exists a sizable difference between the two estimates, it is likely that the actual impact of air quality regulations lies somewhere between the two, resulting in a significant number of dislocated workers.

Although there has been no substantial analyses on the secondary impacts of environmental regulations on Latinos, an extensive literature exists documenting the effects of economic dislocation on Latinos. In general, Latino men are displaced at a higher rate than all other groups of workers (Hamermesh, 1987). During periods of economic disruption, Latinos also suffer larger losses in earnings than other racial or ethnic groups. For example, Latinos who were displaced from Silicon Valley's high-technology industries suffered losses in earnings that were twice as large as those for NH whites; this was true after accounting for differences in age, previous occupation, gender, and prior earnings (Ong, 1991).

Job displacements associated with environmental regulations will likely produce the same racial outcomes described above. Latino workers will be laid off at a higher rate because of their overrepresentation in the industries most affected by environmental regulation and because of their economically marginal position in the labor market. Unemployed Latinos will have a difficult time finding new employment and will experience substantial losses in wages. Unless mitigated, the impact of environmental policies, then, may well reproduce and reinforce existing racial inequality.

In periods of economic decline, studies suggest that the fate of Latino-owned firms will parallel that of Latino workers. The small size of minority firms indicates that they are less well capitalized and more marginal than firms of NH white owners; thus minority firms are less able to absorb or pass along the additional costs of regulatory compliance. In 1982, the most recent year for which there are data, only 16% of Latino-owned firms in California were large enough to have employees.

Even among firms with employees, Latino-owned firms are smaller than average. Table 9.4 lists the average number of employees and

Table 9.4 Firm Averages in California, 1982

	Manufacturing		Services	
	Employees	Sales	Employees	Sales
Latino	13.3	0.582	4.0	0.161
All Firms*	42.1	4.193	9.0	0.394
All Firms**	48.1	NA	12.3	NA

SOURCE: U.S. Bureau of the Census (1984, 1984-1985, 1986).
* Based on County Business Patterns.
** Based on Census of Manufactures and Census of Services. Sales in millions of dollars; based on firms with employees.

average annual sales in two industries that are likely to be directly affected by new environmental regulations. In manufacturing, average employment per minority firm was only one third of the average for all firms in the state, and average sales per minority firm was only one eighth of that for all firms in the state. The averages for minority firms in the service sector are closer to the averages for all firms, but are nonetheless only a fraction of that for all firms in the state. Small Latino firms are hardly the type of businesses that can easily accommodate the extra costs required for pollution controls. Their problems are compounded by the fact that Latino firms have less access to financial capital than NH white firms, even after accounting for differences in personal characteristics (Bates, 1989).

The bias of environmental policies extends to the beneficiaries of improvements in air quality. It will be impossible to restore our air to a pristine state. Even the most ambitious plan will not eliminate air pollution, but merely lower the contaminant level. SCAQMD's projections show that after the implementation of air quality regulations, there will still be geographic areas with much higher than average levels of pollution (1989). Although many Latino neighborhoods will experience substantial improvements, there is no reason to believe that today's Latino residents will be able to retain the benefits of cleaner air. We know that the desirability and dollar value of urban sites are influenced by the level of air pollution. As the air clears and land prices increase, it is questionable whether Latinos, many of whom are renters, will be able to capture the benefits of cleaner air. Instead, they may be forced to pay higher rents or be displaced by a gentrification induced by environmental improvements.

The bias in environmental policies, as represented by the above example in the air quality area, will not likely be eliminated soon. The question of who will be hurt and who will benefit from public policy decisions is ultimately a political one. Technical knowledge can guide us toward effective and efficient measures, but fundamental policies should be made by citizens and their elected officials because the choices involve significant trade-offs between competing goals, generate substantial disruptions, and produce enormous benefits. Ideally, the decision-making process will provide everyone a meaningful voice so that the outcome will be fair. Greater democratic participation would enable Latinos to take proactive positions and would force policymakers to address the issues that confront Latino neighborhoods.

REPRESSIVE GROWTH CONTROLS

The difficulties with traditional regulatory and electoral politics have contributed to the emergence of populist environmental activities. One of the most controversial elements of environmental politics centers around the issue of growth control. Growth control is an approach that is not directed toward eliminating any particular pollutant, but rather as a means of preventing environmental problems from becoming worse. Growth control limits or precludes new activities that would generate additional externalities and that would further tax natural resources.

The number of growth control measures enacted throughout California exploded in the late 1980s, growing from an average of fewer than 30 a year at the beginning of the decade to nearly 150 in 1988 (Glickfeld & Levine, 1990, p. 144). In the late eighties, a majority of the enacted growth control measures came through ballot initiatives, a tool widely used by the populist movement among Californian voters to counter what they perceive as a failure of local and state government to govern adequately. As impressive as the statistics are, the numbers underestimate the strength of the growth control movement because they do not include efforts by community groups to control development by tightening zoning and other land use regulations at the neighborhood level. The number of successes is not known, but these actions undoubtedly have contributed greatly to the overall effectiveness of the slow-growth and no-growth movement.

Table 9.5 California Unemployment and Earnings

| | March Unempl Rates | | | Annual Mean Earnings | | |
	1982	1988	Change	1982	1987	Change
NH Whites	8.2	3.9	−4.3	24.2	27.0	+12%
African Americans	14.2	9.8	−4.4	17.2	20.8	+21%
Latinos	15.7	8.2	−7.5	15.7	17.2	+ 9%
Asians/Others	7.9	5.6	−2.3	20.2	22.8	+13%

SOURCE: U.S. Bureau of the Census, CPS (1982, 1983, 1988).
NOTE: Unemployment rates are calculated for all those who were active in the labor market, either working or actively looking for employment. Wages reported in 1987 dollars × 1,000 for workers between the ages of 24 and 65 with at least $1,000 in wages.

Growth control creates a dilemma for Latinos. Economic restructuring has made Latinos increasingly dependent upon economic growth for jobs and decent wages. The dilemma is rooted in a link between economic growth and the employment status of Latino workers. Their status improved during the last expansionary period, as indicated by the unemployment rates and annual wages reported in Table 9.5. (Nineteen eighty-two was a recessionary year, and 1987 and 1988 were expansionary years.) The racial hierarchy does not disappear over the business cycle because NH whites also experience lower unemployment and earn higher wages during peak business periods. Even in the best of times, Latinos are two times more likely to be unemployed as NH whites, and Latinos earn only 64 cents for every dollar earned by NH whites. Moreover, there is no guarantee that growth will produce meaningful employment opportunities for Latinos. As we noted earlier, industrial jobs with decent wages were a major avenue of upward mobility for minorities, but can no longer serve this function. Nonetheless, the persistency of racial inequality does not negate the fact that many Latino workers are dependent on economic growth, in this case short-run growth, for better employment opportunities.[4] Growth lessened but failed to eliminate the hardship.

The problem of limited economic gains from growth is compounded by the negative impacts of growth. The cost of living has been pushed up by the escalation of housing costs. In Los Angeles, rents have increased faster than the Consumer Price Index, and the supply of low-rent housing has declined (Ong, 1989). Growth also generates enormous externalities in the form of more air pollution. As we have argued earlier, Latinos bear a disproportionately larger share of the additional externalities.

Despite the problems of growth, Latino dependency on economic growth has made many Latinos leery of growth control, as can be seen in opinion polls. Results of from the 1989 Field poll indicate that "Blacks (67%) and other minorities (72%), comprised primarily of Latinos, were more favorably disposed toward future commercial growth in their communities than whites and Asians (both 59%)" (LeGates, 1989, p. 12). A similar difference in attitudes was reported in a 1987 *Los Angeles Times* poll: 45% of NH whites disagreed with Mayor Bradley's progrowth position, whereas only 25% of Latinos did (*Los Angeles Times*, 1987).

Not all growth control measures, however, need to be regressive. The 1986 Proposition M in San Francisco is a case in point. The fairness of this initiative rests in part on the fact that development had provided few benefits to minorities. The expansion of high-rise downtown office buildings disrupted surrounding low-income neighborhoods and failed to expand employment and housing opportunities for minority residents. More important, the proposition contained provisions that directly tied land use decisions to the creation of blue-collar jobs, affordable housing, and neighborhood preservation. As a result of both these factors, Proposition M garnered the support of middle-class, African-American, and Latino voters (DeLeon & Powell, 1988).

Unfortunately, Proposition M is the exception rather than the norm. At the other extreme, growth control politics is being coopted by reactionary forces to implement social control. Some proposed policies are not overtly racist, but nonetheless would have a de facto impact on Latinos. This is particularly true for the growing movement for "population stabilization," which includes organizations ranging from the zero population growth people to mainstream environmental groups. Because much of the population growth in California has come from Latinos, population controls, if rigidly enforced, would slow the "Hispanization" of the state's population.

The danger of growth control politics being used as social control goes deeper than the actions of a few organizations. This danger, embedded in the attitudes of NH whites, is the key to this problem. Their feelings toward a growing Latino population have been ambivalent at best. An analysis of the 1982 California Field Poll shows that nearly three quarters of NH whites believe that immigration to California, which is the major source of growth among Latinos, should be decreased. The same poll indicates the level of public concern centered around undocumented aliens, with nearly all NH whites (96%) stating that the problems caused by illegal immigration are either very serious or somewhat serious. This is not to deny that Latino immigration, legal and illegal, contributes to the state's economy. In the February 1988 California Field Poll, a large majority of the NH white sample (73%) agreed with the statement that the growing number of Latinos is providing labor to fill new jobs. But approximately three quarters also felt that a growing Latino population is also creating unemployment, increasing the number of people anxious to work hard, and increasing crime. Consequently, whatever positive opinions regarding Latinos exist, they are offset by negative sentiments.

Growth politics has taken on a social control aspect aimed at precluding certain classes of people from some communities. Forty-four percent of NH whites in the April 1989 California Field Poll acknowledged that "the concern about having too many minorities in their community" is either a very important or somewhat important factor in motivating people to favor slowing growth, and that 63% thought that "the concern about having too many lower income people in their community" is either a very important or somewhat important motivating factor. Growth controls are de facto, if not de jure, ways to promote racial and economic segregation.

Much of the exclusionary element of social control is being played out at the very local level in the form of NIMBYism (Not In My Backyard), a growing form of grass roots protest against growth and environmental problems at the neighborhood level. Although NIMBYism has surfaced in a broad cross section of communities, including in Latino communities, there are major racial differences in its form. NIMBYism in Latino communities is a struggle against the historical and existing practice of locating obnoxious facilities in neighborhoods that are economically and politically weak. For example, the Mothers of East Los Angeles (MOELA), an active, well-respected, Latino community organization on Los Angeles's eastside, is organizing to stop the siting of the Vernon Hazardous Waste Incinerator, which threatens the safety of their community (Pansing, Rederer, & Yale, 1989). NIMBYism in white affluent communities is a fight to preserve their privileged status. The disparate objectives of minority and NH white communities is reinforced by disparities in the technical, economic, and political resources, which translate into systematic differing abilities of each group to achieve its goals and objectives. When NIMBY politics degenerates into one of governing the location of the problem rather than eliminating its causes, low-income Latino neighborhoods will on the average lose.

CONCLUDING REMARKS

Although this chapter focuses on environmental problems facing Latinos in California, it also sheds light on the broader phenomenon of the generation of social inequality during times of economic restructuring. Of the many injustices in this country, racism has been one of the most enduring and pernicious (Omi & Winant, 1986). Several of the chapters in this volume examine the subordination of Latinos in the labor market. For us, this entails a process of reproduction because labor market inequality is in part an institutional inheritance, historical discriminatory employment practices that have been adapted to the contemporary setting and graphed onto an increasing polarized economic structure. In a very real sense, the forces that now disadvantage Latino workers existed in much earlier times. Economic restructuring since the 1970s has not generated market forces to undermine the institution of racism, but instead has generated market forces that have made racial practices useful in allocating workers into the disparate economic segments and in filling the demand for cheap labor.

The analysis of environmental issues reveals how social inequality is generated in an emerging economic and political arena where racist practices and values must be created, or at least rearticulated. The formation of inequality in the environmental arena should not be surprising because environmental problems are embedded in the larger socioeconomic structure. At a very abstract level, the production of a new form of inequality is a transplanting of preexisting social and economic inequalities to a new arena, a process that propagates racial injustice throughout society. Consequently, the groups most economically marginalized, such as Latinos and other minorities, are also the groups most exposed to environmental hazards.

Given the social embeddedness of the environment, we should not be surprised that environmental politics is far from being racially neutral. The "color-blind" policies are inherently biased against communities of color. Differences in economic and political resources across racial groups generate parallel differences in the distribution of the benefits and burdens of these policies. We have the makings of a tragic outcome because "benign neglect" of the adverse impacts of policies constitutes an acquiescence of the processes that reproduce and reinforce racial inequality. Equally important, environmental politics provides a platform for the groups within the dominant population to push for new forms of social controls in the form of population stabilization and

Table 9.6 California's Population by Voting Status, 1986 (in percent)

	Population	Eligible	Voters
NH White	62	75	81
Latinos	22	12	8
African Americans	7	7	7
Asians/Others	9	6	4

SOURCE: U.S. Bureau of the Census, CPS (November 1986).
NOTE: Eligible includes U.S. citizens, 18 years and older.

exclusionary residential regulations. The unfortunate lesson is that the daily operations of our basic institutions recreate racial inequality.

Although racial inequality in the environmental arena is a predictable outgrowth of our societal structure, this form of inequality should not be dismissed as an unimportant epiphenomenon. Given the extensive harm to people's health and quality of life, and the continued deepening of the environmental crisis, the problems facing Latinos in the environmental arena will become as important as the problems in the areas of employment, housing, education, and health care. Environmental inequality is an inescapable aspect of modern racial inequality in the United States. The material reality makes the environmental arena a major contestable terrain in the struggle for racial justice.

The struggle is political. Unfortunately, as of this writing in 1992, Latinos do not have a viable political voice statewide or within cities. Although they are an increasing proportion of California's population, the political system dilutes the significance of their numbers (Table 9.6). Latinos comprised approximately one quarter of the state's population in 1986 but less than 8% of the state's voters and only 6% of the state's elected officials (Guerra, cited in Clifford, 1990). On the local level, until the recent election of a Latina, the Los Angeles County Board of Supervisors was entirely NH white though one half of its constituency are minorities. In Huntington Park, nearly 90% of the population is Latino, yet until April 1990 every city councilmember was NH white. Latinos are also underrepresented on the emerging regional institutions that influence and shape environmental and growth policies. The governing board of the SCAQMD, for example, is entirely NH white; and although there are minorities on the board of directors for the San Francisco Bay Area AQMD, they constitute a small minority.

Without a meaningful voice in politics, Latinos have little access to influencing the issues that affect their communities.

The fight for environmental justice is no different from the struggle for other forms of racial justice. The ends are the same—the elimination of racism in its many forms. Many of the means are also the same—organizing at the grass roots, promoting participatory politics, building coalitions with other minority groups, advocating for progressive policies, and electing officials who represent minority communities. At the same time, the emergence of environmentalism as a Latino and minority issue is redefining social activism. The changes may not all be positive. There is a danger that this issue can dilute Latino activism by diverting scarce resources away from what some see as more fundamental economic and political struggles. To preclude this, Latinos (and other minorities) find ways to integrate environmentalism into their traditional concerns over jobs, housing, basic services, and political rights. Just as environmental inequalities are embedded in society's larger system of racial inequality, Latino and minority environmentalism must be embedded in the larger struggle for racial justice. The integration, however, is not simple. Merely adding a demand for fairness in environmental policies to the list of other demands is not enough. We must develop a fuller understanding of the web of causal relationships between the environmental sphere and other spheres, and use that understanding as a guide to formulating alternative policies.

NOTES

1. These statistics are for the working population surveyed in March 1988.

2. Although these statistics represent *all* job accidents, they are likely to correlate with exposure to chemical-related illnesses.

3. The South Coast Air Quality Management District (SCAQMD) adopted a comprehensive plan to attain federal air quality standards in the Los Angeles Basin. The first series of regulations includes 120 measures designed to control the use of coatings and solvents; the production, refining, and distribution of petroleum and gas; industrial and commercial processes; residential equipment and public services; agricultural sources; other stationary sources; motor vehicles, transportation systems, and land use; and other mobile sources.

4. It should be noted that minorities are also more vulnerable to economic downturns, suffering from a disproportionate share of the unemployment and lost income during a recession.

10

Critical Theory and Policy
in an Era of Ethnic Diversity:
Economic Interdependence
and Growing Inequality

Frank Bonilla
Rebecca Morales

The economic and social reversals of the last two decades have, paradoxically, left Latinos in strategic positions, both as key protagonists in global, regional, and local restructuring and as informed critics of the intellectual and policy discourse elicited by these new realities. For Latinos, objective placement at the active frontiers and shifting boundaries of key social processes has imposed heavy costs but has also given impulse to a thoughtful questioning of prevailing orthodoxy, academic and political. As Latino voices challenged reigning theory and depictions of changes under way, glaring omissions, costly simplifications, and tacit concessions to things as they are in the main body of research and policy debate have been exposed (H. D. Romo, 1990).

Latinos, for example, have been quick to grasp the renewed pertinence of transnational economic and political processes in fixing new parameters for U.S. as well as Latin American economic development. With this goes an appreciation of the centrality of cooperation along with competitive capability in assuring a constructive role for the United States in promoting its own economic growth along with that of its neighbors. The idea of interdependence, which for many in the United States connotes loss of hegemony and privilege, enters more readily into a Latino worldview searching for greater reciprocity and more balanced power over decisions that necessarily transcend national boundaries and capabilities.

As prototypical immigrants and mobile labor reserves, Latinos also have a very practical fix on the crucial significance of access to jobs and adequate incomes as the foundations of a sense of community and social cohesiveness. Whether as a consequence of the narrowness of alternative social supports, more modest wage expectations, or the survival of traditional values, Latinos, especially recent immigrants from Mexico and Central America, manifest a readiness to work for wages at and below U.S. poverty standards that has been invoked by some in questioning the applicability to them of the underclass concept (Moore, 1988). Logically, and as our results confirm, the structure of labor demand and associated wage scales weigh heavily on social outcomes for this population. In fact, policy issues bearing on job generation and job quality, the regulation of rights in work and access to employment for all workers, citizens or not, work-related language rights, and protection against job hazards—all loom large in the Latino research and advocacy agenda (National Council of La Raza, 1990a). "Mainstream" research on Latinos and work, especially immigrants, has by contrast focused almost exclusively on whether Latinos compete unfairly with native, chiefly black workers, or depress working conditions and wage scales simply by their presence (Commission for the Study of International Migration and Cooperative Economic Development, 1990).

Latinos have long been painfully conscious of the ways in which the complex forces shaping U.S. stratification lock them out of the more rewarding job sectors. Having become in recent decades an overwhelmingly urban population, Latinos now also stand at the epicenter of social transformations that dramatize the social pathologies of big city decline. Beyond the misuse and underuse of human resources, urban fiscal distress, and the deterioration of physical and social infrastructures, lie more subjective concerns about social polarization, fragmentation, and the quality of city life (Berkman et al., 1992). For Latinos the bad news continues to come in. They are now reported to be the most discriminated against group in housing markets across the country (Lueck, 1991). Latino workers are also the most exposed to the severest job hazards (Kilborn, 1992). Yet, we begin to hear as well that newness to the society and social isolation may temporarily shield some Latinos, especially those freshly arrived, from the perverse effects of extreme poverty in postindustrial U.S. cities (Hayes-Bautista et al., 1988). Despite more modest human capital endowments, for example, Mexican immigrants in major cities are perceived by employers as more willing and disciplined low-wage workers than African Americans. Their stronger attachment to family and community are also said to protect the poverty areas in which they are clustered from the more destructive patterns of "underclass" behavior (Taub, 1991). New immigrants have been hailed not only for their willingness to fill the demand for low-wage service workers, but for their entrepreneurial energies in the informal economy and small enterprise (Waldinger, 1991). Recent immigrants, in contrast to settled blacks and Puerto Ricans, are now credited with producing for New York City "a low cost equivalent of gentrification" (Sassen, 1991).

There are complexities as well on the racial front. U.S. Census publications now routinely note that "Hispanic people can be of any race." This is, of course, chiefly a statistical signal that some double counting has been done. The statement nevertheless points to some challenging intricacies in the interaction of race and class in Latino communities and among those in the society at large who, at least by U.S. standards, are judged as less ambiguously defined racially. With the main body of social research and policy inquiry deeply immersed in untangling the balance of tensions between class interests as against race as sources of social polarization and conflict, the impulse to bypass or treat mechanically how Latinos fit into U.S. racialist norms has been pervasive, even among Latinos themselves. Yet the "Latinization" of major regions and cities has brought fresh dimensions into the "American dilemma" that will endure into coming decades, both drawing into alliance and pitting against one another elements of new and old minorities as well as former majorities (Bell, 1987; F. Bonilla, 1988; White, 1984). Contrasting patterns in this interplay, especially between Latinos and African Americans, make headlines around the country in places beyond those treated in this volume as well as in the nation's capital. Indifference or active opposition among African-American leaders and organizations is seen by some Latinos as contributing to persisting imbalances in Latino political representation, access to jobs and social services, and civil rights enforcement. Nevertheless, the urgency of the need to rise above divisive tendencies is acknowledged on both sides, and concrete initiatives to forestall potential ruptures figure in most public statements on the issue (Kamasaki & Yzaguirre, 1990).

In addition, although the 1980s proved to be a decade of significant reversals and sluggish advance in economic and social conditions for Latinos, modest but encouraging gains were registered in political representation at city, state, and federal levels. Though still less than 1% of all in the nation, the number of Latino elected officials doubled in the 1980s, reaching over 4,200 in 1990 (National Association of Latino Elected Officials, 1991). Advocacy groups gained in effectiveness and established a recognized presence at the national and regional levels. Litigation over civil rights—especially with regard to voting, immigration, and language issues—contributed to a clearer articulation and validation of Latino claims that foreshadow major adjustments of social relations, especially in our largest cities. All of these advances were undergirded by a substantial outpouring of fresh research drawing in large part on newly institutionalized public and private data keeping and research programs now staffed principally by Latinos themselves (Inter-University Program for Latino Research, 1992). As the constitutionally mandated redistricting processes for the 1990s get under way, Latinos are better situated than ever to play a meaningful role in these operations all around the country, both in those states where their growing numbers provide a base for larger congressional delegations (California, Arizona, Texas, Florida) and in those, such as New York, that have lost population despite a growing Latino presence (Mexican American Legal Defense and Educational Fund [MALDEF], 1992; Vidueira, 1992).

This account of ongoing changes that inform and provide a growing political thrust for Latino critical policy perspectives could be extended (e.g., Latino strides in the world of business, the community's growth as a consumer market, the proliferation of Spanish-language print and visual media). The point here is that these emergent capabilities, institutional resources, and political orientations have an immediate and objective grounding in the direct experience of ongoing major transformations in U.S. society in which Latinos are central actors. Theory building or policy formulation on *any* national concern that is not attentive to these emergent realities will inevitably fall short of intellectual and political objectives.

Social research, along with science in general, must satisfy cognitive, logical, historical, and social demands. U.S. social science now needs, perhaps more than ever, accounts of disciplined inquiry that highlight

the positive contribution to reasoned knowledge of the social component, including distinctive motivations and insights linked to ethnicity
and identities in multicultural national formations (Gooding, Pinck, &
Shaffer, 1989). Informed consensus and active participation on a broad
scale are perhaps even more fundamental to effective policy than to the
social legitimation of scientific results. Few aspects of human activity
are more demanding in this respect than the organization of productive
activity and the fixing of appropriate rewards for human effort. If our
research sets out to highlight structures and policies with respect to jobs
and wages, it must penetrate both to the active agents keeping these in
place. In this and other matters, policies not convincingly sensitized to
the needs and social contexts of targeted populations will continue to
be experienced as externally imposed subordination (F. Bonilla, 1991).

THE POLICY CONTEXT

This volume set out to document the particulars of the dynamic of
recent economic restructuring within the diverse regional contexts in
which Latinos figure prominently. Taken together, however, the chapters reveal as well an unexpectedly clear convergence in the course of
the eighties of the forces at work and main tendencies shaping labor
market outcomes in every region. With market and state on a downward
course on many fronts, the 1990s thus open as an acutely problematic
conjuncture for the framing of economic and social policy. The capacities of the very individuals, communities, organizations, and institutions that need to mobilize themselves or be mobilized in support of
viable policy solutions seem to be those most directly undercut and
rendered impotent or self-defeating by recent change (Goldsmith &
Blakely, 1991).

Although contention over the competitive standing of the United
States vis-à-vis such countries as Germany and Japan continued to
divide economists, 1991 forced acknowledgment that the United States
was in a genuine depression rather than in a state that could any longer
usefully be tagged as some intermediate state on the way to recovery
(Silk, 1991). Official unemployment figures, widely regarded as underestimates, pushed to 7.1% nationally and closer to 10% in several key
states: Illinois, 9.3%; Michigan, 9.1%; Massachusetts, 8.4%; New York,
8.1%; California, 7.7%; Florida, 7.3% (U.S. Bureau of Labor Statistics,
1992). A sharp increase in permanent layoffs between 1989 and 1991

shook white-collar and service sectors as widely publicized programmed dismissals in manufacturing and construction renewed anxieties on those fronts. According to official projections, levels of job growth attained between 1975 and 1990 are not expected to be matched between 1990 and 2005 (U.S. Bureau of Labor Statistics, 1991). The volatility of the new service economy also partly explains successive shortfalls around the country in projected tax collections of every sort (business, property, sales, and personal income). In many cities and states, debt and deficits have ballooned, further compromising public sector jobs, basic services, and infrastructure maintenance.

Parallel processes and conditions in the countries of origin of Latinos, now irreversibly intertwined with the forces generating economic crisis and social polarization in the United States, also converge to cast a distinctive stamp on the 1980s and the decade ahead. The UN Secretary General's 1988 report on the socioeconomic outlook for the world economy to the year 2000 provides a somber reading of the recent past and immediate future of trends in the hemisphere. Slow growth, stagnation, and further economic polarization are the dominant features of prospective development. Falling per capita incomes and standards of living are tied directly to the dynamic of an oppressive debt (then put at $1.2 trillion), the volatility of money markets, growing protectionism, and creditor-imposed austerity in public spending. Long neglect and waste of human resources and social infrastructures means that the situation has built-in, long-term effects that it will take decades to overcome (F. Bonilla, 1990, p. 82). Though the political relationships between the countries of origin of the three Latino peoples we have highlighted and the United States could hardly be more different, the underlying economic dynamic of North-South relations is essentially that described immediately above.

In the United States the stubborn resistance of White House officials, the political parties, and policy specialists to acknowledge the depth of the economic and social crisis at home and abroad, as well as its roots in structural changes shaped by deliberate policy and the privileging of corporate interests, have given unprecedented scope to a sense of gridlock and impotence beyond the economic arena. From early in the 1980s, a sense of impasse and ideological polarization in U.S. academic and policy circles has been routinely projected in the reports of technical and advisory bodies whose competence, probity, and political disinterest had rarely been challenged in earlier economically straitened or uncertain periods. The 1960s Kerner, Eisenhower, and Katzenbach commission reports are perhaps landmarks in this connection. Yet by 1984, Herbert Stein, probably the most thorough chronicler of the advice economists have provided to presidents since World War II, had this to say:

> Economists do not know enough even to say with much confidence and precision what the effects of different economic policies would be. Even if one is able to describe what effects are desired, he cannot be sure of the prescription or policy that would yield those effects. . . . Even if it were possible to identify the policy that would be best, or probably best, from the standpoint of most of the persons concerned, it might not be possible to get that policy adopted. (p. 323)

Nor do those speaking more recently from more global and techno-logical perspectives seem better prepared to approach the issues of the moment more confidently. A key element of any post-Cold War "peace dividend" might have been a shift of scientific concern from production for military defense and command of space toward a focus on produc-tivity to meet social needs within a global framework of interdepend-ence and pluralism. Yet the Harvard economist Raymond Vernon, ad-dressing a 1986 forum on world technologies and national sovereignty sponsored by the National Academy of Engineering, conveyed early on the reigning skepticism in this regard among scientists themselves:

> Upon identifying the main issues, one is propelled to a basic conclusion: Given the nature of the issues, better data and closer analysis are unlikely to have more than a marginal effect on the behavior of the U.S. government and other governments. *The problems are too large and too conjectural, and the domestic and international mechanisms too feeble to generate more than a marginal impact* [italics added]. (Guile & Brooks, 1987, p. 170)

In short, despite passing allusions to the growing problems of in-equality within and among nations and the urgency of arresting a decline in the real incomes of U.S. workers, there is little ethical or substantively reformist content in the ongoing debate within official circles about productivity, competitiveness, and the place of the United States in the world economy. Grave doubts about the shortness of vision, the efficacy of proposed remedies, and the political will to implement them dominate this discourse. Moreover, as we move more directly into the 1990s, the assertion, unheard in earlier crises, that the nation's wealthy and successful no longer feel genuine responsibility for the poor and marginalized, especially minorities and newcomers, is voiced from more diverse and respected quarters. Individuals in a position to know point to secessionist impulses among business elites now thoroughly cosmopolitan and rejecting the burden of any taxation or other claims on them by U.S. workers (A. Ehrenhalt, 1991; R. Reich, 1991). White working-class voters are said to have operationalized "capital's agenda of restructuring the U.S. economy at the expense of the working class, including *the white working class,*" by falling in with a white ruling-class strategy of appearing to be "hard on race and soft on class" (Kushnick, 1992; Roediger, 1991). "A politics purposively permeated by race has consolidated enough white Americans as a self-conscious racial majority," writes one sympathetic liberal observer. This white middle- and working-class voting bloc stands directly in the way of any racially or ethnically targeted social reform or services, even though, as the same observer notes, "This is not to say that they are bigots or reactionaries. It is rather that they are threatened, not always in ways they understand" (Hacker, 1992).

Heightened racial tensions directly implicate Latinos in forms of racial contention that are both familiar and alien. As in all cultures dominated by Europeans, Latinos have been schooled to experience blackness as a misfortune. Social pressures in the United States encourage at once both a distancing from African Americans and a merging of identities as "minorities" and "nonwhites." How these long-standing ambivalences are resolved in the coming decade will decisively mark the course of U.S. social relations.

Latinos thus enter the economic and political arenas in growing numbers, better informed and better organized to strive for a place and a voice in policy at a moment perhaps unique in this century. The challenges to market and state, the disjunctures between the political and the economic, the weight of external forces on the national economy, and the depth of class and racial polarization seem to have peaked at the very moment that the triumph of capitalism is hailed around the world (Heilbroner, 1989).

LATINO POLICY PERSPECTIVES

Context and conjuncture thus combine to place Latinos in a unique position that demands that they think and act creatively in the necessary bringing into being of both a national and hemispheric economic order that is at once more productive and more equitable. That is, of course, not the path on which current, presidential free trade designs are moving nor that favored by the Latin American governments in the forefront of these initiatives, notably Mexico. In that discourse, interdependence and integration now mean the privileged rather than the simply unfettered movement of capital and commodities, privatization of state enterprises, and further deregulation of the economy. They also mean, as has been noted, limited adjustments of a draining debt service, continued austerity in public spending, further volatility in money markets, and extended stagnation of incomes and living standards. In much of Latin America, development in this mode in the 1980s has come to symbolize capitalism at its most brutal and irrational (Branford & Kucinski, 1988; J. Brecher & Costello, 1991; George, 1988).

The present redeployment of development strategies in the fresh guise of free trade compacts occurs, thus, against the background of some somber and no longer much disputed realities at home and abroad. These are not the heady decades of Operation Bootstrap or the Alliance for Progress. Whatever the short-run outcome of the present economic downturn, the United States must itself still negotiate a range of unprecedented economic and political hurdles. These include, as has been seen, stagnant productivity and savings levels, massive indebtedness and deficits, a fiscal disarticulation among the several levels of government that has major cities on the verge of bankruptcy, increasing social inequality and absolute poverty, and rising racial and ethnic tensions permeating the entire society. These internal setbacks and failures of market and state necessarily raise serious doubts about the U.S. capacity to contribute to the development of productive forces in friendly countries and external dependencies. The overarching contraposition of social promise and denial in market systems figures profoundly in the recent historical experience of Latinos and in the long-term relations between their countries of origin and the United States.

The political scientist Frances Fox Piven has recently suggested that the 1930s depression paved the way for the partial emancipation and social advance of white, European immigrant workers, and the 1960s war on poverty served an equivalent function for many African Americans. The 1990s recession, in her view, should spark another surge of economic and social reforms more directly targeted on Latinos along with African Americans. Of course, as she notes, in those earlier crises reforms were substantially driven by the tumultuous demands of those most affected (Berkman et al., 1992, p. 53).

Lest the emphasis here on the potential transnational capacities and interests of Latinos overshadow their role within the United States, it is worth stressing once more the centrality, permanence, and assured growth of the Latino presence in the United States. Two thirds of the more than 12 million persons of Mexican origin in the United States are U.S.-born citizens, many with several generations of local forebears. Although these percentages are reversed for Puerto Ricans (that is, about two thirds of those on the mainland are island-born), the 2.5 million in the United States as well as the 3.5 million in Puerto Rico are U.S. citizens. The half million or so Cuban-origin persons in the country have one of the highest rates of naturalization among recent entrants. Poll evidence suggests that both Mexican- and Cuban-origin citizens are firmly rooted here and that even a regime change in Cuba would draw only a small proportion of the latter back to the island. In fact, in one view,

> When Castro falls, Miami will become the second city of Cuba, much closer to Havana and more densely settled by a variety of Cubans than Santiago or Camaguey and with commercial flows twenty times more intense. That future Cuba will have to do all within its reach (dual nationality, academic reciprocity, genuine hospitality and human warmth) so that Miami Cubans (*miacubanos*) may strengthen their ties to their country of origin. (Montaner, 1992)

Puerto Ricans seem more disposed than other Latinos to move freely between island and mainland locales, but these remain technically internal changes of residence within U.S. territories (de la Garza & Falcon, 1992).

In short, internationalization is setting in motion new flows of worker circulation that start out as temporary but generate conditions in which families and whole communities are compelled to anchor economic survival simultaneously in more than one national space. The outlook for the hemispheric economy suggests that the forces driving migration toward the United States will persist and probably intensify in the coming decade. The present pace and diversification of Latino demographic growth (10 times that of non-Hispanic whites and 4 times that of African Americans) means in the long run a substantial expansion of Latinos permanently settled here and in a position to act politically on individual and group interests.

Two features of that political affirmation are worth emphasizing here. As reported by the Mexican American Legal Defense and Educational

Fund's Leadership Program, 1991 proved to be a pivotal turning point in the affirmation of Latino political rights:

> Equipped with the latest technological hardware, the practical understanding of the complex redistricting process, and an understanding of their voting rights, Latinos waged their most important battle for equal representation at all levels of government. (MALDEF, 1992)

Second, all stocktaking of political advances in the 1980s threw into sharp relief the vanguard role of Latinas in the gains achieved in both elected and appointive positions. Women were prominent not only in traditional fields such as education and social work but in the legal and medical professions, in fiscal and economic development posts, in city and state legislative bodies, and in the full gamut of advocacy and community-based organizations promoting Latino concerns and their projection in the mass media, cultural production, and academic research.

A LATINO POLICY AND RESEARCH AGENDA

The reach and thrust of the decisive entry of Latinos into the U.S. policy arena in the 1990s is well exemplified by the recent activities of the National Hispanic Leadership Agenda (NHLA). This coalition of Hispanic organizations and individuals undertook an ambitious project in 1991 aimed at producing a national agenda for Hispanics building on public hearings in 14 U.S. cities between September 1991 and March 1992 (National Hispanic Leadership Agenda, 1992). Calling on Latino community leaders, elected officials, scholars, and policy specialists to unite around a program providing Latinos "a clearer vision and stronger voice" in national policy, NHLA invited testimony in five issue areas. Timed for an election year in which the Latino vote might plausibly prove a swing factor in several locales, this exercise promises to mark a historical benchmark (NALEO Educational Fund, 1992). The NHLA hearing themes, identified through an extensive review of earlier Latino policy initiatives, provide a useful reference point for a summary of some research and policy implications of the work presented in this volume. Though our findings bear unevenly on NHLA's announced agenda, they may help to pinpoint the magnitude and complexity of the challenges and opportunities facing Latinos and the United States as a whole in the coming decade. NHLA themes include: economic opportunity, education, empowerment and civil rights, health, and housing.

Economic Opportunity. A considerable body of research and policy analysis concurrent with that in this volume confirms the substantial weight of structural changes in shaping labor market outcomes for U.S. Latinos. Macro shifts in labor demand are now shown to have had negative impacts during economic upturns as well as periods of decline (De Freitas, 1991, pp. 125, 161; Meléndez, 1993; Tienda, Cordero, & Donato, 1991). Most such work also confirms the continuing significance of human capital attributes as well as discrimination in the contemporary treatment of distinctively marked pools of labor. The historical sketches provided here of successive episodes in the incorporation of Latino workers, especially in San Antonio and Chicago, add some depth and sense of continuity concerning the operation of these processes.

More elusive in this body of work is a pressing beyond the vague abstraction of "structures" to the practices and policies as well as social agents that transform these structures and channel their effects. As the Miami instance demonstrates, when the political demand and will are in place, the necessary supports can be provided to accommodate newcomers and partially shield them from the shocks of displacement and risks of unequal exploitation. More important, as the sense of economic crisis has deepened and reaches more directly into middle America, ideological and policy postures prevailing during the 1980s are coming into question. The Family Support Act of 1988 and some polls taken around the time of its enactment showed a public more open to support for the poor. Yet according to numerous key analysts, a combination of factors—budget deficits, distrust of government, and rage at the "underclass"—stood in the way of any national program based on targeting and an enlarged role for government in job creation or social services (Weir, Orloff, & Skocpol, 1988). However apparent it may be that without targeting, sustained economic growth and liberalized social supports will still leave social groups aligned pretty much in keeping with their present endowments, these observers argued that the only viable strategy for aiding the minority poor was for very low profile targeting under an ideological cloak of universalism. These considerations, of course, bore chiefly on racial targeting and did not even address the barriers to targeting for Latinos.

By 1992, however, white rage seemed to be shifting toward government and party inaction as well as the technocratic and authoritarian impulses underlying economic strategies that mandate incentives and maximum freedoms for entrepreneurs and greater effort with reduced rewards for workers. There were even murmurs of a coming liberal turn-around. Serious work affirming economic rights to decent jobs and income is surfacing along with concrete designs for full employment programs that seek to document their cost-effectiveness and capacity to stimulate growth in present economic and political conditions (Harvey, 1992; Wyckle, More-house, & Dembo, 1992). Full-employment legislation that languished in the Congress throughout the 1980s is being linked to and recharged within broader initiatives demanding renewed responsiveness to the needs of major cities at the federal level. Despite the political advances that have been noted, however, Latinos remain on the sidelines of these emergent movements. Latino "invisibility" and contradictory myths about our political leanings—Latinos voters are locked into Democratic party machines; Latinos are traditionally conservative and will gravitate toward Republican agendas—feed into the complacency of politicians and intellectuals on the right and left about our absence in these circles (NALEO, 1992, p. 24). Breaking this isolation and establishing a presence and voice on these many fronts is a major undertaking for the 1990s.

One consequence of the low Latino profile in the burgeoning move-ments for economic rights and urban redevelopment is the marginal consideration given to international dimensions of trade, investment, and people flows in the main body of these initiatives, with separate arrays of actors taking on the challenges of globalization of the econ-omy and hemispheric interdependence. The U.S.-Mexico free trade agreement, the renewed call in the Congress for a final definition of the Puerto Rican status issue, the need to frame a new relation with a Cuba no longer tied to the Soviet Union, the restoring of peace and a chance for economic stability and democracy in Central America are only the most immediate of the pressing international issues in which U.S. Latinos have major stakes and responsibilities. Grasping the essential unity and centrality of these seemingly disparate and potentially divi-sive concerns poses yet another challenge in the theorization of the Latino condition and the future of hemispheric economic integration on more principled and egalitarian grounds. Here as well, emergent move-ments now driven principally by labor organizations, environmental-ists, religious groups, and others concerned with immigrant rights clamor for informed involvement by U.S. Latinos together with their counterparts in Latin America (Brecher & Costello, 1991).

Education. As the national data in Chapter 2 show, modest and uneven gains in schooling among the several national-origin Latino groups failed to close the gaps in educational attainment between them and non-Hispanic whites. Evidence of unequal returns in earnings for roughly equivalent levels of education also suggest perceived or objective differences in the quality of schooling or school performance. Fiscal crises across the country heighten the pressures toward unequal outcomes reflected in dropout rates and difficulties in school to job transitions, especially for those not going beyond high school. Compensatory programs of all kinds become the first targets of rationalizers of austerity measures, with the most powerful backlash probably directed now at bilingual education and diversification of curricula. Despite the legal sanctions supporting the former, English Firsters rail against instruction in any other language. Tribalism, separatist designs, a naive inflation of foreign cultural accomplishments are among the milder misdemeanors imputed to the self-serving professionals said to have burdened their communities with unwanted obstacles to quick assimilation (Gutmann, 1992). Moralizing liberals and conservatives, assuming the mantle of national unity, true universalism, and cultural cosmopolitanism propagandize on a massive scale against any effort to preserve native language skills or cultural traditions within the framework of the school system. Ironically, the most extensive survey data recently gathered on the subject show that Latinos of all national origins are (a) predominantly bilingual; (b) commonly use both English- and Spanish-language media, with a moderate tilting toward the former; (c) overwhelmingly support bilingual education, which they see as a path to bilinguality that contributes to cognitive skills valuable to the United States (De la Garza & Falcon, 1992). Next to the generation of jobs worth having, access to effective, high-quality schooling remains the most indispensable resource for individual and collective negotiation of place within an increasingly complex and volatile economy.

Empowerment and Civil Rights. Latino strides on the political front in the course of the 1980s have already been noted. A surge in the number of elected officials, a strengthening of advocacy groups, successful litigation around civil rights, and effective participation in redistricting processes on the heels of the 1990 Census evidence new capabilities. Effective empowerment will require much more by way of self-study and policy analysis. Efforts toward voter mobilization and coalition building, leadership and candidate development and monitoring, efficient generation and deployment of research at every level of national and international government all remain in an embryonic state. If as some allege, voters are fed up with laissez-faire, it is now time on this as on other fronts to move from solidly grounded critiques to concrete steps and designs for change.

Health and Housing. Detailed examination of these issues was not central to the research undertaken here. Still, their importance has been brought home at various points—with respect to the spatial deployment of jobs and residential patterns, and in the revealing chapter by Ong and Blumenberg on the place of environmental hazards in social inequality (Chapter 9). In the course of this research federal studies have established that Latinos are among the most discriminated against groups in housing markets and the most poorly served by the health service system. In the latter instance as in others, concern has now shifted from "folk illness models," concerned with cultural barriers to health care utilization, to a generalized awareness that the nation's health care system as a whole is in deep trouble. Fortunately, Latino health care providers are among the best organized and capable professional sectors in our communities and well poised to advance research and enter into movements for reform in the field.

At its 20th anniversary conference in 1992, the National Association for Chicano Studies reaffirmed its research mission in terms that should resonate for all those engaged in disciplined inquiry with emancipatory social objectives:

> We recognize that mainstream research, based on an integrationist perspective which emphasized consensus, assimilation, and the legitimacy of societal institutions, has obscured and distorted the significant historical role which class conflict and group interests have taken in shaping our existence as a people to the present moment. Our research efforts are aimed at directly confronting the structures of inequality based on class, racial, and sexist privileges in this society. . . . Dominant theories, ideologies and perspectives play a significant part in maintaining structures of inequality. It is imperative that Chicano scholars struggle against these structures on a theoretical as well as on a policy level. . . . Since ideas can point to possible directions for our people, they are of fundamental importance in defining and shaping our future. (Cordova, 1992)

Latinos thus enter the 1990s positioned to talk to one another as well as to natural allies in both more scientifically informed and politically conscious ways. To prove effective, the critical perspectives and organized research infrastructure developed over the past 20 years must remain as demandingly focused on our own work as on that we would like to redirect or complement. There is no point in replacing a system of knowledge production that has served us so poorly with a second-rate clone.

References

Acuna, R. (1984). *A community under siege: A chronicle of Chicanos in East of the Los Angeles River, 1945-1975.* Los Angeles: Chicano Studies Research Center, UCLA.

Addison, J. T., & Portugal, P. (1987). The effect of advance notification of plant closing on unemployment. *Industrial and Labor Relations Review, 42,* 3-16.

Alba, R. (1984). *The impact of migration on New York State.* State University of New York.

Alexander, D. (1989, March). Chronic lead exposure. *AAOHN Journal, 37*(3), 105-108.

Alvarado, A. J., Riley, G. L., & Mason, H. O. (1990). *Agricultural workers in central California in 1989* (A report from a study by the California State University, Fresno for the California Employment Development Department).

Alvarez, R. (1985). The psycho-historical and socioeconomic development of the Chicano community in the United States. In F. B., C. Bonjean, R. Romo, R. Alvarez, & R. de la Garza (Eds.), *The Mexican-American Experience: An interdisciplinary anthology* (pp. 920-942). Austin: University of Texas Press.

Año Nuevo Kerr, L. (1976). *The Chicano experience in Chicago: 1920-1970.* Unpublished doctoral dissertation, Graduate College, University of Illinois at Chicago.

Applebaum, E., & Schettkat, R. (1989, July). Employment and industrial restructuring: A comparison of the U.S. and West Germany. In E. Matzner (Ed.), *No way to full employment?* (Research Unit Labor Market and Employment, Discussion Paper FSI 89-16, pp. 394-448).

Argüelles, L. (1982, Summer). Cuban Miami: The roots, development and everyday life of an emigré enclave in the U.S. national security state. *Contemporary Marxism, 5,* 27-43.

Bach, R. L., & Meissner, D. (1990). *America's labor market in the 1990's: What role should immigration play?* Washington, DC: Carnegie Endowment for International Peace.

Bailey, T. (1990). Black employment opportunities. In C. Brecher & R. Horton (Eds.), *Setting municipal priorities 1990.* New York: New York University Press.

Ballinger, K. (1936). *Miami millions: The dance of the dollars in the great Florida land boom of 1925.* Miami, FL: Franklin Press.

Banco Nacional de Cuba. (1960). *Memoria 1958-1959.* Havana: Editorial Lex.

Barnet, R. J. (1990, July 16). Reflections: The age of globalization. *The New Yorker.*

Barrera, M. (1979). *Race and class in the southwest: A theory of racial inequality.* South Bend, IN: Notre Dame University Press.

Bates, T. (1989). Small business viability in the urban ghetto. *Journal of Regional Science,* *29*(4), 625-643.

Baumol, W. (1989). Is there a U.S. productivity crisis? *Science, 243*(2891), 611-615.

Bean, F. D., & Tienda, M. (1987). *The Hispanic population of the United States.* New York: Russell Sage Foundation.

Becker, G. (1975). *Human capital: A theoretical and empirical analysis, with special reference to education.* New York: National Bureau of Economic Research, distributed by Columbia University Press.

Bell, D. (1987). The world and the U. S. in 2013. *Daedalus, 116*(3), 1-31.

Bell, L., & Freeman, R. B. (1987, May). The facts about rising industrial wage dispersion in the U.S. *Proceedings,* Industrial Relations Research Association.

Bergman, E., & Goldstein, H. (1983). Dynamics and structural change in metropolitan economics. *American Planning Association Journal, Summer,* 263-279.

Bergmann, B. (1974, April/May). Occupational segregation, wages and profits when employers discriminate by race or sex. *Eastern Economic Journal, 1,* 103-110.

Bergmann, B. (1986). *The economic emergence of women.* New York: Basic Books.

Berkman, R., Brown, J. F., Goldberg, B., & Mijanovich, T. (Eds.). (1992). *In the national interest: The 1990 urban summit.* New York: Twentieth Century Fund Press.

Bienstock, H. (1977). New York City's labor market. *City Almanac, 12*(4).

Bluestone, B., & Harrison, B. (1982). *The deindustrialization of America: Plant closings, community abandonment, and the dismantling of basic industry.* New York: Basic Books.

Bluestone, B., Stevenson, M. H., & Tilly, C. (1992). *An assessment of the impact of "deindustrialization" and spatial mismatch on the labor market outcomes of young white, black, and latino men and women who have limited schooling.* The John McCormack Institute of Public Affairs, University of Massachusetts—Boston.

Blumberg, P. (1981). *Inequality in an age of decline.* New York: Oxford University Press.

Bogen, E. (1987). *Immigration in New York.* New York: Prager.

Bonilla, F. (1988, January 18). *From racial justice to economic rights: The new American dilemma.* Dr. Martin Luther King, Jr., Birthday Celebration, Smithsonian Institution, Washington, DC.

Bonilla, F. (1990). Migrants, citizenship and social pacts. *Radical America, 23*(1), 81-89.

Bonilla, F. (1991, January 26). *Building a Hispanic research agenda: Participants, processes, pitfalls* (Presentation at King's Legacy: Our Unfinished Agenda, A Commemerative Symposium, University of Michigan).

Bonilla, F., & Campos, R. (1981, Spring). A wealth of poor: Puerto Ricans in the new economic order. *Daedulus, 110,* 133-176.

Bonilla, F., & Campos, R. (1986). *Industry and idleness.* New York: Centro de Estudios Puertorriqueños, Hunter College, CUNY.

Bonilla, F., & Torres, A. (1989). *Latinos in a changing regional economy: New York.* New York: Center for Puerto Rican Studies.

Bonilla, R. C. (1983). *Escritos económicos.* Havana: Editorial de Ciencias Sociales.

Borjas, G. (1990). *Friends or strangers: The impact of immigrants on the U.S. economy.* New York: Basic Books.

Borjas, G. J., & Tienda, M. (Eds.). (1985). *Hispanics in the U.S. economy.* Orlando, FL: Academic Press.

Bouvier, L. F., & V. M. Briggs, J. (1988). *The population and labor force of New York: 1990-2050.* Washington, DC: Population Reference Bureau.

Branford, S., & Kucinski, B. (1988). *The debt squads: The U.S., the banks and Latin America.* New Jersey: JED.

Brecher, C., & Horton, R. D. (Eds.) (1989). *Setting municipal priorities 1990*. New York: New York University Press.

Brecher, C., & Tobier, E. (1977). *Economic and demographic trends in New York City: The outlook for the future*. New York: Temporary Commission on New York City Finances.

Brecher, J., & Costello, T. (1991). *Global village vs. global pillage: A one world strategy for labor*. Washington, DC: International Labor Rights Education and Research Fund.

Browning, H., & Singelman, J. (1978). The transformation of the U.S. labor force: The interaction of industry and occupation. *Politics and Society, 8*, 481-509.

Burtless, G. (1991). *Trends in the distribution of earnings and family income: Effects of the current recession*. Testimony for the Senate Budget Committee.

California Department of Finance. (1988). *Projected total population for California by race/ethnicity*. Sacramento: Population Research Unit.

California Department of Industrial Relations. (various years). *Urban Labor in California*.

California Employment Development Department. (1989, June). *Annual planning information, Los Angeles-Long Beach*.

California Employment Development Department, Bureau of Labor Statistics. (various years). *Employment and Earnings*.

Cardoso, F. H., & Faletto, E. (1979). *Dependency and development in Latin America*. Berkeley: University of California Press.

Carnoy, M., Daley, H., & Hinojosa, R. (1989). *The changing economic position of Hispanic and Black Americans in the U.S. labor market since 1959*. Stanford University: Inter-University Program in Latino Research.

Carnoy, M., Daley, H., & Hinojosa Ojeda, R. (1990a). *The changing economic position of Latinos in the U.S. labor market: 1939-1989*. New York: Inter-University Project for Latino Research.

Carnoy, M., Daley, H., & Hinojosa Ojeda, R. (1990b). *Latinos in a changing U.S. economy: Comparative perspectives on the U.S. labor market since 1939*. New York: Research Foundation of the City University of New York.

Carter, D. J., & Wilson, R. (1992). *10th annual status report on minorities in higher education*. Washington, DC: American Council on Education.

Castellanos, E., Echavarria, L., & Galindo, Y. (1989). Educational inequality. In *The widening divide: Income inequality and poverty in Los Angeles*.

Castells, M. (1989). *The informational city*. London: Blackwell.

Castells, M., & Portes, A. (1989). World underneath: The origins, dynamics, and effects of the informal economy. In A. Portes, M. Castells, & L. Benton (Eds.), *The informal economy: Studies in advanced and less developed countries*. Baltimore, MD: Johns Hopkins University Press.

Catalano, J. (1988). *The Mexican Americans*. New York: Chelsea House.

Caughey, J. (1973). *To kill a child's spirit: The tragedy of school segregation in Los Angeles*. Itasca, IL: F. E. Peacock.

Center for Advanced International Studies. (1967). *The Cuban immigration, 1959-1966, and its impact on Miami-Dade County, Florida* (A study conducted for the Department of Health Education and Welfare, HEW WA 66 05). Coral Gables: University of Miami, Research Institute for Cuba and the Caribbean.

Center for Advanced International Studies. (1969). *Psycho-social dynamics in Miami* (Report of a summer study conducted for the Department of Housing and Urban Development, HUD H 983). Coral Gables: University of Miami.

Center for Puerto Rican Studies. (1986). *Characteristics of persons, families and households living in New York City*. New York: City University of New York, Hunter College.

Center on Budget and Policy Priorities. (1988). *Shortchanged: Recent developments in Hispanic poverty, income and employment.* Washington, DC.

Centro de Estudios Puertorriqueños. (1979). *Labor migration under capitalism: The Puerto Rican experience.* New York: Monthly Review Press.

Chapa, J., & Cardenas, G. (1991). *The economy of the urban ethnic enclave* (Lyndon B. Johnson School of Public Affairs Policy Research Project Report No. 97). University of Texas at Austin.

Chiswick, B. R. (1978). The effect of Americanization on the earnings of foreign-born men. *Journal of Political Economy, 85*(5), 897-922.

City of New York Commission on Human Rights. (1989). *Tarnishing the golden door.* New York: Commission on Human Rights.

Clifford, F. (1990, May 7). Barriers for power to minorities. *Los Angeles Times,* Sect. A.

Cohen, S. S., & Zysman, J. (1987). *Manufacturing matters: The myth of the post-industrial economy.* New York: Basic Books.

Columbia University. (1987). *The informal economy and low-income communities in New York City.*

Commercial Club of Chicago. (1984). *Make no little plans.* Chicago: R. R. Donnelly.

Commission for the Study of International Migration and Cooperative Economic Development. (1990). *Unauthorized migration: An economic development response.* Washington, DC.

Community Service Society. (1987). *Poverty in New York City: 1980-1985.* New York: Community Service Society.

Community Service Society. (1989). *Worlds apart: Housing, race/ethnicity and income in New York City, 1978-1987.* New York: Community Service Society.

Community Service Society. (1991). *The New York fiscal crisis: Establishing priorities to protect the quality of life.* (Working Paper). New York: Community Service Society.

Cordova, T. (Ed.). (1992). *Chicano studies: Critical connection between research and community.*

Cortina, R. J., & Moncada, A. (1988). *Hispanos en los Estados Unidos.* Madrid: Ediciones de Cultura Hispanica.

Corwin, A. F. (1978). Causes of Mexican migration to the United States: A summary view. In D. Fleming & B. Bailyn (Eds.), *Perspectives in American history.* Cambridge, MA: Charles Warren Center for Studies in American History.

Cross, H. E., & Sandos, J. A. (1981). *Across the border: Rural development in Mexico and recent migration to the United States.* University of California, Institute of Governmental Studies.

Dagodag, W. T. (1984). Illegal Mexican aliens in Los Angeles: Locational characteristics. In *Patterns of undocumented migration: Mexico and the United States* (pp. 199-217). Totowa, NJ: Rowman & Allanheld.

Daniels, P. W. (1985). *Service industries.* London: Methuen.

De Freitas, G. (1991). *Inequality at work: Hispanics in the U.S. labor force.* New York: Oxford University Press.

de la Garzia, & Falcon, A. (1992). *Identity, policy preferences and political behavior: Preliminary results from the Latino National Political Survey.* New York: Latino National Political Survey.

DeLeon, R., & Powell, S. S. (1988, October). *Growth control and electoral politics in San Francisco: The victory of Proposition M in 1986* (Working Paper No. 3).

Denison, E. (1979). *Accounting for slower economic growth: The U.S. in the 1970's.* Washington, DC: Brookings Institute.

Drennan, M. (1988, June 11-13). *Deconstruction of the New York economy* (Prepared for a meeting of the Dual City Working Group).

Edgewood Independent School District v. Kirby. (1988).

Ehrenhalt, A. (1991). *The United States of ambition.* New York: Random House.

Ehrenhalt, S. M. (1987). *Looking to the 1990's: Continuity and change.* New York: U. S. Bureau of Labor Statistics, Middle Atlantic Region.

Ellwood, D. T. (1986). The spacial mismatch hypothesis: Are there teenage jobs missing in the ghetto? In R. B. Freeman & H. J. Holzer (Eds.), *The black youth employment crisis.* Chicago: University of Chicago Press.

Enchautegui, M. E. (1990). *Geographical differentials in the socioeconomic status of Puerto Ricans: The role of migration selectivity and labor market characteristics* (PSC Report #90-188).

Escobar, E. J., & Lane, J. B. (Eds.). (1987). *Forging a community: The Latino experience in northwest Indiana, 1919-1975.* Chicago: Cattails.

Fainstein, N. I. (1987). The underclass/mismatch hypothesis as an explanation for black economic deprivation. *Politics and Society, 15*(4), 403-451.

Fainstein, S., Fainstein, N., Hill, R. C., Judd, D., & Smith, M. P. (1986). *Restructuring the city: The political economy of urban redevelopment* (rev. ed.). New York: Longman.

Farley, J. E. (1987a, April). Disproportionate black and Hispanic unemployment in U.S. metropolitan areas. *American Journal of Economics and Society, 46*(2), 129-150.

Farley, J. (1987b). Segregation in 1980: How segregated are America's metropolitan areas? In G. A. Tobin (Ed.), *Divided neighborhoods: Changing patterns of racial segregation.* Beverly Hills, CA: Sage.

Feagin, J. R. (1985). The global context of metropolitan growth: Houston and the oil industry. *American Journal of Sociology, 90,* 1204-1230.

Federal Reserve Bank of New York. (1981, Summer). *Quarterly Review.*

Federal Reserve Board. (1992, January). Changes in family finances of 1983 to 1989: Evidence from the Survey of Consumer Finances.

Fernandez-Kelly, M. P., & Garcia, A. M. (1986). *Advanced technology, regional development, and Hispanic women's employment in Southern California.*

Fogelson, R. M. (1967). *The fragmented metropolis: Los Angeles 1850-1930.* Cambridge, MA: Harvard University Press.

Forment, C. A. (1989, January). Political practice and the rise of an ethnic enclave: The Cuban-American case, 1959-1979. *Theory and Society, 18,* 47-81.

Forsyth, A. (1989). Immigration and economic assimilation. In *The widening divide: Income inequality and poverty in Los Angeles.*

Freedman, M. (1983). The labor market for immigrants in New York City. *New York Affairs, 4,* 94-111.

Freeman, R. (1976). *Black elite.* New York: McGraw Hill.

Freeman, R. B., & Holzer, H. (1986). The black youth employment crisis: Summary of findings. In *The black youth employment crisis.* Chicago: University of Chicago Press.

Friedman-Jimenez, G. (1989, February). Occupational disease among minority workers. *AAOHN Journal, 37*(2), 64-70.

Friedmann, J., & Salguero, M. (1988). The barrio economy and collective self-empowerment in Latin America. In M. P. Smith (Ed.), *Power, community and the city.* New Brunswick, NJ: Transaction Books.

Garcia, P. (1985). Immigration issues in urban ecology: The case of Los Angeles. In *Urban ethnicity in the U.S.: New immigrants and old minorities* (pp. 73-100). Beverly Hills, CA: Sage.

Garofalo, G., & Fogarty, M. S. (1979). Urban income distribution and the Urban Hierarchy-Inequality Hypothesis. *Review of Economics and Statistics, 61,* 381-388.

George, S. (1988). *A fate worse than debt: The world financial crisis and the poor.* New York: Grove.

Georges, E. (1984). *New Immigrants and the political process: Dominicans in New York.* New York: Center for Latin American and Caribbean Studies, New York University.

Ginzberg, E., & Vojta, G. (1981, March). The service sector of the U.S. economy. *Scientific American, 244,* 48-55.

Glazer, N. (1988). The new New Yorkers. In P. D. Salins (Ed.), *New York unbound.* New York: Basil Blackwell.

Glickfeld, M., & Levine, N. (1990). The relationship between local growth controls and production of affordable housing: A California case study. In *Regulatory impediments to the development and placement of affordable housing* (Hearings Before the Sub-Committee on Policy Research and Insurance, Committee on Banking, Finance and Urban Affairs, House of Representatives).

Glickman, N. J., & Glasmeier, A. K. (1989). The international economy and the American South. In L. Rodwin & H. Sazanami (Eds.), *Deindustrialization and regional economic transformation: The experience of the United States.* Winchester, MA: Unwin Hyman.

Glickman, N., & Wilson, R. (1985). *The emerging economic base and local development policy issues in the Austin-San Antonio corridor* (Lyndon B. Johnson School of Public Affairs Policy Research Project Report No. 71). Austin: University of Texas.

Goldsmith, W. W. (1992). *Separate societies: Poverty and inequality in U.S. cities.* Philadelphia: Temple University.

Goldsmith, W., & Blakely, E. J. (1991, February). *Generations of poverty: America's underclass as an economic and political dilemma* (Monograph 39). University of California, Institute of Urban and Regional Development.

Gooding, D., Pinck, T., & Shaffer, S. (Eds.). (1989). *The uses of experiment.* New York: Cambridge University Press.

Grasmuck, S. (1984). Immigration, ethnic stratification and native working class discipline: Comparisons of documented and undocumented Dominicans. *International Migration Review, 18,* 3.

Greenwood, M. J., & McDowell, J. M. (1986, December). The factor market consequences of U.S. immigration. *Journal of Economic Literature, 24,* 1738-1772.

Grier, E. S., & Grier, G. (1988, March). *Minorities in suburbia: A mid-1980's update* (Report of the Urban Institute Project on Housing Mobility). Washington, DC.

Guile, B. R., & Brooks, H. (Eds.). (1987). *Technology and global industry.* Washington, DC: National Academy Press.

Gutierrez, M. (December, 1988). Desaliento y esperanza: La comunidad Dominica en Manhattan. *Arieto.*

Gutmann, P. M. (1979). Statistical illusions, mistaken policies. *Challenge, 22,* 5-13.

Gutmann, S. (1992). The bilingual ghetto: Why New York schools don't teach immigrants English. *City Journal, 2*(1), 29-39.

Hacker, A. (1992). *Two nations: Black and white, separate, hostile, unequal.* New York: Scribner.

Hamermesh, D. (1987). *What do we know about worker displacement in the U.S.?* (Working Paper No. 2402).

Hanson, C., & Falcon, A. (1992). *Latinos and the redistricting process in New York City.* New York: Institute for Puerto Rican Policy.

Hanushek, E. (1981). *Sources of black-white earnings differentials.* Stanford University, Institute of Educational Finance and Governance.

Harrison, B. (1988, December). *Individual wages and the growth of the black middle class.* Paper delivered to the Winter Meetings of the Allied Social Science Associations (combined session of the Industrial Relations Research Association and the National Economic Association), New York City.

Harrison, B., & Bluestone, B. (1987). *The dark side of labour market 'flexibility': Falling wages and growing income inequality in America* (Labour Market Analysis and Employment Planning Working Paper No. 17).

Harrison, B., & Bluestone, B. (1988). *The great u-turn: Corporate restructuring and polarization of America.* New York: Basic Books.

Hartmann, H. (1981). *Women, work and wages.* Washington, DC: National Academy Press.

Harvey, P. (1992). Employment as a human right. In W. J. Wilson (Ed.), *Sociology and the public agenda.* New York: Russell Sage.

Hauser, P. M. (1981). The census of 1980. *Scientific American, 245,* 53.

Hawley, C. T., Long, J., & Rasmussen, D. W. (1978). Income distribution, city, size and urban growth. *Urban Studies, 15,* 1-7.

Hayes-Bautista, D., Schink, W. O., & Chapa, J. (1988). *The burden of support: Young Latinos in an aging society.* Stanford, CA: Stanford University Press.

Heilbroner, R. (1988). The coming meltdown of traditional capitalism. *Ethics and International Affairs.* New York: Carnegie Council on Ethics and International Affairs.

Heilbroner, R. (1989). Reflections: The triumph of capitalism. *The New Yorker.*

Hernández, R. (1989). Notes on the incorporation of Dominican workers in the New York labor market. *Punto 7 Review, 2*(1).

Hill, R. C. (1989). Comparing transnational production systems: The case of the automobile industry in the United States and Japan. *International Journal of Urban Reg Res, 13*(3), 462.

Hinojosa Ojeda, R. (1989). *The political economy of north-south interdependence: Debt, trade and class relations across Mexico and U.S.* Unpublished doctoral dissertation, University of Chicago.

Hirsch, B. (1982). Income distribution, city size and urban growth: A re-examination. *Urban Studies, 19,* 71-74.

Hoffman, A. (1974). *Unwanted Mexican Americans in the great depression: Repatriation pressures, 1929-1939.* Tucson: University of Arizona Press.

Hoffman, A. (1978). Mexican repatriation during the great depression: A reappraisal. In A. F. Corwin (Ed.), *Immigrants—and immigrants' perspectives on Mexican labor migration to the United States.* Westport, CO: Greenwood.

Hughes, M. A. (1987). Moving up and moving out: Confusing ends and means about ghetto dispersal. *Urban Studies, 24,* 503-17.

Inter-University Program for Latino Research (IUP). (1992). *The inter-university program for Latino research 1988-1991.* New York: Author.

Jaynes, G. D., & Williams, R. M., Jr. (Eds.). (1989). *A common destiny.* Washington, DC: National Academy Press.

Johnston, W. (1987). *Workforce 2000.* Indianapolis, IN: Hudson Institute.

Kamasaki, C., & Yzaguirre, R. (1991, September). *Black-Hispanic tensions: One perspective.* Paper presented for the 1991 convention of the American Political Science Association.

Kasarda, J. D. (1985). Urban change and minority opportunities. In P. E. Peterson (Ed.), *The new urban reality.* Washington, DC: Brookings Institute.

Kasarda, J. D. (1988). Jobs, migration and emerging urban mismatches. In J. Michael, G. H. McGeary, & L. E. Lynn (Eds.), *Urban changes and poverty.* Washington, DC: National Academy Press.

Kasarda, J. D. (1989, January). Urban industrial transition and the underclass. *Annuals of the American Academy of Political and Social Science, 501,* 26-47.

Kennickell, A., & Shack-Marquez, J. (1992, January). Changes in family finances of 1983 to 1989: Evidence from the Survey of Consumer Finances. *Federal Reserve Board Bulletin.* Washington, DC.

Kilborn, P. T. (1992, February 28). For Hispanic immigrants, a higher job-injury risk. *New York Times,* p. A1.

Kirstein, P. N. (1977). *Anglo over bracero: A history of the Mexican worker in the United States from Roosevelt to Nixon.* San Francisco: R & E Research Associates.

Kiser, G. C., & Kiser, M. W. (Eds.). (1979). *Mexican workers in the United States: Historical and political perspectives.* Albuquerque: University of New Mexico Press.

Kolbert, E. (1991). Senator pothole. *New York Times Magazine, 6*(28), 1.

Kushnick, L. (1992). The construction of a racialized working class. *Sage Race Relations Abstracts.*

Larson, T. (1990, Fall). *Hispanic employment by the County of Los Angeles.* Unpublished manuscript, Los Angeles.

Lawrence, R. Z. (1984, Fall). Sectoral shifts and the size of the middle class. *Brookings Review.*

Ledebar, L. C. (1991). *City fiscal distress: Structural, demographic and institutional causes.* Washington, DC: National League of Cities.

LeGates, R. T. (1989, September). *Public opinion gridlock on California growth issues* (Working Paper No. 89-16).

Leonard, J. S. (1986). Comment on David Ellwood's: The Spatial Mismatch Hypothesis. In R. B. Freeman & H. Holzer (Eds.), *The black youth employment crisis.* Chicago: University of Chicago Press.

Levy, F. (1987). *Dollars and dreams: The changing American income distribution.* New York: Sage Foundation.

Levy, F. (1988). *Dollars and dreams: The changing American income distribution.* New York: Norton.

Levy, F., & Murnane, R. J. (1992, September). U.S. earnings levels and earnings inequality: A review of recent trends and proposed explanations. *Journal of Economic Literature, XXX,* 1333-1381.

Lieberson, S. (1980). *A piece of the pie: Blacks and white immigrants since 1880.* Berkeley: University of California Press.

Light, I., & Bonacich, E. (1988). *Immigrant enterprise.* Berkeley: University of California Press.

Linares, G. (1989). Dominicans in New York. *Centro, 2*(5).

Lipietz, A. (1986). New tendencies in the international division of labor: Regimes of accumulation and modes of regulation. In A. Scott & M. Storper (Eds.), *Production, work, territory.* Boston: Allen & Unwin.

Los Angeles County. (1988, February 5). *Affirmative action: Special report to the board of supervisors.* Office of Affirmative Action Compliance.

Los Angeles Times. (1987, June 13-17). L.A. Times Poll.

Lueck, T. J. (1991, November 3). U. S. study finds Hispanic minority most often subject to victimization. *New York Times,* p. R1.

MALDEF, see Mexican American Legal Defense and Educational Fund.

Maldonado, E. (1987). Contract labor and the origins of Puerto Rican communities in the United States. In E. J. Escobar & J. B. Lane (Eds.), *Forging a community: The Latino experience in Northwest Indiana, 1919-1975* (pp. 201-212). Chicago: Cattails.

Markusen, A. R. (1983). *High tech jobs, markets and economic development prospects* (Working Paper No. 403). Berkeley: University of California.

Markusen, A. (1987). *Region building: The politics and economics territory.* Totowa, NJ: Rowman & Allenheld.

Massey, D. (1983). *The demographic and economic position of Hispanics in the United States: The decade of the 1970's.* Washington, DC: National Commission for Employment Policy.

Massey, D. S. (1984). *Spatial divisions in labor.* London: MacMillan.

Massey, D., & Denton, N. Trends in residential segregation of blacks, hispanics, and Asians, 1970-1980. *American Sociological Review 52*(6), 802-825.

Matos Cintrón, W. (1980). *La politica y lo politico en Puerto Rico.* Mexico: Serie Popular Era.

Maume, D. S. (1983). Metropolital hierarchy and income distribution: A comparison of explanations. *Urban Affairs Quarterly, 18,* 413-429.

McCarthy, K., & Burciaga Valdez, R. (1985). *Current and future effects of Mexican immigration in California.* Santa Monica, CA: Rand Corporation.

McCrate, E. (1990, Spring). Labor market segmentation and relative black/white teenage birthrates. *Review of Black Political Economy, 18*(4), 37-53.

McDonald, J. F. (1984). *Employment location and industrial land use in metropolitan Chicago.* Champaign, IL: Stipes.

Mead, W. R. (1990). *The low-wage challenge to global growth.* Washington, DC: Economic Policy Institute.

Mead, W. R. (1991, April 14). Why the roller coaster only goes one way: Down. *The Los Angeles Times.*

Meléndez, E. (1987). *Vanishing labor: The effects of industrial restructuring on LFPR of Puerto Rican women in New York City.* Paper presented at the Conference on American Wages, Incomes and Public Policy, University of Massachusetts, Boston.

Meléndez, E. (1988). *Labor market structure and wage inequality in New York City: A comparative analysis of Hispanics, non-Hispanic blacks and whites.* Cambridge, MA: Massachusetts Institute of Technology, Department of Urban Studies and Planning.

Meléndez, E. (1993). Latino poverty in Massachusetts. In E. Meléndez & M. Uriarte (Eds.), *Latinos, poverty and public policy in Massachusetts.* Boston: University of Massachusetts Press.

Merrion, P. (1990, April 30). Manufacturing heads south. Mexico's maquiladoras lure local companies with cheap labor costs. *Crains Chicago Business.*

Mexican American Legal Defense and Educational Fund National Leadership Program. (1992, January). Latino participation in 1991 redistricting charts course for political empowerment. *Leading Hispanics, 6*(1).

Miller, R. J. (Ed.). (1983, November). Robotics: Future factories, future workers. *Annals of the American Academy of Political and Social Science*, p. 470.

Mincey, R. G. (1988). *Industrial restructuring, dynamic events and the racial composition of concentrated poverty.* Paper prepared for the SSRC, Comm.

Mishel, L., & Frankel, D. M. (1991). *The state of working America.* Armonk, NY: M.E. Sharpe.

Mohl, R. A., & Betten, N. (1987). Discrimination and repatriation: Mexican life in Gary. In E. J. Escobar & J. B. Lane (Eds.), *Forging a community: The Latino experience in Northwest Indiana, 1919-1975* (pp. 161-186). Chicago: Cattails.

Montaner, C. A. (1992, March 13). Pasion y destino de los Miacubanos. *El Nuevo Dia,* p. 59.

Montejano, D. (1987). *Anglos and Mexicans in the making of Texas, 1836-1986.* Austin: University of Texas Press.

Moore, J. (1988). *An assessment of Hispanic poverty: Does a Hispanic underclass exist* (Tomas River Center Report, 2, 1).

Moore, J. (1989, June). Is there an Hispanic underclass? *Social Science Quarterly, 70*(2), 265-284.

Morales, R. (1983, Winter). Transitional labor: Undocumented workers in the Los Angeles automobile industry. *International Migration Review, 17*(4), 570-596.

Morales, R. (1991, September). *Redefining borders: Labor migration and national sovereignty.* Paper presented at the Impact of the International Order on the Nation State, Cambridge, UK.

Morales, R. (1992). Transitional labor in the Los Angeles automobile industry. In W. A. Cornelius (Ed.), *The changing role of Mexican labor in the U.S. economy: Sectoral perspectives.*

Morales, R., & Mines, R. (1984). *San Diego full-service restaurants: A view from the back-of-the-house* (unpublished paper). Berkeley, CA.

Morales, R., Ong, P. M., & Payne, C. (1988). New entrants into the Los Angeles economy. In J. Fijalkowski (Ed.), *Transnationale Migration in der Arbeitswelt—Studien zur Auslaenderbeschaeftigung in der Bundesrepublik und zum Vergleich (Transnational migrants in the employment system—Studies on the employment of foreign workers in the Federal Republic of Germany and in international comparison).* Berlin: Rainer Bohn Verlag.

Morales, R., Ong, P. M., & Payne, C. (1990). New entrants into the Los Angeles economy. In J. Fijalkowski (Ed.), *Transnationale Migranten in der Arbeitswelt* (pp. 223-250). Berlin: Sigma Bohn.

Morales, R., & Tamayo, J. (1991). Urban development along the U.S.-Mexican border. In L. A. Herzog (ed.), *Changing boundaries of the Americas.* Boulder, CO: Westview.

Morales, R., & Tamayo, J. (1992, April). Urbanization and development of the United States-Mexico border. In L. A. Herzog (Ed.), *Changing boundaries in the Americas: New perspectives on U.S.-Mexican, Central American and South American borders* (Contemporary Perspectives Series, No. 4). La Jolla: Center for U.S.-Mexican Studies, University of California at San Diego.

Moses, M. (1989, March). Pesticide-related health problems and farmworkers. *AAOHN Journal, 37*(3), 115-130.

Muir, H. (1953). *Miami, U.S.A.* Coconut Grove, FL: Hurricane House.

Mullis, I., & Jenkins, L. (1990). *The reading report card, 1971-88.* National Assessment of Educational Progress (NAEP), Educational Testing Service for U.S. Department of Education. Washington, DC: Government Printing Office..

Murgia, E. (1975). *Assimilation, colonialism and the Mexican American people* (Mexican American Monograph Series No. 1). Austin: Center for Mexican American Studies, University of Texas.

Myrdal, G. (1944). *An American dilemma.* New York: Random House.

NACLA. (1992, July). *The NACLA report: Coming north: Latino and Caribbean immigration, xxvi*(1). New York: NACLA.

NALEO, see National Association of Latino Elected Officials.

National Association of Latino Elected Officials Educational Fund. (1992). *The Latino vote in 1992* (NALEO Background Paper #19).

National Center for Educational Statistics. (1988). *Digest of educational statistics 1988.* U.S. Department of Education.

National Center for Educational Statistics. (1990). *Digest of educational statistics 1990.* U.S. Department of Education.

National Center for Educational Statistics. (1991). *Digest of educational statistics, 1991.* U.S. Department of Education, Office of Educational Research and Improvement (NCES 91-697), Table 171.

National Council of La Raza. (1990a). *The decade of Hispanics: An economic retrospective.* Washington, DC.

National Council of La Raza. (1990b). Hispanic poverty: How much does immigration explain? *Proceedings from the National Council of La Raza's Poverty Project Roundtable.*

National Hispanic Leadership Agenda. (1992). *1992 Policy Summary.* Washington, DC.

National Safe Workplace Institute. (1988). *Failed opportunities: The decline of U.S. job safety in the 1980's.* Chicago.

Nelson, J. I., & Lorence, J. (1985). Employment in service activities and inequality in metropolitan areas. *Urban Affairs Quarterly, 21*(11), 106-125.

New York City Department of City Planning. (1985). *The Puerto Rican New Yorkers.* New York: New York City Department of City Planning.

Noyelle, T. J. (1987). *Beyond industrial dualism.* Boulder, CO, and London: Westview.

Noyelle, T. (1989). New York's competitiveness. In T. Noyelle (Ed.), *New York's financial markets.* Boulder, CO: Westview.

Noyelle, T. J., & Stanback, T. M. (1985). *The economic transformation of American cities.* Totowa, NJ: Rowman & Allenheld.

Offe, C. (1984). *Contradictions of the welfare state* (J. Keane, Ed.). Cambridge, MA: MIT Press.

Oficina Nacional de los Censos Demográfico y Electoral. (1955). *Censos de población, viviendas y electoral: Informe general.* La Habana: P. Fernández y Cía, S. en C.

Omi, M., & Winant, H. (1986). *Racial formation in the United States: From the 1960's to the 1980's.* New York: Routledge & Kegan Paul.

Ong, P. M. (1988, December). *The Hispanization of L.A.'s poor.* Paper presented at the Roundtable on Hispanic Poverty, sponsored by the National Council of La Raza, Washington, DC.

Ong, P. M. (1989). Neighborhoods, poverty and race. In *The widening divide: Income inequality and poverty in Los Angeles.*

Ong, P. M. (1990). Uncertain economic progress: Racial inequality among Californian males, 1940-1980. In S. Chan (Ed.), *Income and status differences between white and minority Americans: A persistent inequality* (Mellen Studies in Sociology, Vol. 3). Lewiston, NY: Edwin Mellen.

Ong, P. M. (1991, Spring). Race and post-displacement earnings among high-tech work-
     ers. *Industrial Relations.*
Ong, P. M., Lawrence, J., & Davidson, K. (1991). *Pluralism and residential patterns in
     Los Angeles.* Unpublished manuscript.
Ong, P. M., & Morales, R. (1988). Mexican labor in Los Angeles. In J. Johnson & M.
     Oliver (Eds.), *Proceedings of the Conference on Comparative Ethnicity.* University
     of California at Los Angeles, Institute of Social Science Research.
Ong, P. M., & Morales, R. (1992). Mexican labor in Los Angeles. In M. Romero & C.
     Candelaria (Eds.), *Community empowerment and Chicano scholarship* (pp. 63-84).
     Berkeley, CA: National Association for Chicano Studies.
Orfield, G. (1985). Ghettoization and its alternatives. In P. E. Peterson, *The new urban
     reality.* Washington, DC: Brookings Institute.
Organization for Economic Cooperation and Development. (1985). *1985 OECD Employ-
     ment Outlook.* Paris: OECD.
Ortiz, V. (1986, Fall). Changes in the characteristics of Puerto Rican migrants, from
     1955-1980. *International Migration Review, 20,* 612-628.
Padilla, E. (1947). *Puerto Rican immigrants in New York and Chicago: A study in
     comparative assimilation.* Unpublished doctoral dissertation, Department of An-
     thropology, University of Chicago.
Padilla, F. (1985). *Latino ethnic consciousness: The case of Mexican Americans and
     Puerto Ricans in Chicago.* South Bend, IN: University of Notre Dame Press.
Padilla, F. (1987). *Puerto Rican Chicago.* South Bend, IN: University of Notre Dame
     Press.
Padilla, S. (1990, February 7). Coalition sees high costs, lost jobs in AQMD clean air
     plan. *Los Angeles Times,* Section F.
Pansing, C., Rederer H., & Yale, D. (1989, August 20). *A community at risk: The
     environmental quality of life in East Los Angeles* (Client project for the Graduate
     School of Architecture and Urban Planning, University of California, Los Angeles).
Partnership for Hope. (1991). *Pride and poverty: A report on San Antonio.* Partnership
     for Hope, 3737 Broadway, Suite 100, San Antonio, TX 78209.
Pedraza-Bailey, S. (1985). *Political and economic migrants in America: Cubans and
     Mexicans.* Austin: University of Texas Press.
Pérez-Stable, M. (1993). *The Cuban Revolution: Origins, course, and legacy.* New York:
     Oxford University Press.
Peterson, P. E. (1985). *The new urban reality.* Washington, DC: Brookings Institute.
Piore, M. J., & Sabel, C. (1984). *The second industrial divide: Possibilities for prosperity.*
     New York: Basic Books.
Piore, M. J., & Sabel, C. F. (1984). *The second industrial divide: Possibilities for
     prosperity.* New York: Basic Books.
Piven, F. F. (1977). The fiscal crisis: Who got what and why. In R. Alcaly & D.
     Mermelstein (Eds.), *The fiscal crisis of American cities.* New York: Vintage.
Planning Institute. (1988, December 5). *The economic and social impacts of: The Air
     Quality Management Plan, the Regional Mobility Plan and the Growth Manage-
     ment Plan.* University of Southern California, Los Angeles.
Port Authority of New York and New Jersey. (1980). *The regional economy.* New York:
     Port Authority of New York and New Jersey.
Port Authority of New York and New Jersey. (1984). *The regional economy.* New York:
     Port Authority of New York and New Jersey.

Port Authority of New York and New Jersey. (1987). *Comprehensive annual financial report.* New York: Port Authority of New York and New Jersey.

Porter, M. E. (1990). *The competitive advantage of nations.* New York: Free Press.

Portes, A. (1987, October). The social origins of the Cuban enclave economy in Miami. *Sociological Perspectives, 30,* 340-372.

Portes, A., & Bach, R. L. (1985). *Latin journey: Cuban and Mexican immigrants in the United States.* Berkeley: University of California Press.

Portes, A., Castells, M., & Benton L. (Eds.). (1989). *The informal economy: Studies in advanced and less developed countries.* Baltimore, MD: Johns Hopkins University Press.

Portes, A., & Jensen. L. (1989, December). The enclave and the entrants: Patterns of ethnic enterprise in Miami before and after Mariel. *American Sociological Review, 54,* 929-949.

Portes, A., & Manning, R. D. (1986). The immigrant enclave: Theory and empirical examples. In S. Olzak & J. Nagel (Eds.), *Comparative ethnic relations.* Orlando, FL: Academic Press.

Portes, A., & Sassen-Koob, S. (1987). Making it underground: Comparative material on the informal sector in western market economies. *American Journal of Sociology, 93,* 30-61.

Prohías, R., & Casal, L. (1973). *The Cuban minority in the U. S.: Preliminary report on need identification and program evaluation.* Boca Raton: Florida Atlantic University.

Psycho-social dynamics in Miami. (1969, January). Coral Gables, FL: University of Miami.

Ranney, D. (1985). *Factory closings and early warning indicators* (Research Report #3).

Regional Plan Association. (1986). *Outlook for the tri-state region through 2000.* New York: Regional Plan Association.

Regional Plan Association. (1988). *The growing Latino presence in the tri-state region.* New York: Regional Plan Association.

Reich, M. (1981). *Racial inequality.* Princeton, NJ: Princeton University Press.

Reich, R. (1991). *The work of nations.* New York: Alfred Knopf.

Reimers, C. (1985). A comparative analysis of the wages of Hispanics, blacks, and non-Hispanic whites. In G. J. Borjas & M. Tienda (Ed.), *Hispanics in the U.S. economy* (pp. 27-75). Orlando, FL: Academic Press.

Rein, M., Anderson, G. E., & Rainwater, L. (1987). *Stagnation and renewal in social policy: The rise and fall of policy regimes.* Armonk, NY: M. E. Sharpe.

Reisler, M. (1976). *By the sweat of their brow: Mexican immigrant labor in the United States, 1910-1940.* Westport, CT: Greenwood.

Research Group on the Los Angeles Economy. (1989). *The widening divide: Income inequality and poverty in Los Angeles.*

Ricketts, E. R., & Sawhill, I. V. (1988). Defining and measuring the underclass. *Journal of Policy Analysis Management, 7*(2), 316-325.

Rivera-Batiz, F. L. (1987). Is there a brain drain of Puerto Ricans to the United States? *Puerto Rico Business Review, 12,* 1-5.

Roan, S. (1990, August 30). High number of lead poisoning cases found. *Los Angeles Times,* p. A3.

Robinson, J. (1989, February). Trends in racial inequality and exposure to work-related hazard, 1968-1986. *AAOHN Journal, 37*(2), 56-63.

Rochin, R. I., & de la Torre, A. (1992). Rural issues pertaining to the rise of Hispanics in America. In G. Johnson & J. Bonner (Eds.), *Agricultural agendas for the rural and basic social social sciences.* East Lansing: Michigan State University Press.

Rodríguez, N., & Feagin, J. R. (1986, December). Urban specialization in the world-system: An investigation of historical cases. *Urban Affairs Quarterly, 22,* 187-220.

Roediger, D. R. (1991). *The wages of whiteness: Race and the making of the American working class.* London and New York: Verso.

Rogg, E. (1974). *The assimilation of Cuban exiles: The role of community and class.* New York: Aberdeen.

Rohatyn, F. (1990, November 8). The fall and rise of New York. *The New York Review of Books.*

Romo, H. D. (1990). *Latinos and blacks in the cities: Policies for the 1990's.* Austin, TX: Lyndon B. Johnson Library and School of Public Affairs.

Romo, R. (1983). *East Los Angeles: History of a barrio.* Austin: University of Texas Press.

Rosales, F. A., & Simon, D. T. (1978). Los trabajadores Chicanos en la industria siderurgica y el sindicalismo en el Medio Oeste de 1919 a 1945. In J. G. Quiniones, & L. L. Arroyo (Eds.), *Origenes del moviemiento obrero Chicano.* Mexico, D. F.: Ediciones Era.

Rosenberg, S. (Ed.). (1989). *The state and the labor market.* New York: Plenum.

Ross, R., & Trachte, K. (1983). Global cities and global classes: The peripheralization of labor in New York City. *Review, 6* (3), 393-431.

San Antonio Independent School District v. Rodriguez. (1971).

San Antonio Light. (1990, November 15-18). Special report: A thousand lives.

Sánchez Korrol, V. (1983). *From colonia to America: The history of Puerto Ricans in New York.* Westport, CT: Greenwood.

Santiago, A. M. (1989). *Patterns of residential segregation among Mexicans, Puerto Ricans, and Cubans in U.S. metropolitan areas* (Working Paper No. 1).

Sassen, S. (1988). *The mobility of labor and capital: A study in international investment and labor flow.* Cambridge, UK: Cambridge University Press.

Sassen-Koob, S. (1989). New York City's informal economy. In A. Portes, M. Castells, & L. Benton (Eds.), *The informal sector: Theoretical and methodological issues.* Baltimore, MD: Johns Hopkins University Press.

Sassen, S. (1991). *The global city: New York, London, Tokyo.* Princeton, NJ: Princeton University Press.

Sassen, S., & Grover, W. (1986). *Unregistered work in the New York metropolitan area.*

Savitch, H. (1988). *Post-industrial societies.* Princeton, NJ: Princeton University Press.

Schaller, B. (1983). *The employment outlook for mnorities in a changing economy: Evidence from New York City's financial services sector.* New York: New York City Office for Economic Development.

Scott, A. J., & Paul, A. S. (1988). Industrial development and regional growth in southern California, 1970-1987. In *Can California be competitive and caring?* UCLA Institute of Industrial Relations.

Scott, A. J., & Storper, M. (Eds.). (1986). *Production, work, territory.* London: Allen & Unwin.

Sheets, R. G., Nord, S., & Phelps, J. J. (1987). *The impact of service industries on underemployment in metropolitan economies.* Lexington, MA: D. C. Heath.

Shefter, M. (1985). *Political crisis, fiscal crisis: The collapse and revival of New York City.* New York: Basic Books.

Silk, L. (1991, October 18). Economic scene. *New York Times,* p. D2.

Silver, H. (1984). *Regional shifts, deindustrialization and metropolitan income inequality.* Paper presented at the Annual Meeting of the American Sociological Association, San Antonio, TX.

Simon, J. (1989). *The economic consequences of immigration.* Cambridge, MA: Basil Blackwell.

Smith, J., & Welch, F. (1986). *Closing the gap: Forty years of economic progress for blacks.* Santa Monica, CA: Rand Corporation.

Smith, J., & Welch, F. (June, 1989). Black economic progress after Myrdal. *Journal of Economic Literature, 27,* 519-564.

Smith, L. (Ed.). (1988). *The Cuomo Commission report: A new American formula for a strong economy.* New York: Simon & Schuster.

Smith, M., & O'Day, J. (1991). Educational equality, 1966 and now. In D. Verstegen (Ed.), *Spheres of justice in American schools.* New York: Harper & Row.

Soja, E., Morales, R., & Wolf, G. (1983). Urban restructuring: An analysis of social and spatial change in Los Angeles. *Economic Geography, 59,* 195-230.

South Coast Air Quality Management District. (1989, March). *Air quality management plan, South Coast air basin.*

Southern California Social Survey. (1988). Institute for Social Science Research, UCLA, Compter data file.

Squires, G. D., Bennett, L., McCourt, K., & Nyden, P. (1987). *Race, class and the response to urban decline.* Philadelphia: Temple University Press.

Stafford, W. (1985). *Closed labor markets: The underrepresentation of blacks, Hispanics and women in New York City's core industries.* New York: Community Service Society.

Stafford, W. (1990). *Employment segmentation in New York City municipal agencies.* New York: Community Service Society.

Stanback, T. M., Jr., Bearse, P. J., Noyelle, T. J., & Karasek, R. (1981). *Services: The new economy.* NJ: Allenheld Osmon.

Standing, G. (1986, June 16). *Labour flexibility: Cause or cure for unemployment?* (Public Lecture No. 25). Geneva.

State of California Department of Industrial Relations. (various years). Urban Labor in California.

States in Profile. (1990). McConnelsburg, PA: Brazius & Foster and State Policy Research, Inc.

Stein, H. (1984). *Presidential economics.* New York: Simon & Schuster.

Strazheim, M. (1980). Discrimination and the spatial characteristics of the unio labor market for black workers. *Journal of Urban Economy, 7*(1), 119-140.

Tanzi, V. (1982). *The underground economy in the United States and abroad.* Lexington, MA: D. C. Heath.

Taub, R. P. (1991). *Differing conceptions of honor and orientations toward work and marriage among low income African Americans and Mexican Americans.* Chicago Urban Poverty and Family Life Conference, Irving B. Harris Graduate School of Public Policy and the Social Science Research Council.

Taylor, P. S. (1987). Mexican labor in the Calumet region. In E. J. Escobar & J. B. Lane (Eds.), *Forging a community: The Latino experience in northwest Indiana, 1919-1975* (pp. 33-79). Chicago: Cattails.

Thurow, L. (1987, May). A surge in inequality. *Scientific American, 256*(5), 30-37.

Tienda, M. (1988). Looking to 1990: Immigration, inequality and the Mexican origin people in the United States. *Ethnic Affairs* (Center for Mexican American Studies, University of Texas at Austin), (2), 1-22.

Tienda, M., & Borjas, G. (1986). *The economic consequences of immigration.* Madison: University of Wisconsin, Institute for Research on Poverty.

Tienda, M., Cordero Guzman, H., & Donato, K. (1991). *Queues and consequences: Labor force activity of minority men and women* (Discussion Paper Series).

Tobier, E. (1984). *The changing face of poverty: Trends in New York City's population in poverty—1960-1990.* New York: Community Service Society.

Torres, A. (1988). *Human capital, labor segmentation and inter-minority relative status.* Unpublished doctoral dissertation, New School for Social Research.

Torres, A. (1991, Summer). Labor market segmentation: African American and Puerto Rican labor in New York City: 1960-1980. *Review of Black Political Economy, 20*(1).

Torres, A., & Bonilla, F. (1991, May). *Decline within decline: Latinos in New York.* New York: Center for Puerto Rican Studies.

Torres-Saillant, S. (1989). Dominicans as a New York community: A social reappraisal. *Punto 7, II*(1),

Tyson, L. D., & Zysman, J. (1989). Developmental strategy and product innovation in Japan. In L. D. Tyson, J. Zysman, & C. Johnson (Eds.), *Politics and productivity: The real story of why Japan works* (pp. 59-140). New York: Ballinger.

U.S. Bureau of the Census. (1970). *Public use microdata samples* (PUMS, 15% 1/100 sample). Washington, DC.

U.S. Bureau of the Census. (1980). *Public use microdata samples* (PUMS, 5% sample). Washington, DC.

U.S. Bureau of the Census. (1984). *County business patterns, 1982 (No. 6). California.* Washington, DC: GPO.

U.S. Bureau of the Census. (1984-1985). *Survey of minority-owned business enterprise.* Washington, DC: GPO.

U.S. Bureau of the Census. (1986a). *Current population survey, March 1986.* Washington, DC.

U.S. Bureau of the Census. (1986b). *State and metropolitan area data, 1986.* Washington, DC: GPO.

U.S. Bureau of the Census. (1988a, August). *The Hispanic population in the United States: March 1988* (Current Poplation Reports, Series P-20, No. 431). Washington, DC.

U.S. Bureau of the Census. (1988b, January 6). *Hispanic women have 12 percent of all births, census bureau says* (Press Release CB88-SP.01). Washington, DC.

U.S. Bureau of the Census. (1988c). *Money income and poverty status in the United States: 1987 (Current Population Reports).* Washington, DC.

U.S. Bureau of the Census. (1991a, September 26). *1990 median houshold income dips, census bureau reports in annual survey* (Press Release, CB91-288). Washington, DC.

U.S. Bureau of the Census. (1991b, March). *Current Population Survey.* Washington, DC.

U.S. Bureau of the Census. (1991c). *Statistical Abstract of the United States.* Washington, DC.

U.S. Bureau of Census. (various years). *County business patterns* [CBP].

U.S. Bureau of the Census. (various years). *Current population survey* [CPS].

U.S. Bureau of Labor Statistics. (1968). *The labor force experience of the Puerto Rican worker.* Washington, DC: GPO.

U.S. Bureau of Labor Statistics. (1989). *Occupational injuries & illnesses in the United States by industry, 1987* (Bulletin 2328). Washington, DC: GPO.

U.S. Bureau of Labor Statistics. (1991, November). *Outlook 1990-2005* (Monthly Labor Review, 114, 11, 11/91).

U.S. Bureau of Labor Statistics. (1992, March). *Monthly labor review.*

U.S. Bureau of Labor Statistics. (various years). *Wage differences among metropolitan areas.*

U.S. Census of Manufacturers. (various years).

U.S. Congressional Budget Office. (1987, June). *Contract out: Potential for reducing federal costs.* Washington, DC: Government Printing Office.

U.S. Department of Commerce. (1955). *Investment in Cuba.* Washington, DC.

United Church of Christ. (1987). *Toxic wastes and race in the United States: A national report on the racial and socio-economic characteristics of communities with hazardous waste sites.*

Urban Summit 1990. (1990). New York: Urban Summit Planning Committee.

Van Dyk, J. (1990, May 5). Growing up in East Harlem. *National Geographic, 177.*

Van Houten, H. (1989). The cost of not being Anglo. In *The widening divide: Income inequality and poverty in Los Angeles.*

Vartabedian, R. (1992, January 30). 200,000 state jobs seen periled by defense cuts. *Los Angeles Times,* pp. A1, A16.

Vidueira, J. (1992, March 18). The quest for empowerment. *VISTA, 7*(8).

Vrooman, J., & Greenfield, S. (1980). Are blacks making it in the suburbs? *Journal of Urban Economy, 7,* 155-167.

Wacquant, L. J. D., & Wilson, W. J. (1989, January). The cost of racial and class exclusion in the inner city. In W. J. Wilson (Special Ed.), *The underclass: Issues, perspectives and public policy, 501,* 182-192.

Waldinger, R. (1991). Changing ladders and musical chairs: Ethnicity and opportunity in post industrial New York. *Politics and Society, 15*(4), 369-401.

Waldinger, R. (1990). Race and ethnicity. In C. Brecher & R. D. Horton (Eds.), *Setting municipal priorities 1990.* New York: NYU Press.

Waldinger, R. (1989a). Immigration and urban change. *Annual Review of Sociology, 15,* 211-232.

Waldinger, R. (1989b). In C. Brecher & R. D. Horton (Eds.), *Setting municipal priorities 1990.* New York: New York University Press.

Waldinger, R. (1986). *Through the eye of the needle: Immigrants and enterprise in New York's garment trade.* New York: New York University Press.

Weintraub, S. (1990). *A marriage of convenience.* New York: Oxford University Press.

Weitzman, P. (1989). *Worlds apart: Housing, race/ethnicity and income in New York City, 1978-87.* New York: Community Service Society.

White, T. H. (1984, March). New powers, new politics. *New York Times Magazine.*

Wilson, K., & Portes, A. (1980). Immigrant enclaves: A comparison of the Cuban and black economies of Miami. *American Journal of Sociology, 86*(2), 295-319.

Wilson, W. J. (1985). The urban underclass in advanced industrial societies. In P. E. Peterson (Ed.), *The new urban reality.* Washington, DC: Brookings Institute.

Wilson, W. J. (1987). *The truly disadvantaged: The inner city, the underclass and public policy.* Chicago: University of Chicago Press.

Wolff, R. P. (1945). *Miami: Economic pattern of a resort area.* Coral Gables, FL: University of Miami.

Word, D. L. (1989, May). *Population estimates by race and Hispanic origin for states, metropolitan areas, and selected counties, 1980-1985* (Series P-25, No. 1040-RD-1).

Wyckle, L., Morehouse, W., & Dembo, D. (1992). *Worker empowerment in a changing economy: Jobs, military production and the environment.* New York: Apex.

Author Index

Subject Index

About the Authors

John J. Betancur received his Ph.D. from the University of Illinois at Chicago in 1986 in public policy analysis. He is currently teaching at the University of Illinois at Chicago in both the School of Urban Policy and Planning and the Latin American Studies Department as well as doing research at the Center for Urban Economic Development. His research interests include labor and economic development for minority communities and international development and its effects on less developed countries and cities.

Evelyn Blumenberg is a Ph.D. candidate in urban planning at the University of California, Los Angeles, and is specializing in labor issues. She has a bachelor's degree in political science from the University of California, Berkeley, and a master's degree in urban planning from UCLA. Prior to entering graduate school, she directed several voter registration and election campaigns in low-income, minority communities.

Frank Bonilla is Thomas Hunter Professor of Sociology at Hunter College, City University of New York, and Director of CUNY's Centro de Estudios Puertorriqueños. He is also Professor in CUNY's Ph.D. programs in sociology and political science. Currently, he is Managing Director of the Inter-University Program for Latino Research (IUP), a consortium of eight university-based research centers concerned with the situation of Latinos in the United States. Within IUP he is the principal coordinator of the working group, Latinos in the Changing U.S. Economy.

Susan Burek holds an M.A. in sociology (1991) from the University of Texas at Austin, where she specialized in the study of stratification, labor, minorities, and social problems. She worked for 10 years with poverty programs at the Texas Department of Human Services. She conducted socioeconomic and labor market research on Mexican Americans for the University of Texas at Austin Center for Mexican American Studies. She also conducted unemployment and work value research on Mexican Americans for the University of Texas Health Science Center in San Antonio. She currently conducts research on children's mental health programs for the Texas Department of Mental Health and Mental Retardation.

Gilberto Cardenas was born in Los Angeles, California. He received his Ph.D. in sociology from the University of Notre Dame. Currently he is Associate Professor of Sociology and Director of the Center for Mexican American Studies, The University of Texas, Austin, as well as Co-Director of the Inter-University Program for Latino Research. He has published and lectured widely on international migration and border studies.

Martin Carnoy was born in Warsaw, Poland, in 1938. He attended the California Institute of Technology and the University of Chicago, where he received his Ph.D. in economics in 1964. He worked at the Brookings Institution on Latin American trade issues before coming to Stanford in 1969. He is a Professor in the School of Education and also teaches courses in the Department of Economics. He writes about U.S. and international political economics and the economics of education and labor markets and is the author of many articles and books, including *Education as Cultural Imperialism, Economic Democracy* (with Derek Shearer), *The State and Political Theory, Schooling and Work in the Democratic State* (with Henry Levin), and *Education and Social Transition in the Third World* (with Joel Samoff). His recent research has focused on African Americans and Latinos in the U.S. labor market and on the impact of the new information technology on developing countries' economies.

Jorge Chapa, Assistant Professor at the Lyndon B. Johnson School of Public Affairs, was born in Monterrey, Mexico, and was raised in Chicago, Illinois, and the surrounding area. He received his bachelor's degree in biology from the University of Chicago, and upon graduation, studied and traveled in Latin America. As a result of his travels and personal experiences, he developed a deep interest in the welfare of Latinos, particularly those living in the United States. He obtained master's degrees in demography and sociology and a Ph.D. in sociology from the University of California, Berkeley, and in 1988 co-authored *The Burden of Support,* an analysis of the policy implications of population trends in areas with large Hispanic populations. His current teaching, research, and publications focus on the low rates of Hispanic educational, occupational, and economic mobility and on the development of policies to improve these trends.

Teresa Cordova received her Ph.D. from the University of California, Berkeley, and is currently Assistant Professor at the School of Architecture and Planning at the University of New Mexico. She is the author of "Community Intervention Efforts" (appearing in *Challenging Uneven Development,* edited by Wiewel and Nyden) and edited *Chicana Voices: Intersection of Class, Race and Gender.* She has conducted research on neighborhood change, community development, affordable housing, and land use conflicts. She is an active member of the National Association for Chicano Studies and the Third World Conference Foundation.

Hugh M. Daley is Research Associate with Sociometrics Corporation, Los Altos, California. He received his M.S. from Syracuse University and is a Ph.D. candidate at Stanford University. He has authored and co-authored technical and scientific reports in areas of information technology assessment. His principal research interest is the economic and organizational impacts of the growth of the information sector in the U.S. economy. He is co-author of *Latinos in a Changing Economy: Comparative Perspectives on the U.S. Labor Market Since 1939,* and was principally responsible for organization and analysis of the national economic data on which the monograph is based. Since joining Sociometrics, he has provided technical support to the Data Resources Program of the National Institutes of Justice and is currently working on the development of search and retrieval software for sociodemographic data and statistical program objects.

Raul Hinojosa Ojeda is Assistant Professor of Planning in the Graduate School of Architecture and Urban Planning at the University of California, Los Angeles. He received his B.A. (economics), M.A. (anthropology), and Ph.D. (political science) at the University of Chicago. He is the author of various articles on political economy of regional integration dynamics in various parts of the world, including debt, trade, and migration relations between the United States and Mexico and other Latin American countries. He is currently writing a book on the political economy of U.S.-Mexico relations in the 20th century, including the recent move toward a free trade agreement. He is co-author of *Latinos in a Changing U.S. Economy: Comparative Perspectives on the U.S. Labor Market Since 1939,* and co-editor of *Labor Market Interdependence between the United States and Mexico.*

Rebecca Morales is Associate Professor at the Center for Politics and Policy, Claremont Graduate School, Claremont, California, and Research Policy Director, The Tomas Rivera Center. She holds a Ph.D. from M.I.T. in urban and regional development. Her publications focus on Latinos, immigrants, community development, and international industrialization. She is the author of a forthcoming book titled *Flexible Production: Restructuring of the International Automobile Industry.*

Paul M. Ong is Associate Professor of Urban Planning at the University of California, Los Angeles. He holds a master's degree in urban planning from the University of Washington, Seattle, and a Ph.D. in economics from the University of California, Berkeley. His research focuses on immigrant and minority workers.

Marifeli Pérez-Stable is Associate Professor of Sociology at the State University of New York, College of Old Westbury. She is the author of articles on Cuba published in *Cuban Studies/Estudios Cubanos, Latin American Research Review, Latin American Perspectives,* and several anthologies. She is the author of *The Cuban Revolution: Origins, Course, and Legacy* (1993). During 1991-1992, she held a National Science Foundation Visiting Professorship for Women at the New School for Social Research in New York City.

Saskia Sassen is Professor of Urban Planning and Director of the Ph.D. program in planning at Columbia University, currently on leave at the Russell Sage Foundation. She is the author of *The Mobility of Labor and Capital: A Study in International Investment and Labor Flow* and *The Global City: New York, London, Tokyo.* She is completing a book with Maria Patricia Fernandez-Kelly about the impact of economic restructuring on the employment of immigrant women.

Andres Torres is Research Director of the Labor Studies Program at the University of Massachusetts/Boston. Previously he served as Research Director at the Center for Puerto Rican Studies, Hunter College of the City University of New York. He received his doctorate in economics from the New School for Social Research.

Maria de los Angeles Torres is Assistant Professor of Political Science at DePaul University in Chicago. She has published and conducted research in the area of Cuban Americans and U.S. foreign policy. She was Director of the Mayor's Advisory Commission on Latino Affairs during the Harold Washington administration.

Miren Uriarte is a Sociologist on the Faculty of the College of Public and Community Services and Senior Researcher at the Mauricio Gastón Institute for Latino Community Development and Public Policy at the University of Massachusetts/Boston. She conducts research on the formation and institutional development of Latino communities in the United States. She is the co-editor (with Edwin Melendez) of *Latinos Poverty and Public Policy* (forthcoming).

DATE DUE